A2-Level
Business
Studies

The Revision Guide

Editors:
Gemma Hallam, Katherine Reed

Contributors:
P. M. Brockbank, John Grant, Peter Gray, Jeff Harris, Nagu Rao,
David Morris, Adrian Murray, Lynda Turner, Keith Williamson

Proofreaders:
Keri Barrow, Claire Fiddaman, Susan Harrison, Lynda Turner

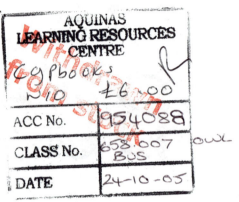
Published by Coordination Group Publications Ltd.

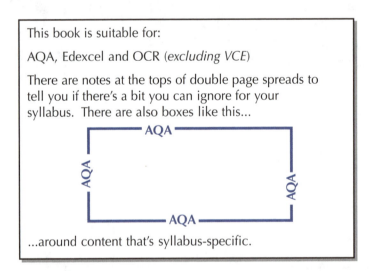

This book is suitable for:

AQA, Edexcel and OCR (*excluding VCE*)

There are notes at the tops of double page spreads to tell you if there's a bit you can ignore for your syllabus. There are also boxes like this...

AQA

...around content that's syllabus-specific.

ISBN: 1 84146 349 3
Groovy website: www.cgpbooks.co.uk
Jolly bits of clipart from CorelDRAW
Printed by Elanders Hindson, Newcastle upon Tyne.

Contents

We deliberately haven't put any _essay_ answers in this book, because they'd just be repeating what's in the revision guide. Instead, we've put in a section about how to write good essay answers, and do well. Answers for the _numerical_ questions are included though, on page 138.

Marketing

You've covered some marketing at AS level — there's more to learn for A2, though.
*These two pages are for **AQA and OCR**.*

The **Role** of **Marketing** is to **Identify** and **Satisfy** customer **Needs** and **Wants**

1) Market research and analysis finds out what customers **need and want**. Marketing also tries to **anticipate** what they'll want in the future so that the business can get an advantage over its competitors.

2) Marketing tries to ensure that the business supplies goods and services that the customer **wants**, in order to **maximise profit**. It's mutually beneficial for the business and the customer — the customer gets something they like, the business makes a profit.

3) Remember, marketing covers **market research**, **market analysis**, **market planning** and the "**marketing mix**" — the four big Ps of product, price, promotion and place (distribution).

Marketing affects all **Departments** and **Functions** in a business

1) Most larger businesses have a specialised **marketing department** — but marketing affects **all departments**.

2) **Market analysis** can tell the **finance** department **how much** the business is likely to make in **sales**. Market analysis tells the business how **big** the market for a product is, so they know if they can **expand** and make more profits without having to **diversify** into supplying new products.

3) Market research and analysis tells the **research and development** people what kind of products to **research** and **design**, in order to meet **future needs**.

1) Marketing is also **influenced** by other business functions.

2) For example, the business' **marketing budget** is influenced by its overall **financial position** — when money's tight, the marketing budget will be small.

3) Also, any changes in production capacity or human resources affect the business' **strengths** and **weaknesses**, which affect the **marketing strategy** it chooses to follow.

Marketing objectives may **conflict** with the objectives of other departments. For example, the production department may want to continue with the same processes that they've always used, while the marketing department might want to diversify and make new products using new processes.

Marketing approaches can be **Product**, **Market** or **Asset Oriented**

1) **Product oriented** businesses start by deciding what they can **produce**. They put the product ahead of customer needs or budget constraints.

2) Product orientation is a **risky** strategy, because it **assumes** that customers will love the product. Customers might want or need a **different product** altogether.

3) The product-led approach only really works when there's very **little competition** in the market, or when the product is something that customers really want.

1) **Market oriented** businesses start by finding out what the **customer wants**.

2) A **market-led** approach is more likely to **succeed** than a product-led approach.

3) The market-led approach has **risks** — it chases customer needs even when the firm doesn't have the right **resources** to meet them. Market-led strategies can push the firm into new markets where it doesn't have enough **experience**. This can end in failure, with disappointed customers leaving the brand.

1) **Asset-led marketing** combines **consumer wants** with the **strengths** (assets) of the business.

2) For example, when developing the **new Mini**, **BMW** linked the **market desire** for a new small car with their **reputation** for **reliability** and engineering expertise. Customers were happy to pay a **premium price** for the new Mini because it combined these two things.

3) **Asset-led marketing** is now seen as the best route to long term **customer satisfaction** and **brand loyalty**. It helps businesses ensure that they're **capable** of making a product customers need before they start the manufacturing process.

AQA   *AQA*   *AQA*

Marketing

The **Law** has an impact on **Marketing**

1) The Government regulates the activities of businesses to make sure they act in the **public interest**. It does this by passing new laws.

2) Legislation **protects consumers**, but it often leads to **increased costs** for businesses and it may **stifle innovation**.

3) Legislation can **open up markets**, for example the laws that opened up the utilities (gas and electricity) market in the UK, and the laws governing the EU single market. It can also **close markets** through **protectionist** measures, for example tariffs on imports.

4) Legislation also protects businesses through **patents**, **trademarks** and **copyright**.

The **Law** directly affects the **Marketing Mix**

1 — Product

- Some products are **plain illegal** under UK law, e.g. handguns.
- The **Sale of Goods Act** means that goods must be "of **merchantable quality**".

2 — Price

- **Predatory pricing** (cutting prices to force a competitor out of business) is illegal in the EU and in the US. It's difficult to **prove** that a business is trying to kill competition, though.
- Consumers must **know the price** before they buy — e.g. pubs must display drink prices next to the bar.
- The word "sale" can only be used if the product has been sold at higher prices previously.

3 — Place / Distribution

- Some products can only be sold in certain places by certain people — e.g. some medicines can only be bought with a doctor's **prescription**, not over the counter or off the supermarket shelf.
- **Licences** are required to sell some products, e.g. **alcohol** or firearms.
- **Sunday trading** is limited. The sale of **alcohol** is limited to certain hours in the day.

4 — Promotion

- The **Trade Descriptions Act** regulates promotion. Businesses can't lie about their products. They can't "bait and switch" by advertising a nice product and supplying a crummy one. Product **labelling** is regulated — for example, you can't make claims of medical benefits without proper medical evidence.
- **Offensive adverts** can be **banned**. The Advertising Standards Agency regulates adverts.
- Advertising of some products is **restricted**. **Prescription medicine** can't be advertised on TV, and **tobacco** products can barely be advertised anywhere any more. Advertising of alcoholic drinks is restricted.
- **Advertising hoardings** need planning permission.

Practice Questions

Q1 How does marketing affect the finance department?

Q2 What's the difference between market-led marketing and asset-led marketing?

Q3 State two examples of how legislation can open up markets.

Q4 Give three ways in which the law would affect the marketing of a new alcopop.

Exam Question

Q1 Demand for personalised T-shirts is increasing. KB Garments produce T-shirts in bulk. How should they adapt their marketing plan to make the most of this change in the market? (10 marks)

Marketing — even educated fleas do it...

OK, being honest here, some of this will be familiar from the AS book. Thing is that some boards cover asset-led marketing etc. for AS level, and AQA leaves it until A2. So, if you're doing AQA, focus on the stuff on page 2 about the role of marketing, and relating customer tastes to business strengths. If you're doing OCR, concentrate on the law bits on page 3.

Market Analysis and Buyer Behaviour

*Market analysis tells firms about the size of the market and the customers within the market. Firms also like to know why customers within the market buy what they buy. These pages are for **AQA** and **OCR** and are helpful for **Edexcel**, too.*

Market Analysis *tells firms about* Market Size *and* Growth

1) **Market size** is the **total** of all the **sales** within the market. It's measured by either the **volume of sales** (the **number of units** sold) or the **value of sales** (the total sales **revenue**).

2) Businesses need to know if the market is **growing** or **shrinking**.

3) **Competition** in a **shrinking** market is **heavy** — there are fewer customers to go around. Firms may want to get out of a market that's getting smaller.

4) In a **growing** market, **several** firms can **grow easily**.

Looks like a big one.

Market Analysis *tells firms about* Market Share

1) Market share is the **percentage** of sales in a market that is made by **one firm**, or by **one brand**.
Market share = sales ÷ total market size × 100 %

2) For example, if **1 out of 4** PCs bought was a Dell, this would give Dell a **25% market share** (in terms of volume). If **£1 out of every £10** spent on perfume was a Chanel purchase, this'd give Chanel a **10% market share** (in terms of value). It's easy to work out.

3) It's important to look at **trends in market share** as well as trends in sales revenue. Letting your market share slip is not good — it means that **competitors** are **gaining advantage** over you.

> **Example**: Say the mobile gaming market has grown by **15%** from one year to the next. A software company selling games for mobile devices would not be happy if they'd only increased sales by **5%** from £200 000 to £210 000 — they're failing to grow at the **same rate** as the market, so their **market share** has gone down. That 5% growth isn't looking so good now that they know that someone's muscling in on their market share.

Markets *are* Segmented *into groups of* Similar Customers

Different groups of customers have different needs. **Analysing** different **segments** of a market allows a firm to focus on the needs of **specific groups** within a target market. A market can be segmented in several ways:

1) **Income.** Luxury products are aimed at high income groups.

2) **Socio-economic class.** Businesses can segment their market based on the kind of jobs people have — from senior professionals to unemployed people.

A	Higher managerial, administrative and professional, e.g. hospital consultant, MD of big firm, barrister.
B	Intermediate managerial, administrative and professional, e.g. teacher, accountant.
C1	Supervisory or clerical, junior managerial/administrative/professional, e.g. production supervisor.
C2	Skilled manual, e.g. plumber, electrician, chef, hairdresser, gas fitter.
D	Semi-skilled and unskilled manual, e.g. bus driver, waiter/waitress, postman/woman, cleaner.
E	Casual labourers, state pensioners, the unemployed.

3) **Age.** Businesses target products at specific age groups — pre-teens, teens, 25-35 year olds, the over 55s etc.

4) **Gender.** For example, chocolate manufacturers target some bars at women (Flake) and some at men (Yorkie).

5) **Geographical region.** Some products have a regional market — e.g. Welsh cakes, haggis.

6) **Amount of use.** For example, mobile phone suppliers market differently to heavy users and light users.

7) **Ethnic grouping.** New ethnic minority digital TV channels make it easier for firms to target ethnic groups.

8) **Family size.** New houses are built with a number of bedrooms to suit the target consumer. Large "family packs" of breakfast cereal, loo roll etc. are aimed at large families.

9) **Lifestyle.** Busy young workers buy lots of microwaveable ready meals, so ready meals are targeted at them.

All the above methods focus on a **characteristic of the customer**. In addition, new segmentation methods categorise markets according to the **reasons** for buying a product — as an essential, as a luxury, as a gift, etc.

Market Aggregation *lumps all segments together as a* Mass Market

Market aggregation tries to appeal to **everyone**, by marketing a product with **general appeal**, that everyone will hopefully like. It's the **opposite** of **market segmentation**, which markets products to some market segments and deliberately ignores or excludes others. Marketing has moved increasingly **away** from mass market aggregation.

Market Analysis and Buyer Behaviour

Businesses need to *Know Their Customers* — *Why* they buy *What* they buy

1) Understanding **why** a customer buys a product allows a business to **respond** to the **customer's needs**.

2) Psychologists study the **science of behaviour**, so psychology can provide insights into motivation. Businesses can use psychology in their marketing to subtly persuade people to buy.

3) Businesses aim to identify and anticipate **cultural shifts** which influence buying behaviour. A move towards **healthier lifestyles** has prompted growth in sales of low fat foods, gym memberships and exercise equipment.

4) Purchasers go through several **stages** when they buy something: 1) **recognising** the **need**, 2) **finding information**, 3) considering **alternatives**, 4) **purchasing** the product, and 5) **evaluating** the purchase.

5) For **low value** purchases (also called "**low involvement**" purchases), this all happens very quickly and purchasers may skip steps 2 and 3. For **high involvement**, high cost industrial contracts, the process could take **years**.

Customer Personality affects New Product Uptake

1) "**Innovators**" are the **very first** to buy the shiny new thing when it comes out. There are only a very few innovators.

2) "**Early adopters**" buy the new product **soon** after it's released. They're the sort of people who others go to for **advice** on what digital camera to buy, what sort of espresso maker to get, etc.

3) "**Early majority**" buyers buy **fashionable** stuff before it goes out of fashion, but they're more conservative than early adopters.

4) "**Late majority**" buyers are **sceptical** of new technology and want to be sure that it'll work and that it won't break.

5) "**Laggards**" are **behind** everyone else — **everyone's** got one by now, **except** this lot. For example, they couldn't imagine what they'd want a mobile phone for. They tend to be nostalgic about the past.

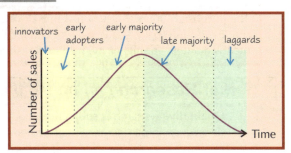

Customers can play Different Roles in Purchasing

> There can be more than one customer in each purchase — purchaser and decision maker both count as customers.

In any purchase, a customer plays **one or more** of these **roles**.

1) The **initiator** gets the ball rolling, and decides that there's a need to buy.

2) The **influencer** tries to influence the decider or the purchaser. **Kids** are often influencers.

3) The **gatekeeper** is the person who stands in between a sales person and a decision maker. For example, a **secretary** can decide whether to give a photocopier rep an **appointment** with the boss.

4) The **decision maker** makes the decision to buy, obviously.

5) The **purchaser** is the one who actually does the buying. In a **domestic** purchase, the decision maker and purchaser are usually the **same person**. In an **industrial** purchase, a **manager** usually makes the decision to buy, and a **purchase clerk** does the actual purchase order.

6) The **user** is the one who actually uses the thing. If they're lucky, they'll have some input into the purchase.

Practice Questions

Q1 Give examples of four different ways that markets are segmented.

Q2 What's the difference between market segmentation and market aggregation?

Q3 What are the five stages a buyer goes through when making a purchase?

Q4 What are the six roles identified in a purchase?

Exam Questions

Q1 Knowledge of customers is the most important factor for small businesses. Discuss.   (12 marks)

Q2 Analyse the use of psychology in marketing reduced calorie chocolate bars.   (8 marks)

The orange market — all too easily segmented...

Blimey, there's a lot on these pages. Some of it follows on from AS work, so it shouldn't be totally new. Market segmentation and buyer behaviour kind of go together. You can segment based on gender, age, class etc, and you can make assumptions about the buyer behaviour of those segments. You can also segment based on psychology.

Market Research

*Every business needs to know what people want, and how much they'd be willing to pay for it. For **OCR** and **Edexcel**.*

Market Research finds out about Markets, Customers and Competitors

1) Market research analyses the **size**, **geography**, **segmentation**, and **potential** of markets.

2) Market research also finds out about **products** and **product development**.

3) Analysis of sales includes finding out about **sales methods**, **territories** (where things are sold), and **outlets** (the shops, catalogues or websites which do the selling).

4) **Promotional activities** can be analysed — adverts, special offers, point of sale displays.

5) Analysing the **economy** is also part of market research.

6) **Customer motivation** is an important area of market research. Businesses need to know **why** customers buy their product, why they buy **competitors'** products, and what their **perceptions** are of products on the market.

7) It's really important to research **competitors'** **actions** and **products**. Market research can tell you about the **competitors' market share** and about the unique selling points (**USPs**) of their products.

> The **purpose** of market research is to **reduce risk**. It's become more and more important as **business** has become more and more **risky** — the **pace of change** has increased, product development is more **costly**, globalisation means markets are **bigger** (with more consumers and more competitors), and **consumer attitudes** change frequently.

Market Research can be Qualitatitive or Quantitative

1) **Qualitative** research is **subjective** and attempts to find out why customers make purchasing decisions. In particular, it's concerned with customer behaviour, motivation, tastes and preferences.

2) **Quantitative** research is **factual** and consists of "what" and "who" type questions, e.g. "What market share does Hellman's mayonnaise have?" "Who buys Pop Tarts?".

Field Research gathers Primary Data

1) **Primary data** is information that doesn't already exist. It's collected for a specific purpose.

2) **Surveys** (face-to-face, telephone or postal), **observation** (watching customer reactions), **loyalty cards**, panel and group **discussions** and **test marketing** are used to collect primary data.

3) **Loyalty cards** (e.g. Tesco Clubcard, Nectar card) provide rewards for customers and also **collect information** about what they buy. This information is used to **target** ads and special offers to the customer's buying pattern.

4) **Panel** and **group discussions** find out about **customer attitudes** and changing **tastes** and **behaviour**. The **Delphi** technique (see p.17) assembles a panel of **experts** to discuss an issue and provide a consensus view.

5) **Test marketing** involves a **small-scale test** of a new product. This reduces costs, allows the business to learn lessons before a national launch and lets them solve any problems. However, test marketing gives **competitors** a **preview** of the product, and they may react by counter-marketing or developing rival products.

6) Primary data is taken from a small **sample** of the market. There's more on sampling on the next page.

Desk Research uses Secondary Data

1) **Secondary data** is **second-hand** information, which has been gathered by someone else.

2) **Secondary data** includes data from the Department of Trade and Industry and **government statistics** such as the Census and the Social Trends report.

3) **Market intelligence reports** are produced by market research organisations like Mintel and AC Nielsen. **Trade associations** and **trade journals** are also good sources.

Primary and Secondary market research data have Pros and Cons

Advantages of primary data	It's **targeted** at a specific issue. It can assess **buyer psychology**. It's **up-to-date**.
Disadvantages of primary data	It's **expensive**. There's a risk of **bias** if it isn't done correctly.
Advantages of secondary data	It can often be obtained for **free**. It may provide a good **overview** of the market. Secondary data is often based on **accurate**, **reliable** figures, e.g. from the Census.
Disadvantages of secondary data	It's **not tailored** to meet a specific need. **Market intelligence** reports are **expensive**. Information may be **outdated**. The original data may be biased.

Market Research

Probability Sampling involves Random Selection

1) **Probability** sampling involves picking names out of a "sampling frame" at **random**. A sampling frame is a **complete list** of the population being sampled, which needs to be **accurate**, **complete** and without any **duplicate** entries. Easier said than done. **Random**, **systematic** and **stratified random** are all kinds of probability sampling.

2) In **random sampling** each member of the population has an equal chance of selection. This means that sampling error can be determined statistically. ⟵

3) **Systematic** sampling involves choosing a **starting point** in the sampling frame and selecting every *n*th value, e.g. every fifth name. There may be bias, if there's an underlying pattern in the sampling frame.

4) In **stratified random sampling** the population is put into **segments** called "**strata**" based on things like age, gender or income — for example age 18-24, age 25-34, age 35-44, age 55-64, age 65+. Names are selected at random from within each segment.

Population means the bunch of people you're surveying, not all 60 million people in the UK.

See p.8 for sampling errors. In short, they're what happens when the sample doesn't represent the population properly.

Non-Probability Sampling involves Human Choice

1) **Non-probability sampling** isn't random. It isn't possible to work out a sampling error. Non-probability sampling can be reliable, though, provided the population data is up-to-date and the respondents are carefully selected. Quota, cluster and convenience are different types of non-probability sampling.

2) In **quota sampling**, the selection is made by the **interviewer**, who'll have a quota to meet — e.g. "interview 20 women between 25 and 34". It's a bit like stratified random sampling, but it's not random — interviewers tend to pick people who look "nice", which introduces bias. It's quick and useful, though.

3) **Cluster sampling** selects groups (clusters) rather than individuals. For example, instead of sampling 400 homes from a town of 10 000 homes, you could divide the town into geographical clusters of 100 homes, and sample four clusters. This greatly reduces the **time** and **legwork** needed to do the survey.

4) In **single stage cluster sampling**, **everyone** in the cluster is interviewed. **Multi-stage cluster sampling** is often used when each cluster is too large. It's random sampling from within successive stages — for example picking a local authority, then picking postcodes within that local authority and then picking houses from those postcodes.

5) New businesses with limited funds often use **convenience sampling**, which samples consumers who are most easily contacted. Bias is clearly a problem with convenience sampling.

Market Research is a Trade-Off between Cost and Accuracy

1) No market research is **perfect**. Bias may be introduced by untruthful responses, poor sampling and bad analysis.

2) The **more you spend** on market research, the **better** your sampling process can be, the better your questionnaire can be designed, the more data you can collect via loyalty cards or whatever. But you may not make as much money from your findings as it costs to do the research. So, firms often **settle for second best**.

Practice Questions

Q1 What is the purpose of market research?
Q2 List five methods of gathering primary data.
Q3 What are the advantages and disadvantages of primary and secondary data?
Q4 What's quota sampling?
Q5 A market research interviewer visits all households in one council ward of a city. What kind of sampling is this?

Exam Question

Q1 Andrew is thinking of leaving teaching and setting up as a private tutor.
a) Discuss which method of research, primary or secondary, is likely to be better for Andrew. (11 marks)
b) Explain two reasons why Andrew might want to use sampling to gather data. (6 marks)
c) Is random or quota sampling likely to be most appropriate for Andrew? Explain your answer. (6 marks)

Who in the heck does buy Pop Tarts, anyway? Beats me...

Market research is A Big Thing in A2 Business Studies — it's a tool used to help plan and budget for marketing activities. You'll probably be expected to mention it in a Marketing question, even if you don't get a straightforward "what kind of sampling should this guy use?" question. Make sure you can evaluate different research techniques.

Market Research Analysis

*Once a business has done market research, they need to analyse the data. For **OCR** and **Edexcel**.*

Surveys can have **Sampling Errors**

1) Errors in surveys can come from **sampling errors** and **non-sampling errors**.

2) A **sampling error** is the difference between the **sample's mean value** and the **population's true mean value**. For example, if the sample value is 19 and the actual value is 20, then the sampling error is 1. Generally, the **larger** the sample, the **smaller** the sampling error.

3) **Non-sampling errors** come from various sources. For example, respondents may give answers to **please** the **interviewer**, they may give **socially acceptable** answers instead of the truth, or they may just fail to **understand** the question. Respondents may fail to **return** a postal survey. Errors can also get into the data when it's being **typed up** and prepared.

Managers need to **Make Sense** of Data

1) Marketing people need to turn raw market research data into something that's **easy** for managers to use and understand. It's very useful to figure out the **central tendency** of a set of data. The central tendency is another word for the **average** of a set of data — it's one single representative figure that managers can use.

2) **Mean**, **median** and **mode** are measures of central tendency. The **mean** is all the results ÷ the number of results, the **median** is the **middle** value when the figures are placed in ascending order, and the **mode** is the **value that occurs most often** in the data. All basic maths.

3) A **normal distribution** is a **symmetrical** bell curve. The mean, median and mode are all the same, and they're all slap bang in the middle.

4) With a **skewed** distribution, the mean, median and mode aren't all the same.

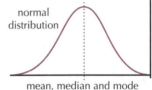

normal distribution

mean, median and mode

skewed distribution

mean | mode
median

The **Range** is the **Difference** between the **Highest** and **Lowest** Values

1) It's **easy to calculate**. It should be viewed with some caution, though, because the highest and lowest values might not be typical.

2) The **interquartile range** is the difference between the **top 25%** (quarter) and **bottom 25%** (quarter). It covers the **middle half** of the set of values. It's often **more useful** than the range.

Example: This **cumulative frequency table** shows the days of absence taken by **41 employees**.

Days absence	0	1	2	3	4	5	6	15
Number of employees	15	5	9	6	1	2	2	1
Cumulative frequency	15	20	29	35	36	38	40	41

To calculate the upper boundary of the **lower quartile** use the formula $\frac{n+1}{4}$ where n is the number of values, i.e. 41. Therefore, the upper boundary of the lower quartile is (41+1)÷ 4 = **10.5**. This is between the 10th and 11th values, in the range 0-15, so you can tell that the people in the lower quartile had **no absences**.

To find the **upper quartile**, use the formula $\frac{3(n+1)}{4}$. This is 31.5, between the 31st and 32nd value, i.e. 3 days absent. The interquartile range = **between 0 and 3** = **3 days**. This is a more useful figure than the range which is 15 days.

The **Standard Deviation** is a measure of the data's **Spread** around the **Mean**

1) The **standard deviation** is a **really important** measure.

2) The **formula** for calculating standard deviation is:⟶ $\sigma = \sqrt{\dfrac{\Sigma\,(x - \mu)^2}{n}}$ where x = each piece of data, μ = the mean, and n =the number of pieces of data. (OCR only). Σ means "the sum of".

So, it's the <u>square root of</u>... (the <u>sum of</u> the <u>square of the differences</u> between each piece of data and the mean) <u>divided by the number of bits of data.</u>

Example: The weekly sales of a product are 34, 32, 14, 25 and 24 units.
The mean is (34 + 32 + 14 + 25 + 24) ÷5 = 129÷5 = **25.8 units** per week.

The variance is just the sum divided by *n*.

Work out the standard deviation as follows:

Yes, you do have to work out (x-μ) for each value, then <u>square</u> it, then <u>add up all the squares</u> and <u>divide by the number of values</u>. Life is tough on occasions.

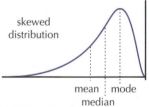

x	34	32	14	25	24			
x−μ	8.2	6.2	-11.8	-0.8	-1.8	sum	variance	SD
(x−μ)²	67.24	38.44	139.24	0.64	3.24	248.8	49.76	7.05

Market Research Analysis

The **Standard Deviation** of a **Normal Distribution** is very useful for **Analysis**

The standard deviation of a **normal distribution** graph is very useful for **analysis** and **problem solving**.

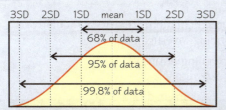

One standard deviation either side of the mean   = **68%** of the distribution.
Two standard deviations either side of the mean   = **95%** of the distribution.
Three standard deviations either side of the mean = **99.8%** of the distribution.

These facts are true for all normal (unskewed) distributions.

Check out these **Examples** of using **Standard Deviations**

Example 1: A battery lasts on average **250 hours** with a **standard deviation** of **30 hours**.
68% will last between **220-280 hours** (one SD either side of the mean),
95% will last between **190-310 hours** (two SDs either side of the mean) and
99.8% will last between **160-340 hours** (three SDs either side of the mean).

These percentages come from up there. Learn them.

Example 2: You can also work out the probability of one of those batteries lasting for **more than 290 hours**.

1) 290 hours is **40 hours above the mean** (250 hours). The SD is 30, so this is 40÷30 = **1.33 standard deviations from the mean**. This is called the Z score.

2) Using the Z score table for a normal distribution, convert the Z score of **1.33** into a **percentage**: it works out to **0.4082**, which is **40.82%** of the area under the curve.

3) The **mean average** battery life is **250 hours**, and you've just worked out that **40.82%** of them have a life between **250 and 290 hours**.

4) **50%** of them have a life of between **0 and 250 hours** So... that gives you 50% + 40.82% = 90.82% which have a lifetime of **290 hours or less**.

5) One last simple step — 100% – 90.82% = **9.18%** have a lifetime of **more than 290 hours**.

A Section of a Z Scores Chart

Z	area	Z	area
1.22	0.3888	1.28	0.3997
1.23	0.3907	1.29	0.4015
1.24	0.3925	1.30	0.4032
1.25	0.3944	1.31	0.4049
1.26	0.3962	1.32	0.4066
1.27	0.3980	1.33	0.4082

In the exam, you'll be given the Z scores.

You can just read the Z score from the chart. For example, A Z score of 1.31 tells you 40.49% of the area under the curve lies between the mean and Z.

(How do I know that — because the mean is 250 hours, that's how. 50% of them last longer than that, 50% last less time than that.)

Practice Questions

Q1   What is a sampling error?

Q2   Give three reasons why non-sampling errors may occur.

Q3   Explain the term "interquartile range".

Q4   What proportion of a normal distribution graph lies 2 standard deviations from the mean?

Exam Questions

Q1   Calculate the range and interquartile range for the following data: (9 marks)

Number of cans of limeade bought per week	0	1	2	3	4	5	6	14
Number of respondents	20	16	6	5	3	0	1	1

The answers to these questions are on p.138.

Q2   The weekly sales of a product are as follows: 20, 18, 14, 12 and 24 units. Calculate the standard deviation. (8 marks)

It's devious, alright...

These pages build on AS work. You've met the Standard Deviation in AS, but this time OCR people are expected to be able to work it out, with a nasty looking formula, and what's worse, use it to work out probabilities. Terrifying, no doubt. But terror won't get you anywhere, so get used to using that formula. Just plug the numbers in and work that little bleeder out.

Marketing Analysis

Businesses need to be able to analyse market data, to figure out what it all means.
*These two pages are for **AQA**, **OCR** and **Edexcel**.*

Marketing analysis uses Qualitative Techniques

1) **Qualitative** techniques involve **human judgement** rather than maths and calculation. They're particularly useful when there's **not much data** to go on, and when the time frame being investigated is long.

2) The main qualitative techniques used are **panel consensus** (See **Delphi** technique on p.17), **personal insight** and using **historical analogies** — i.e. drawing on past experiences.

Causal Methods are Quantitative Techniques which use Maths and Correlation

1) **Causal** methods use **mathematical models** and **correlation** to figure out a **cause and effect** relationship. An example of something that suits this technique is price elasticity of demand, which measures how demand for goods responds to a change in price (see p.20).

2) Using **mathematical models** managers can establish a **statistical relationship** between variables and forecast how changes in one variable affect another.

3) **Correlation** is a measure of how **closely** two variables are **related**, for example the pay of employees and their absenteeism. Correlation may be **strong** (high), **weak**, or there may be no apparent correlation at all.

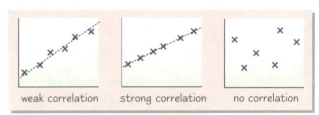
weak correlation   strong correlation   no correlation

4) It's a **useful tool**, but correlation **doesn't prove** cause and effect by itself. **Other variables** may be important — e.g. newspapers are delivered in the morning, but the sunrise doesn't make the paper fall on the doormat.

Time Series Analysis records data over Time

1) **Time series analysis** is used to reveal **underlying patterns** by recording and plotting data over time, for example the recording of **sales** over a year.

2) **Trends** are the long-term movement of a variable, for example the sales of a particular product over a number of years. Trends may be **upward**, **constant** or **downward**, but there are usually **fluctuations** around the trend.

3) **Seasonal** fluctuations repeat on a **regular** daily, weekly or yearly basis, e.g. the use of electricity over a 24-hour period, or the sale of ice lollies over a year.

4) **Cyclical** fluctuations are regular repetitions over a **medium term** period, often many years. The business cycle of boom and bust has a cyclical pattern.

upward trend   seasonality   seasonality with upward trend

5) **Random** fluctuations can be completely random. They also include the results of **major disturbances** — things like **war**, changes of government and sudden **unpredictable events** like the terrorist acts of 9/11, the outbreak of foot and mouth disease or the 2004 Asian tsunami.

Data can be Extrapolated to Predict the Future

1) The pattern revealed by data can be **extended** into the **future**.

2) Managers identify the **trend**, and **assume** the trend will carry on into the future.

3) For example, a graph of sales figures over time can show correlation between sales and time — say an upwards trend. All you do to **extrapolate** is draw a line of best fit on the graph to show the trend, and keep the line going to project the trend into the future. Then you read off the predicted sales figures. Easy.

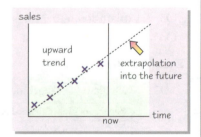

4) Extrapolation works great with **constant trends**. Unfortunately, the **pace of change** in the market can be very fast. **Customer desires** and **technological advances** change quickly. This means that extrapolations from the past don't always predict the future very accurately.

5) **Sudden unexpected events** are the biggest pitfall for extrapolation. Random fluctuations in the market due to things like **natural disasters** make extrapolation from past data look completely useless. For example, extrapolation from sales of beef in the UK in the 1980s would predict a healthy, growing market. In the 1990s, the BSE crisis meant that everything turned belly up.

Marketing Analysis

A *Moving Average* is *Updated* as *New Information* is received

1) A **moving average** is one which is recalculated as new information comes in. An example is the **inflation** rate, which is an **average** of the previous **twelve months'** price rises. The inflation rate is **updated every month**.

2) The effect of a moving average is to **smooth out data** and isolate underlying **trends** from seasonal, cyclical and random **fluctuations**. Once the trend has been isolated it can be **extrapolated** on a graph.

An example of *Moving Averages* — pay attention because it's *Tough*

Step 1 Work out the total for the **first 4 quarters**. Put it in the **4 quarter moving total** column, in the **Q4 of 2001** row.

Step 2 Work out the total for the **next 4 quarters** (2001 Q2 to 2002 Q1), and put it in the 4 quarter moving total column, beside Q1 of 2002. **Repeat** this process for the next 4 quarters, and the next, 'til you're done.

Step 3 Add the **4 quarter moving total for 2001 Q4** and the 4 quarter moving total for **2002 Q1** and put it in the **8 quarter moving total column**, in the 2002 Q1 row. **Repeat** for the rest of the 4 quarter totals.

You do this because the average calculated in <u>Step 1</u> doesn't <u>line up</u> with any of the quarters — it lines up with a point <u>between</u> Q2 and Q3 of 2001. Adding the two 4 quarter totals together takes data from <u>5 quarters</u>, with quarters 2001 Q2, Q3 and Q4 appearing twice. Because it covers 5 quarters, it's got a <u>proper midpoint</u>. If you were doing a 3 month moving average, you wouldn't have to bother with this.

Year	Quarter	Sales revenue (thousand £s)	4 quarter moving total	8 quarter moving total	Quarterly moving average
2001	1	243			
	2	250			
	3	289			261.00
	4	256	1038		264.63
2002	1	255	1050	2088	268.38
	2	267	1067	2117	270.00
	3	302	1080	2147	271.50
	4	256	1080	2160	274.25
2003	1	267	1092	2172	276.50
	2	277	1102	2194	284.88
	3	310	1110	2212	290.13
	4	315	1169	2279	
2004	1	250	1152	2321	

Step 4 **Divide** the 8 quarter total by 8, put the value in the **quarterly moving average** column in the 2001 Q3 row.

Step 5 **Repeat** this process for the rest of the **8 quarter totals**. This gives you your quarterly moving averages.

Moving Averages have Limitations

1) Moving averages are **difficult** to work out over long periods.
2) They're **no use at all** in **unstable** environments.
3) The **past** isn't always a good basis for predicting the future.
4) More recent data should be **weighted** to make it more important.
5) The periods should **match the business cycle** to capture up and down turns.

Practice Questions

Q1 What is correlation?   Q3 What are moving averages?

Q2 What is extrapolation?   Q4 What is time series analysis?

Exam Question

Q1 a) Calculate the quarterly moving average trend for the sales revenue data below (figures are in thousands). (14 marks)

2001 Q1 630   2002 Q1 621   2003 Q1 602   2004 Q1 589
    Q2 567   Q2 578   Q2 550
    Q3 552   Q3 543   Q3 502
    Q4 678   Q4 600   Q4 560

The answers to these questions are on p.138.

b) Plot the Quarterly Moving Average trend on a graph. (4 marks)

These moving averages can reach quite a speed on level ground...

Those moving averages are hard to get your head round, but not impossible. You'll need to really make sure that you genuinely, honestly follow all the steps for calculating them. Don't kid yourself that you get it if you don't. Read the hints for each step, and you <u>can</u> understand it. Honest. It's doable. Don't be tempted to skip it, because it may be in the exam.

Marketing Decision-Making

*These pages are for **AQA**, **OCR** and **Edexcel**.*

Marketing *is about* Making Decisions *to suit the market*

1) Marketing isn't just about market research, or marketing activity. It's about **making decisions** and making sure that all the necessary **resources** are in place to allow the business to take the **right action**.

2) It's often very **hard** for managers to come to the right marketing decisions. Markets are constantly evolving — **consumers' needs** change and develop and the rapid pace of technological change creates **uncertainties**. It's **not easy** to figure out what the market for mobile phones, handheld games or even women's sports shoes will be like in 5 years' time.

Scientific Marketing *is a* Systematic *approach*

1) The **scientific marketing model** attempts to **eliminate guesswork** and **bias**. It does this by emphasising **objective** decision-making and the use of **factual** and **numerical** data.

2) The model consists of a series of **stages**: setting **objectives**, **gathering data**, **analysing** data, forming a **hypothesis** (a **marketing strategy**), **testing** it out, **evaluating** it and then **changing** the strategy if necessary.

3) It's **scientific** because marketers examine a hypothesis, consider alternatives and analyse results, just like **scientists** do.

4) **Market research** is **fundamental** to the procedure — it's impossible to form a hypothesis or test it without **good data**.

5) There's also wide use of **quantitative data**, **statistical analysis** and **mathematical modelling**, for example calculating and modelling price elasticity by looking at the correlation between price and demand.

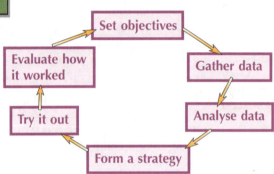

Scientific Marketing *has* Pros *and* Cons *versus* Gut Feeling

1) The scientific method is only as **reliable** as the **data** that it uses. **Dodgy market research** gives **dodgy data**, which gives **dodgy decisions**.

See p.6-9 of this book and p.12-13 of the AS book for more on market research.

2) Market research data can be **difficult** or **expensive** to come up with. It may be more **practical** to rely on **past experience** or **gut feeling**, rather than going to the far end of the earth to find out the data. In a stable market, when there's lots of time to figure out a decision, the scientific method is best.

3) Gut feeling is very **risky** because it isn't based on rational thought or quantifiable data. However, the more **experience** a manager has, the better their decisions are likely to be. **Experience** can fine-tune gut feeling.

4) The scientific method gives more reliable results, but it tends to churn out boring, predictable decisions. When management want an off-the-wall creative solution, it makes sense to make decisions based on hunches.

5) **Small firms** operating in **niche markets** do not have the **resources** or **specialist skills** to properly make use of the scientific model. New small businesses don't have enough **experience** to fall back on, either. This "double whammy" is one of the reasons for the high **failure** rate of new businesses.

Marketing Managers *use the* AIDA Model *to develop* Promotional Campaigns

1) The **AIDA** model is used to develop promotional campaigns. It's mainly applied to **above-the-line** activities such as **advertising** through the media, although it can be applied to below-the-line promotion.

2) The idea behind the **AIDA** model is that **effective advertising** goes through **four stages**:

Below-the-line = special offers, direct mail, PR etc. See p.21.

1) **A**ttention	First, the advertiser aims to grab the consumer's **attention**. An **amusing** or **controversial** ad campaign works well for this.
2) **I**nterest	Next, the advertiser aims to get the consumer **interested** in the product. The ads try to **differentiate** the brand from rival brands.
3) **D**esire	The focus is on **persuading** the consumer he or she **wants the product**. Advertising may portray a **desirable image**. **Free samples** may be offered.
4) **A**ct	The aim now is to get the consumer to **act** and **actually buy** the product. **Sales promotions** (e.g. low initial price, three for price of two) are often used.

Marketing Decision-Making

DAGMAR is a model for Promotion and Advertising

1) **DAGMAR** stands for **D**efining **A**dvertising **G**oals for **M**easured **A**dvertising **R**esults.

2) DAGMAR aims to **increase awareness** of the product. It's based on the idea that **customers** move through a series of **five stages** when buying a product.

Stage	Consumer	Promotion
Unawareness	**Doesn't know** about the product.	Media advertising.
Awareness	Has a **vague awareness** of the product.	Media advertising.
Comprehension	**Recognises** and **knows about** the product.	Support through product information.
Conviction	**Prefers** the product to others.	Advertising to reinforce brand differentiation.
Action	**Purchases** the product (hooray).	Personal selling.

3) The **promotional mix** is designed to move the customer **smoothly** through the stages.

4) The DAGMAR model follows the psychological pattern of **buyer behaviour**, (see p.5). For **impulse**, or **low-value** sales (e.g. an ice-cream) the customer may blend stages together, and recognise and understand the product as soon as they're aware of it, which lets them take action quickly. For **high value** sales, the process of increasing awareness can take months.

Promotional mix = the different sorts of promotion used.

5) Some things stop the consumer from moving through the five stages — competitor activity, unwillingness to buy and memory lapses can all slow things down.

Ansoff's Matrix is used for Strategic Decisions

1) Ansoff's Matrix is used to analyse a business' **markets** and **products**.

2) **Market penetration** involves selling the same goods to the same market. The aim is to **encourage greater use** amongst existing users, or to prompt users of rival products to **switch brand**. It's not risky.

3) **Product development** is selling **new products** to **existing markets**. It's used when the market has good **growth potential** and the business has high market share, strong R&D and a good **competitive advantage**.

	Products	
	Existing	New
Markets Existing	Market penetration	Product development
New	Market extension or development	Diversification

4) **Market development** is selling **existing products** to **new markets**, for example **new market segments**, or **new geographical areas**. It's particularly relevant to **product-led businesses** with considerable **production assets**, who can easily make lots of identical products and sell them in new areas. Market development can be **risky**, unless the firm has spotted a **clear new market opportunity**.

5) **Diversification** involves selling **new products** to **new markets**. Diversification is a **very risky** strategy. It's appropriate when a business really needs to diversify to reduce dependence on a **limited product range**, when there's promise of **high profits**, or when the company has **cash reserves** to fall back on.

Businesses also use SWOT Analysis for marketing decision-making

The SWOT model is covered in the **AS book**, and it's also covered on **p.116** of this book. So go check it out.

Practice Questions

Q1 List the steps in the AIDA model.

Q2 What are the stages a customer needs to be moved through in the DAGMAR model?

Q3 Outline the 4 parts of Ansoff's Matrix.

Q4 Why might a business seek to diversify?

Exam Question

Q1 Explain two problems a business might face if it makes marketing decisions based solely on the scientific marketing model.

(6 marks)

Follow your gut feeling — my gut says "have a ham sandwich"...

It's a bit odd that you're expected to seriously weigh up "scientific method" versus "oh, well, just guess". Thing is, it isn't as simple as that. The data you'd use for a scientific marketing approach might not be very good. An experienced business person who's been there, done that and bought the T-shirt doesn't always need to work everything out with a pencil.

Marketing Planning and Strategy

Obviously, businesses have to plan everything, especially their marketing activities.
*These pages are for **AQA**, **Edexcel** and **OCR**.*

Marketing Planning is about turning Objectives into Action

1) Marketing planning sets out a **coordinated action plan** for operations, finance and personnel functions, so that they meet the firm's **corporate** and **marketing** objectives. Marketing plans **integrate business functions together**.

2) A marketing plan provides **background information** into the nature of the business and its markets, describes the **marketing strategies** that'll be employed and the **detailed action plans** and **budgets** that those strategies need.

3) Some people describe marketing as the **interface** between the **customer's needs** and the **other management functions**. Marketing is the central, **integrating** function which makes sure that the products provided meet the customer's needs — in terms of **specification**, **price**, **availability** etc.

Everything goes through marketing.

4) There's a **trade-off** between meeting the **customer's needs** and **making profit**. **Asset-led marketing** (see p.2) acknowledges that businesses need to **play to their strengths** and utilise their assets effectively, so it's the best placed to please the customer and the finance department at the same time.

5) Hugh Davidson is a marketing guru who believes that marketing concerns **everybody** within a business and it's **everyone's responsibility** to build **added value** on behalf of the customer. His ideas of what marketing should do to make sure it turns objectives into results are summarised as **POISE**:

Profitable	Marketing must balance value to the **customer** with **profitability**.
Offensive	Marketing needs to be **proactive**, take **risks** and **invest** for the long term.
Integrated	Marketing is **everyone's responsibility**, in **every department** of the business.
Strategic	Marketing should be done after **careful analysis** and evaluation of alternatives.
Effectively communicated	Marketing requires **commitment** and **cooperation** from **all staff** and departments.

A marketing plan Asks Questions... and Answers them

In order to develop a marketing plan a business needs to ask and answer some **key questions** about itself, including:

Question the business must ask...	How to answer it
Where are we **now**?	Do a **market audit**.
Where do we **want** to go?	Set **corporate objectives**. Set **marketing objectives**.
How will we get there?	Devise **strategies** – broad methods. Plan **tactics** – specific, detailed plans.
How do we **know** when we've **arrived**?	**Evaluate progress**, compare progress with **measurable targets**.

"What plan was behind this vile knitwear?" pondered Chandra Funnel, the great marketing detective.

Marketing Plans are Great, but they can Go Wrong

Marketing plans are great because...

Developing a marketing plan **focuses marketing activity**, provides a **plan** for **all departments**, picks out marketing **opportunities** and **anticipates** potential problems.

Strategic marketing planning aims to cope with change — but sometimes it fails to cope.

Strategic planning **anticipates change**, provides clear objectives and **direction** and encourages **effective planning**. The process of **analysis** improves **understanding** of the market. But... the **fast pace of change** may render plans redundant. Also, if strategies are **vague** and the information used is **out of date**, they won't cope well with future changes.

Marketing plans can go wrong when...

The **business functions aren't well integrated**, managers are **short-term in outlook**, **bureaucracy** overwhelms the planning process, there isn't enough good **market research** or **analysis**, the **business culture** resists taking **responsibility** for marketing, there isn't enough **working capital** to pay for the best strategies.

Marketing Planning and Strategy

The marketing planning *Process* is *Cyclical*

1) Setting **goals**:	**Mission statement** and overall **corporate objectives**.
2) **Analysing** the situation:	**Marketing audit**, **SWOT** analysis, marketing **assumptions**.
3) Coming up with **strategy**:	Marketing **objectives** and **strategy**. **Forecast** of expected **results**, **target** setting. **Alternative plans** in case things **change**.
4) **Allocating resources**:	**Marketing budget** and **detailed action plan**.
5) **Monitoring** and **adjusting** strategy:	**Checking performance** against **targets**. **Adjusting** if necessary.

Back to step 3.

Analysis and *Audits* look at *Internal* and *External Factors* and *Trends*

1) A market audit is an appraisal of **internal** and **external** factors affecting the business, e.g:

Business Environment	The Market	Internal Audit	Competition
Political and Legal	Size and growth	Products	Competitor's sales
Economic	Segments	Market share	Their profit margins
Social	Buyer habits	Current marketing mix	Their market share
Technical	Cost of entry	Strengths and weaknesses	Their marketing mix
International	Opportunities	Human resources	Their plans

2) Various **tools** are used in **analysis**, e.g. **PEST**, **SWOT** and **Cost/Benefit analysis**. There's more about these analysis tools on p.116-119, in the Objectives and Strategy section, because they're used for **more** than just marketing.

3) Various **assumptions** about **external factors** are built into the marketing plan. These include the future rate of **growth** of the **economy**, future **tax** rates, **demographics** and **competitor activities**.

Objectives and *Strategies* set out *Marketing Aims* and *Directions*

1) **Market objectives** say which products will be sold in which markets.

2) They can be **qualitative** (**describing** policies, brand image, product quality, product development) and **quantitative** (**specific aims** for market share, sales revenue, market penetration and profitability).

3) Marketing strategies set out the **broad plans** from which action plans and tactics are determined. They specify the **target market** and the **marketing mix**, (product, price, place and promotion).

Action Plans and *Budgets* give *Detail* of how it'll all happen

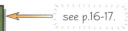 see p.16-17.

1) Action plans are detailed plans for individual marketing activities, e.g. the sales plan and the promotion plan.

2) Budgets are constructed in line with the action plans. Managers must **identify costs**, for example **advertising**, **research**, **distribution** and **personal selling** costs. Budgets are categorised by product, department or activity.

3) The whole plan has to be **monitored constantly**, in order to assess performance, take corrective action, control costs and adapt the plan if it isn't working. It's important to set measurable targets for progress checking.

Practice Questions

Q1   Why is marketing called the central, integrating function?

Q2   What does "POISE" stand for?

Q3   List three factors you'd expect to see in a marketing audit.

Q4   Give examples of two qualitative and two quantitative marketing objectives.

Exam Questions

Q1	Explain the external factors that a business must take into account when developing its marketing plan.	(6 marks)
Q2	Examine the possible benefits of marketing planning to small businesses.	(8 marks)

Plans, plans, plans and more plans, nothing but plans...

All the exam syllabuses are very keen on getting you to see things in terms of analysing, planning and evaluating. Every topic is looked at from the point of view of a business manager deciding the best course of action to take. Marketing is no exception, especially as it's so crucial to getting the big corporate objectives on track — no sales means no money.

Marketing Budget and Sales Forecasting

The marketing budget specifies the finances available for spending on marketing activities, and contains sales targets. These pages are for AQA and Edexcel.

A **Marketing Budget** is a **Quantified Plan** for **Marketing Activities**

1) Before a budget is set, the **market audit** is done — marketing managers analyse information before they set their **marketing objectives** and **strategies**. Then they come up with an **action plan** of what they're going to do, which is where the budget comes in — they need to say how much money they'll **spend** on marketing, and how much money they expect to **make** through marketing.

2) **Sales budgets** contain **sales targets** for the business in terms of volume, market share, sales growth etc.

3) **Expenditure budgets** set out the level of **spending** needed to cover the **costs** of all marketing activities — advertising, market research, distribution, personal selling etc.

4) Budgets may be categorised in terms of **products**, **departments** and **marketing activity**. Above-the-line and below-the-line activities may have separate budgets.

Expenditure Budgets can be Set in various ways

1) **Incremental budgeting** involves adding a small additional amount to the previous year's allocation, to take account of inflation. It's a very common method, because it's easy to understand and easy to do. However, it doesn't plan for unexpected events, so it can leave the firm unable to respond to new opportunities or threats.

2) **Sales-related budgeting** allocates marketing spending based on the sales revenue that the product will generate.

3) In **task-based budgeting**, marketing tasks are costed out and finances shared out accordingly.

4) "**Competitor parity**" budgeting means matching competitor spending. It's difficult to accurately determine what your competitors are spending on their marketing. They aren't likely to fax you their budget first so that you can copy it, after all. Businesses don't tend to base their budget 100% on competitors — competitor action is likely to affect the expenditure budget a bit, though.

5) The **financial state of the business** is a huge factor. Rather obviously, small businesses and new businesses are more likely to be restrained by what they can afford.

Sales Budgets depend on Past Sales, the Market, Objectives and Finances

1) **Sales targets** within sales budgets are set by looking at past figures and **extrapolating** (see next page).

2) Sales targets depend on **market conditions** — the **business cycle** and **competitor** actions can affect demand.

3) The **financial position** of the business and the **expenditure budget** are a factor. Spending a lot on marketing a product means that you'd expect it to **sell** pretty well.

Budget Setting has its Pitfalls

1) It's best to **consult with staff** when setting the budget. Staff **resent** not being involved in setting targets.

2) On the other hand, staff shouldn't have too much control over budget setting, because they'll set targets that are **easily reached**, or ask for more money than they need so that they won't **overspend**. Managers' **egos** are a factor as well — managers may see a large budget as an indicator of **status**.

3) Preparing budgets can be very **time consuming**, especially when there's lots of negotiation.

4) Basing an expenditure budget purely on financial position has its drawbacks. It means that the business spends a lot on marketing when sales are high, and less on marketing when sales are low — when it needs it most.

5) With **incremental budgeting**, managers may be tempted to spend the **whole budget** to make sure they get at least the same amount in next year's budget. This isn't a cost-effective way to behave.

Marketing Budgets need to be Justified by the Product

1) Budgets need to be justified in relation to the finances available, and the likely **return**. A product with a **high predicted rate of return** will earn itself a **bigger expenditure budget**.

2) **Product portfolio analysis** and the **Boston Matrix** (see p.19) are used to determine which products should be supported by extra spending and which "milked" to provide revenue for other marketing activities.

3) The **product life cycle** (p.18) is a useful model. Marketing expenditure is likely to be high during the **launch** and **growth** phases of a product, or when **extension strategies** are being used.

Marketing Budget and Sales Forecasting

Sales Forecasting aims to Predict the Future

1) **Sales forecasting** predicts the **future sales** of a product. This allows managers to set **sales targets**. Sales performance can be measured against those targets.

2) Sales forecasts allow the **finance** department to produce **cash flow** forecasts — once they know how much the business is expected to sell, they can work out how much money is expected to come in.

3) Sales forecasts also allow **production** and **human resources** departments to gear up for the expected level of sales. They can make sure that they have the right amount of machinery, stock and staff.

Backdata and Extrapolation are Quantitative techniques for Forecasting Sales

1) **Backdata** is **data from the past**. Sales backdata from last year can be used to predict likely sales for this year. Managers look for trends in the data and **extrapolate** them forward. Moving averages and time series analysis (see p.10-11) help to identify trends in sales backdata.

2) Extrapolation is a great way of predicting sales as long as trends stay **constant**. When there's a major upheaval in the market (rare, but it does happen), extrapolation will lead you up the garden path.

3) Managers also use **market research data** to predict future sales.

4) **Test marketing** can be used to provide sales forecasts. The product is launched within a limited geographical area. Test marketing gives **accurate data**, and a **reliable** indicator of **demand**. Managers can **learn lessons** from the test marketing exercise and apply them to the full scale national launch.

5) On the other hand, test marketing allows **competitors** to look at the product before the full launch.

Qualitative Techniques such as the Delphi Method are also used

Qualitative techniques call for **human judgement**. They're particularly important when data is scarce. They include personal **insight** (hunches), **panel consensus**, and **experience** (e.g. referring to previous life cycles of similar products).

1) The **Delphi** method asks questions of a **panel of experts** in order to predict the future. The idea is that you get better prediction from human experts than from extrapolating trends.

2) The firm asks each expert **individually** for their opinion of what'll happen in the market. The experts' answers are **anonymous**. The firm puts the experts' opinions together in **summary** form, and sends the summary back to all the experts for their **comments**. The firm then summarises the comments and sends them out a second time for **further comments** and views. They repeat the process as necessary.

3) Because the original responses are **anonymous**, and each expert is asked questions **individually**, the experts won't be **swayed** by reading what the leading industry guru, or their arch-enemy, has to say.

4) The process of repeatedly summarising and asking for more comments is supposed to lead the experts towards a **consensus** view that they all agree on.

Practice Questions

Q1   List the ways budgets can be allocated.

Q2   What's the difference between sales-related budgeting and task-based budgeting?

Q3   What are the advantages of sales forecasts?

Q4   What is backdata?

Q5   What is the Delphi Method?

Exam Questions

Q1   Given that forecasts can be wrong, should firms bother to forecast at all?   (12 marks)

Q2   How might a company in business-to-business sales set their marketing budget?   (8 marks)

Ancient weirdness ahoy...

Interesting (or perhaps not) fact — the Delphi method is named after an oracle from ancient Greek times. There was a priestess at a place called Delphi who would chew laurel leaves (poisonous, by the way) and hallucinate the answers to people's questions. Nowadays researchers ask industry big kahunas to give their opinions instead. That's progress, folks.

The Marketing Mix: Product

Marketing mix = what the product's like, what the price is, how it's sold, and where it's sold. For **OCR**, useful for **Edexcel**.

Value Analysis makes sure that Products are Good Value for Money

1) Businesses try to make their products **good value for money** — both for **themselves** and for the **customer**.

2) Value analysis looks at ways of **reducing costs** of making, warehousing, distributing and selling the product — these costs should be reduced as far as possible, without reducing the product **quality** too much.

Products have a Life Cycle from Development to Decline

1) The product life cycle shows the **sales** of a product over **time**.

2) It's useful for planning **marketing strategies** and changing the **marketing mix**.

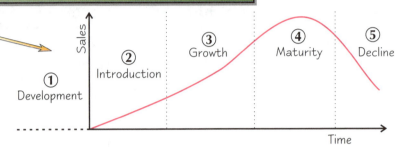

1 — Development

1) The **research and development** (R&D) department **develops** the product.

2) The **marketing** department does **market research**.

3) The **costs** are **high**, and there aren't any sales yet to cover the costs.

4) New product development has a **high failure rate**. This is because there's often **not enough demand**, or because the business can't make the product **cheaply** enough to let them make a profit.

2 — Introduction

1) The product is **launched**, either in one market or in several markets. It's sometimes launched with **complementary** products — e.g. the Playstation was launched with games.

2) Businesses often **promote** the product heavily to build sales — but businesses need to make sure they've got enough **resources** and **capacity** to **meet the demand** that promotions create.

3) The **initial price** of the product may be **high** to cover **promotional costs**. This is called **price skimming** (see p.20).

4) Alternatively, the price can start off **low** to encourage sales. This is called **penetration pricing** (see p.20).

5) Sales go up, but the sales revenue has to pay for the high **fixed cost** of development **before** the product can make a **profit**. Businesses usually ditch products with disappointing sales at this stage.

6) There aren't many **outlets** for the new product yet, and competition is **limited**.

3 — Growth

1) Sales grow fast. There are **new customers** and **repeat** customers.

2) **Economies of scale** mean the price of manufacturing a unit goes down the more you make, so **profits rise**.

3) The **pricing** strategy may change.

4) **Competitors** may be attracted to the market. Promotion points out **differences** from competitors.

5) The product is often **improved** or **developed**.

6) Rising sales encourage **more outlets** to stock the product.

4 — Maturity

1) **Sales** reach a **peak** and profitability increases because the **fixed costs** of **development** have been **paid for**.

2) Sales start to go down. The price is often reduced to stimulate **demand**, which makes it less profitable.

3) At this stage, there aren't many new consumers. Some products are forced out of the market.

5 — Decline

1) The product doesn't **appeal** to consumers any more. **Sales fall** rapidly and profits decrease.

2) On the other hand, the product may just stay profitable if **promotional costs** are **low** enough.

3) If sales carry on falling, the product is **withdrawn** or **sold** to another business. This is called **divestment**.

The Marketing Mix: Product

Businesses need a *Variety* of *Products* — a *Mixed Product Portfolio*

1) The **product portfolio** is the **range** of different products and brands that a business holds. For example, Unilever has a massive portfolio including Marmite, Knorr, Domestos, Timotei, Carte d'Or and Walls Solero.

2) Businesses aim to have a **product portfolio** with a number of **different products**, all at **different stages** of the **product life cycle**.

← *This is the key bit.*

The *Boston Matrix* is a model of *Portfolio Analysis*

Each circle in the matrix represents one product. The size of each circle represents the turnover of the product.

The Boston Matrix compares **market growth** with **market share**.

1) All **new products** are **question marks** (sometimes called **problem children** or **wildcats**) and they have a small market share and high market growth. They aren't profitable **yet** and need **heavy marketing** to give them a chance of success. A business can do various things with question marks — **brand building**, **harvesting** (maximising sales or profit in the short term) or **divestment** (selling the product off).

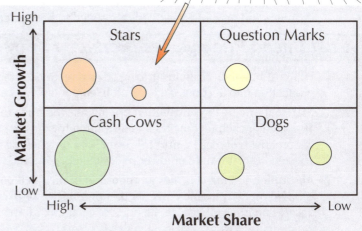

2) **Stars** have high market growth and high market share — they have the best future potential. They're in their profitable **growth** phase — they're future cash cows.

3) **Cash cows** have high market share but low market growth. They're in their **maturity** phase. They've already been promoted and they're produced in high volumes, so costs are low. Cash cows bring in plenty of **money**.

4) **Dogs** have low market share and low market growth. They're pretty much a lost cause. The business will either harvest profit in the short term, or sell them off.

The Boston Matrix lets a business see if it has a good balanced **product portfolio**. A balanced product portfolio means that a business can use money from its **cash cows** to **invest** in its **question marks** so they can become **stars**.

The Boston Matrix **isn't infallible**. A product's **cash flow** and **profit** may be **different** from what the matrix suggests (e.g. a dog may have strong cash flow and be profitable despite falling sales).

When you use the Boston Matrix to evaluate a product portfolio in the **exam**, make sure you do it in the **context** of the **case study in the question**. This means looking at the **current market position** (brand image compared to other brands), the **market share** and **external factors** like the **economy**, or any **future events** mentioned in the question.

Product Differentiation markets products to make them *Stand Out*

1) Bog standard **mass market** products like washing powder or pasta sauce tend to be **all the same**, more or less.

2) They need **product differentiation** to make them stand out from the competition. Clever marketing and branding makes customers see the product as special, or particularly suited to them and their needs.

Practice Questions

Q1 Why is profitability low at introduction, but high at maturity in the product life cycle?

Q2 In which stage of the product life cycle would you find: a) cash cows, b) dogs, c) stars?

Q3 From which element of the product portfolio would a business get money to invest in its question marks?

Exam Question

Q1 A manufacturer makes cathode ray tube TVs, plasma screen TVs, VHS recorders, DVD players and DVD recorders. Evaluate their product portfolio. (10 marks)

They're alive, they're alive...

OK, some of this might look a bit familiar. The thing is, for OCR AS level you're only expected to have a basic understanding of product portfolio analysis, whereas for OCR A2 level, you're expected to have more detailed knowledge of the Boston Matrix. And for Edexcel, you need to know how businesses plan out their marketing mix.

The Marketing Mix: Price

*These pages are for **OCR** and **Edexcel**.*

Price *is an important part of the* Marketing Mix

1) Price determines the **revenue** that businesses get. Price is a **balance** between being **competitive** and being **profitable**. Too high, and people **won't buy**. Too low, and you won't make enough **profit**.

2) In a **competitive** market, customers have lots of **choice** — so price is an **important** factor. In a **monopoly**, there's only one seller in the market, and customers have no choice. A monopoly seller can charge **high** prices.

3) The price must **fit in** with the other aspects of the **marketing mix**. It must fit in with the **product** — the **quality** of the product, the customer's **desire** to have it and the **features** and **benefits** they get. It must fit in with the way that the business intends to **distribute** the product, and the way they intend to **promote** it — some distribution channels and promotion methods are suited to **high price** luxury goods, and others are suited to **discount** goods.

Cost Based Pricing *uses* Production Costs *to work out* Price

1) **Full-cost based** or **cost plus pricing** takes direct and indirect costs of production into account, and adds a **fixed percentage** called the **mark-up**. See p.31 for more on costing.

2) **Marginal pricing** or **contribution pricing** sets the price to be more than the **variable costs** per unit. The price of each unit makes a **contribution** towards the **fixed costs**. If there are **enough sales**, the product will make a **profit** — even if it's only selling for a little bit more than the variable costs. This means that firms can lower prices temporarily, and can offer special low prices for special orders. *Fixed costs = machines, admin wages etc.*

3) **Absorption pricing** allocates a **proportion** of the **fixed costs** to each unit, so the price is based on the **variable costs** per unit plus a slice of **fixed costs** per unit. It's called **absorption** pricing because the price of each unit **absorbs** part of the **fixed costs**. *Variable costs = production wages, raw materials etc.*

4) **Target-based pricing** sets the price based on the **target profit** that the firm decided they needed to make when they set their objectives. The price has to cover variable costs, fixed costs per unit and the target profit.

Market Based Pricing *uses* Market Demand *to work out* Price

1) **Penetration pricing** is when a product has a low initial price to get into the market. As the volume of sales goes up, the price is increased. A magazine might start with a low initial price to get readers buying it.

2) **Price discrimination** is when different prices are charged for the same product — e.g. **plane tickets** vary in price depending on when you travel. Different groups of customers can be charged different prices.

3) **Price skimming**, or **creaming** means starting with a high price and reducing it later. The price can go down when the product has achieved economies of scale. **High tech** goods, e.g. video cameras and digital music players use this pricing strategy. *A product can keep a high price if it has strong brand values, a USP, or if it's meant to be seen as exclusive / luxury.*

4) **Psychological pricing** bases the price on customers' **expectation** about what to pay. For example, a high price may make people think the product is high quality. £99.99 seems better than £100 even though it's only 1p difference.

Competition Based Pricing *sets price based on* Competitors' Prices

1) Market leaders often act as **price maker**, or **price leader**. They set the price, and other businesses follow.

2) Competition reduces prices. In very competitive markets, **buyers dictate the price**, and sellers have to **take whatever price** the buyer is willing to pay — e.g. milk producers selling to supermarkets are **price takers**.

3) **Destroyer pricing** or **predatory pricing** is when a business **deliberately lowers prices** to force another business **out of the market** — e.g. **supermarket price wars**, when supermarkets cut the price of their own brand goods to incredibly low levels. Predatory pricing is a **gamble** — the predatory business usually makes a **loss** on the product. They either need to be making enough profit on other products to **cover the loss**, or the rival business needs to go out of the market pretty darn quick so that the **price can go up** again.

Price Elasticity *is the relationship between* Price *and* Demand

Raising prices reduces the level of **demand**, and vice versa. **Price elastic** products show a **large** fall in demand after a small rise in price (or vice versa). **Price inelastic** products don't have much change in demand after price changes.

Price elasticity of demand depends on level of **competition** and **ease of switching**. When customers can easily switch to a **rival product**, raising your price makes them ditch your product and buy the rival product **instead** — **reducing demand** for your product. So, when you discuss setting or changing prices, bear the **market conditions** in mind.

Marketing Mix: Promotion and Distribution

Above-the-Line Promotion is Advertising through the Media

1) Advertising uses various **media** including print, film, TV, radio, Internet, hoardings, even the sides of buses. The choice of media depends partly on the **number of target customers** and the number of **readers** or **viewers** who'll **see** the ad. Ideally, a business wants its ads to be seen by as **many** of the target market as possible.

2) The **impact** of an ad is very important — especially in the "unawareness" part of the **DAGMAR** model and the "attention" part of the **AIDA** model, where the aim is to **grab the consumer** and make them **aware** of the brand.

3) Advertising **costs** a business **money**. The cost of an advertising campaign must be **worth it** in terms of the **extra sales** it creates. TV adverts at prime-time viewing times are very expensive, but they reach a lot of people.

4) **Specialist media** are used to selectively advertise specialist products to **niche markets**. For example, a manufacturer of fish hooks would advertise in a monthly fly fishing magazine, not in the Telegraph newspaper.

5) **Mass media** are mainly (but not always) used to advertise **mass market consumer** products and services.

Below-the-Line promotion is Everything Else apart from advertising

1) **Sales promotions** are things like "buy one get one free" **special offers** (BOGOF), competitions, free gifts, point of sale displays, sponsorship, and trade-ins (e.g. paying for part of a new car by giving the seller your old car). Sales promotions can be aimed straight at the **customer** to **raise awareness** or **increase sales**. Manufacturers also do sales promotions aimed at the **retailer** to encourage them to **stock** more of their products.

2) **Direct mail** means **mailshots** sent out to customers. The customer usually hasn't **asked** to receive them. Businesses that keep information about their customers on a database can **target** their direct mail to particular consumer groups. Untargeted direct mail or "**junk mail**" is a **waste of money**, and gets thrown away.

3) **Public relations** (**PR**) is a firm's attempt to put out a **good message** about itself and its products or services. PR includes **press releases** sent to the media and special **promotional events**, e.g. new product launch parties.

4) **Personal selling** or **direct selling** is personal communication between a **sales person** and a customer. Personal selling includes **sales assistants** in shops as well as travelling sales people and phone sales people.

5) **Sponsorship** of **events** makes consumers aware of a firm and their product. It also gives the firm a good image.

Businesses choose Distribution Channels to suit both Business and Product

1) **Distribution channels** between manufacturer and consumer can have several **intermediaries** such as importer, wholesaler and retailer — or they can be **direct**, with no intermediaries.

2) It's more **profitable** to **sell direct** — intermediaries take their cut of the selling price. Businesses that sell direct (e.g. over the Internet) can offer **lower prices**, because they don't have to pay for retail premises or staff. Also, the fewer intermediaries in the distribution chain, the more control the manufacturer has over how the product is promoted, and what the final selling price will be.

3) It's a lot less **hassle** to sell through **wholesalers**. Wholesalers can take care of distributing the product to lots of retailers, which **cuts down paperwork**. Wholesalers **break bulk** for businesses — they buy a job lot of goods and pay for them up front, which increases the manufacturer's working capital.

4) Distribution must suit the **product** as well. Everyday, **standard goods** are distributed as widely as possible. **Luxury goods** are sold in a **small** number of **exclusive** shops — this helps preserve a luxury brand image.

Practice Questions

Q1 What is absorption pricing?

Q2 What is penetration pricing?

Q3 Give two examples of below-the-line promotion.

Q4 Why do businesses use wholesalers?

Exam Question

Q1 An electronics manufacturer is about to launch a new range of PDAs (personal digital assistants) aimed at the non-expert consumer, with fewer features and details than their top range. Discuss the factors which influence the price it will set for the new range of PDAs. (12 marks)

Distribute your attention evenly over the pages...

The different aspects of the marketing mix have an impact on each other. For example, price and product must go together to give the right impression to customers — e.g. luxury soap is expensive. Distribution must fit in, too. Packaging can be seen as a blend of promotion and product — it's part of the product in a way, but it also promotes the product.

Accounting Perspective and Concepts

This section builds on the Accounting and Finance section in AS Business Studies.
*These two pages are for **OCR** and **Edexcel**, but they're useful for **AQA** too.*

All businesses need Accounting Data for Decision Making

1) In order for managers to make **informed decisions** they must have access to **accurate** and **recent** financial information. They need to know **how much** their **assets** are worth, how much they **owe**, and **when** money comes in to the business or leaves the business.

2) By **law**, limited companies must produce two sets of **final accounts** — annual **profit and loss accounts** that detail the company's performance over a year, and a **balance sheet** that shows assets and liabilities.

3) In addition, companies produce a **cash flow statement** showing the **flow of money** in and out of the business. The data is used both for planning for the future and controlling the operations of the business.

4) The law requires businesses to give information about their finances, and present their final accounts in a particular way, to make sure they're not hiding anything. This is called the **disclosure requirement**.

> *Balance sheet, profit and loss account and cash flow statement are called final accounts.*

Stakeholders use accounts to measure the performance of the business, and help them make decisions, e.g.

1) **Managers** use all this information to make **internal** decisions. **Employees** can also use the accounts to help them decide whether the business provides good career prospects.

2) The data is also used **externally** for investment decisions by existing and potential **shareholders**.

3) **Suppliers** use a firm's accounts to decide if they want to offer the firm credit.

4) **Competitors** use accounts to see how a business is doing, and to figure out what the business might do next.

Financial Planning can be Short, Medium or Long Term

1) In the **short term** a business needs to be able to **pay the wages** and its **suppliers** in order to survive.

2) **Medium-term** planning is for growth — things like **product** improvements, new products/services, research and development (R&D), expanding the workforce, **training** programmes and improving marketing.

3) **Long term planning** is about working towards the company's **long-term goals**, e.g. gaining a dominant market share, achieving growth over 5 or 10 years etc.

Managers use Other information Alongside financial information

Managers use financial information to help them to make **good decisions** and come up with sensible plans. **Other information** is used to help put the accounting information in **context**.

1) The **marketing** department can generate information on **predicted sales**, **competitor activity** and any changes in the **target market**.

2) The **production** department can supply information on production **capacity**, research and design of **new products** and any changes to the **supply** of raw materials.

3) The **human resources** department can supply information on the current **wage bill**. They can also predict what the wage bill will be if there are **changes** to the workforce — e.g. some of the employees are promoted to a higher pay grade.

Some of the information comes from **internal** sources (recording and predicting events **within the business**) and some is gathered from **external** sources (recording and predicting events in the **market**).

Information Technology is used in Accounting

1) **Accounting software** allows managers to instantly call up the **financial data** they need. They can instantly see data about assets, liabilities, overheads etc.

2) Managers can run **final reports** instantly. They can check the profit and loss statement or the balance sheet **every month** at the touch of a button.

3) Computer software can work out **financial ratios** (see p.40-44) so that managers can **quickly** analyse the financial health of the business.

4) Financial and accounting software also makes it easy to manage **day-to-day** financial activity — e.g. sending out invoices and paying suppliers.

Joe had given up asking for a proper computer system.

5) It's important that financial decisions are made with accurate, up-to-date information. Larger firms use **management information systems** (see p.122) that provide recent, valid data from across the functions of a firm.

Accounting Perspective and Concepts

Accounts *are produced according to* Seven Accounting Principles

① Consistency — all the company's accounts must be done in the same way.
1) This consistency rule allows the user of the accounts to have **confidence** in the information.
2) The company has to formulate an **accounting policy** and **consistently apply it** to all its accounts.

② Going concern — assume the company will keep trading.
1) This rule requires that a company will **continue to exist** for the **foreseeable future**.
2) If the business can't pay its **overheads** and its **debts**, it may be put under a different set of accounting rules and go into **administration**, or even be **liquidated**.

③ Matching — money owed is "matched" to the month of the transaction, not the month when the debt is paid.
1) The date when cash is received may bear **no relationship** to the date when business was done — e.g. a manufacturer sells products to a retailer in February but doesn't receive the cash for that transaction until April. The money owed to the company by the retailer is recorded in February, not April.
2) This lets the company **compare** one period of the year with another in a **fair** manner. It takes away the **coincidence** of when money is actually received — and it is a coincidence, because the debtor could just as easily have paid a month earlier or a month later.

④ Materiality — really small amounts can be ignored.
1) Assets, liabilities or events which make "**no material difference**" to the final account can be ignored.
2) For example, you **needn't bother** to calculate and enter a value for the seven paper clips found in the drawer when completing a stock valuation for a company with £200 000 worth of stock. The value of those paper clips will make **no material difference** to the company's final profit or loss account.

⑤ Objectivity — accounts must be based on fact, not opinion.
1) This rule is to avoid **falsehood** and **bias** in producing final accounts. Assets must be listed as what they're really worth, not what you'd like them to be worth.
2) **Over-optimistic** or **over-cautious** accounts may not be objective.

⑥ Prudence — "if in doubt, overstate your losses and understate your profits".
1) By overstating losses and understating profits, you'll **never** end up with **less** money than you expect, and you might well end up with **more** money than you expect.
2) **Managers** tend to be **over-optimistic** — e.g. they may overstate the ability of a customer to pay, or understate the future level of bad debt. Prudence is designed to **balance out** this tendency.
3) The principle of prudence is also called the principle of **conservatism**.

⑦ Realisation — this is when goods and services change hands.
1) The goods or services are "**realised**" when the **legal title** to them is transferred from seller to buyer.
2) The point in time when this happens may not be the same as the point at which **money** changes hands.

Practice Questions

Q1 Why do companies keep accounts?
Q2 What is meant by "matching" in accounting terminology?
Q3 What is meant by "short term financial planning"?

Exam Question

Q1 Explain why accounts are produced according to the principles of matching, materiality and realisation. (9 marks)

Ah yes, but there's no accounting for taste...

Most of this builds on the AS Accounting and Finance section. Here, the same content is covered, but in plenty more detail, and there's some brand new content too. Learn the accounting principles and why they exist — the underlying idea of all the principles and the disclosure requirement is that firms shouldn't be able to hide the truth about their financial affairs.

Sources of Finance

*Sources of finance have to match up with the type of business, and what the business wants to spend the finance on. These two pages are for **AQA**, **OCR** and **Edexcel**, but mostly **OCR** and **Edexcel**.*

Businesses need Finance for Working Capital and Capital Expenditure

1) **Capital expenditure** means money used to buy **fixed assets**. These are things used over and over again to produce goods or services for sale — e.g. **factories** and **equipment**. Businesses need capital expenditure to **start up**, to **expand** and to **replace** worn out equipment.

2) **Working capital** (or **revenue expenditure**) is the cash needed to pay for the daily running of a business. It's used to pay wages, suppliers, electricity/gas bills, business rates etc. The amount of working capital is predicted using the **cash flow forecast**.

3) **Capital expenditure** allows a business to **grow**. **Working capital** allows a business to **survive**. All businesses need **both** types of finance.

Expenditure is a fancy way of saying "spending".

4) You'll find **capital expenditure** on the balance sheet, in the form of **fixed assets**, and the **capital** used to purchase them. See p.34-36 for more about the balance sheet.

5) You'll find **working capital** (**revenue expenditure**) on the profit and loss account, in the form of **expenses**. See p.32-33 for more about the profit and loss account.

AQA — AQA — AQA

Finance can be Internal or External, Short Term or Long Term, Debt or Equity

1) **Internal** finance is capital made available **within** the firm by cutting costs, or by putting **profits from trading** back into the business. Internal capital is often quite **limited**.

2) **External** finance is capital raised **outside** the business.

3) Ways of raising external capital include **selling shares**, asking the bank for an **overdraft** and getting a **loan** from a bank or a venture capitalist (someone who invests in businesses for a living).

---

1) **Short-term finance** is capital that's raised, used, and paid back quickly. A mechanic using a **bank overdraft** to buy a new car engine then selling the car and repaying the overdraft within a few **weeks** is a good example. Businesses use short-term finance to give them **extra working capital** so that they can pay their bills while they're waiting for their customers to pay up.

2) **Long-term finance** is capital that's paid back over a period of **more** than **one year**.

Here, "long-term" describes when a <u>debt</u> is due to be repaid. But the money may be used to meet medium-term <u>needs</u> — see p.25.

---

1) **Debt** is money **borrowed** from someone. It has to be **paid back**, with **interest**. Borrowing money allows new and small businesses to buy things that they couldn't afford otherwise — a business can grow faster if it doesn't have to save up to buy equipment and raw materials.

2) **Equity** capital is money received from **selling shares**. This can raise large amounts of capital quickly, and it doesn't need paying back. The drawback of raising money by selling shares is that the **shareholders control the business**. It's easier to control a business owned by a few shareholders than a business owned by lots of shareholders. Shareholders get a **slice** of the **profits** too.

3) The proportion of a business that's financed through debt rather than equity is called **gearing**. **Highly geared** firms financed mainly through **debt** can grow quickly — but they'll need to use a lot of their profits to pay back the debt and the **interest** on it. There's more about gearing on p.42.

There are Three Main Ways to raise Internal Capital

1) **Profit** can be retained and built up over the years for **later investment**.

2) Businesses can **sell** some of their **assets** to generate capital. This is called **rationalisation**.

3) A business can find some internal capital by **reducing working capital**. They do this by reducing the amount of **stock** they hold, **delaying** payments to **suppliers** and **speeding up** payments from **customers**. The saving can go towards future spending. The amount of capital a business can get from tightening its belt like this is **limited**.

OCR and Edexcel — OCR and Edexcel

Sources of Finance

External Finance can be for Short, Medium and Long Term needs

External finance can increase working capital in the short term

1) **Trade credit** is where a business negotiates a **delay** between **receiving** raw materials or stock and **paying** for them. **30 days** is a typical credit period. Larger businesses may negotiate longer periods.

2) **Overdrafts** are where a bank lets a business have a negative amount of money in its bank account, up to an overdraft limit. Overdrafts are **flexible** and easy to arrange. Overdrafts are only suitable for **short-term finance**, because banks charge a **lot** of **interest** on them.

3) **Debt factoring** is a service that banks and other financial institutions offer to improve cash flow. They take **unpaid invoices** off the hands of the business, and give them instant **cash** payment (of less than 100% of the value of the invoice). They collect payment from the individual or company who should have paid the invoice, and **keep** some of the money as a **fee**.

External finance is used for medium term needs — usually between 1 and 5 years

1) **Loans** have lower interest charges than overdrafts — they're suitable for **medium-term** finance. Loans are repaid in monthly instalments. Banks need security for a loan, usually in the form of property. If the business doesn't repay the loan, the bank can sell the property from under them to get their money back.

2) Leasing is when a business **rents** fixed assets like cars and office equipment instead of **buying** them. Leasing means paying a smallish amount each month instead of shelling out a lot of money all in one go. Businesses can easily **upgrade** equipment or vehicles that they're leasing. In the **long run**, leasing works out **more expensive** than buying, though.

External finance can also be used for long-term projects

1) **Debentures** are special kinds of long-term **loan** with low **fixed interest rates** and **fixed repayment dates**.

2) **Grants** are money from local government and some business charities. To qualify for a grant, businesses usually have to be creating **new jobs**, setting up in **deprived** areas or being started by **young people**.

3) A limited company can sell **shares** in the business. Shareholders can get a share of the profits, called a **dividend**. The share price goes up if the business does well, so shareholders can sell at a profit. **Ordinary shares** give a **variable** dividend each year that depends on how much profit the company has made. **Preference shares** give a **fixed** dividend each year. Preference shareholders get the first bite at the profits — if profits are low, ordinary shareholders don't get much dividend.

4) **Venture capitalists** provide capital by giving loans and by buying shares. Venture capital is particularly suitable for business start-ups or expansion.

OCR and Edexcel — *OCR and Edexcel*

A company's financial accounting statements give details of where its money came from. You'll find sources of finance like debentures, shares, overdrafts and bank loans detailed on the balance sheet.

Practice Questions

Q1 What's the difference between revenue expenditure and capital expenditure?

Q2 Give an example of a suitable external source of finance for (a) a short term cash flow problem, (b) new machinery.

Q3 What's the difference between an overdraft and a loan?

Q4 What types of businesses are most likely to qualify for grants?

Exam Questions

Q1 Explain three types of finance that might be suitable for financing the launch of a cyber-café business. (6 marks)

Q2 Discuss why most businesses finance growth and expansion with a mixture of internal and external finance. (8 marks)

I don't notice it saying "mum and dad's money" anywhere...

The source of finance depends on what it's going to be used for — fixed assets or working capital. Short term sources of working capital are suitable for plugging short term cash flow gaps. The better a business plans its spending, the more advantage it can take of cheaper long term borrowing like loans and share issues.

Budgeting and Variances

*Budgets and variance control have an impact on management and motivation. These pages are for **OCR** and **Edexcel**.*

A **Budget** is a **Financial Plan** that **Sets Targets**

A **budget** forecasts **future earnings** and **future spending**, usually over a year. Budgets allow managers to **control their spending**. Each budget contains financial **targets** — **objectives** which help **motivate** staff and **monitor performance**.

1) Budget targets should **stretch** the abilities of the business in order to **motivate** staff to do their best.

2) Budgets must be **achievable**. **Unrealistically** high sales budgets or low expenditure budgets will **demotivate** staff. No one likes being asked to do the **impossible**.

3) Staff can get **job satisfaction** from having **responsibility** for a budget. This helps to **motivate** them.

4) Budgets can be used in employee **appraisal** (assessing staff performance — see p.74).

The **Budget Setting** process involves **Research** and **Negotiation**

1) To set the **sales budget** (see p.16), businesses **research** and **predict** how sales are going to go up and down through the year, so that they can make a good prediction of **sales revenue**.

2) To set the **production budget** (expenditure budget), businesses research how labour costs, raw materials costs, taxes and inflation are going to go up over the year. They can then figure out the **costs** of producing the volume of product that they think they're going to sell.

3) Annual budgets are usually agreed by **negotiation** — when budget holders have a say in setting their budgets, they're **more motivated** to achieve them.

Budget holder = the person in charge of setting and meeting a budget.

4) Good budgets need to **establish priorities**. It's important for budget holders and staff to know which **spending targets** are **most important** to meet, and which **sales targets** are most important to meet. Some items on the production budget may be so vital to the business that it's OK if they go slightly over budget.

5) Establishing budget priorities requires **research** and **negotiation**, too.

Budgets can be **Updated Each Year** or done from **Scratch**

- **Historical or incremental budgets** are updated each year based on the **previous** year's figures. For example, a business looking for 10% revenue growth might add 10% to the advertising, wages and raw materials budgets.

- **Zero budgeting** means starting from scratch each year. Budget holders **start** with a budget of **£0**, and have to **plan** all the year's activities, ask for money to spend on them, and be prepared to **justify** their requests to the finance director. Budget holders need good negotiating skills for this. Zero budgeting gives a business more **flexibility** than **historical budgeting**. It takes longer than historical budgeting, but it can be a lot more accurate.

1) Managers need **training** to set and manage budgets properly. This can be **time consuming** and **expensive**.

2) Some managers are very good at arguing for a large budget for their department or team. This could result in money going to them when it should be going elsewhere. Managers with big **egos** may see a large budget as an indicator of **status**.

3) With **historical budgeting**, managers may be tempted to spend the **whole budget** to make sure they get at least that amount in next year's budget. This isn't cost-effective.

Variance is the **Difference** between **Actual** figures and **Budget** figures

1) A **favourable variance** leads to **profits increasing**. If revenue's more than the budget says it's going to be, that's a favourable variance. If costs are below the cost predictions in the budget, that's also a favourable variance.

2) An **adverse variance** is a difference that **reduces profits**. Selling fewer items than the sales budget predicts is an adverse variance. Spending more on an advert than the marketing budget allows is an adverse variance.

3) Variances **add up**. For example, if actual sales exceed budgeted sales by £3000 and expenditure on raw materials is £2000 below budget, there's a combined favourable variance of £5000. Spending £10 000 on raw materials in a month with a £6000 budget would create a £4000 adverse variance.

4) **Small** variances aren't a big problem. They can actually **motivate** employees. Staff try to **catch up** and sort out small **adverse** variances themselves. Small **favourable** variances can motivate staff to **keep on** doing whatever they were doing to create a favourable variance.

5) **Large** variances can **demotivate**. Staff don't work hard if there are large favourable variances — they **don't see the need**. Staff can get demotivated by a large **adverse** variance — they may feel that the task is **impossible**.

Budgeting and Variances

Variances Need Sorting — *even when they say you're doing better than expected*

1) It's extremely important to spot adverse variances as **soon** as possible. It's important to find out which budget holder is responsible — and to take action to fix the problem.

2) It's **also** important to **investigate favourable variances**. Favourable variances mean the budget targets weren't **stretching** enough — so the business needs to set more **difficult targets**. The business also needs to understand **why** the performance is better than expected — if a department is **doing something right**, the business can **spread** this throughout the organisation.

Variances are caused by several factors — *Internal* and *External*

External factors cause variance

1) **Competitor behaviour** and changing **fashions** may increase or reduce **demand** for products.

2) Changes in the **economy** may change the costs of wages.

3) The cost of **raw materials** may go up.

Internal factors cause variance

1) Improving **efficiency** causes **favourable** variances. However, a business might **overestimate** the amount of money it can save by streamlining production methods. This would cause an adverse variance.

2) A business might **underestimate** the **cost** of making a change to its organisation, for example it might not take account of the cost of **training** employees to use a new computer system.

3) Changing the selling price changes sales revenue. A business which cuts the price of its products after it's **already** set the budget creates a **variance** for itself.

4) Internal causes of variance are a **serious concern**. They suggest that the **internal communication** in a business needs improvement.

Variance Analysis means *Catching* variances and *Fixing* them

1) Businesses can either change what the **business** is doing to make it fit the budget, or change the **budget** to make it fit what the **business** is doing. Remember, **flexible** budgets **can** be changed, but fixed budgets **can't**.

2) Businesses need to **beware** of chopping and changing the budget **too much**. Changing the budget **removes certainty** — which removes one of the big benefits of budgets. Altering budgets can also make them **less motivational** — when staff start to expect that management will change targets instead of doing something to change performance, they don't see the point in trying any more.

3) Businesses fix **adverse variances** by either changing the **marketing mix** so they'll sell more products, cutting production **costs**, motivating employees to **work harder** or asking suppliers for a better deal.

4) Businesses act to fix **favourable variances** by making sure that **increased productivity** in one part of the business **spreads** through the business. If the variance is caused by a **pessimistic budget**, they make sure that they set more **ambitious targets** next time.

Practice Questions

Q1 Give two advantages of budgets.

Q2 What is variance?

Q3 Give two internal factors which create variances.

Q4 What do businesses do to fix favourable variances?

Exam Question

Q1 A business budgets £120k expenditure on wages, rent and other costs, and £270k revenue from sales. The actual costs are as follows: £80k on wages, £30k on rent and £22k on other costs. The actual sales revenue is £275k.
(a) What is the total variance? *Answer on p.138.* (4 marks)
(b) What does your answer suggest about the budgeting process within the business? (3 marks)

You should see the variances in my PC game budget...

All businesses need budgets to give them a good idea of how much money they'll be making, and how much money they'll be spending. When the real life results don't quite match up to the budget, there must be something wrong with either the budget-setting process, or the actions of the business. Either way, it needs sorting out, not ignoring. Much like your revision.

Cost and Profit Centres

*Businesses can look at sales budgets and production budgets for the whole of the business — or they can look at one part of the business in isolation and work out how much money it's spending, and how much it's making. These pages are for **OCR** and **Edexcel**. AQA people have already covered this in AS.*

Managers set **Budgets** for **Parts** of the **Business** — **Cost** and **Profit Centres**

1) **Cost centres** are parts of a business that directly **incur costs**. The business can identify costs, measure them, and **monitor** them against a **mini-budget** that applies just to that part of the business.

2) **Profit centres** are parts of a business that directly **generate revenue** as well as costing money. The business can work out the **profit** or **loss** they're making by subtracting the **costs** from the **revenues**.

3) The IT department of a business is an example of a **cost centre**. Managers **can** work out the **costs** of IT technician wages and new computer upgrades. They **can't** work out the **revenue** that the IT department earns, because they **don't charge** other departments for providing IT support.

4) A chain of shops can treat **each shop** as a **profit centre**. The business owner **can** work out the **costs** of stock, rent and staff wages for each shop, and also work out **sales revenue** for each shop.

5) Manufacturers can treat each **product line** as a profit centre. Individual **brands** can also be profit centres. You can figure out how much they cost, how much they make, and then **set a budget** based on how much you **think** they're going to cost and how much you think they're going to make next year.

> All cost and profit centres are is a **way to work out budgets** for a particular **part** of a business. With a **cost centre**, you can work out costs, so you can set a **cost budget**. With a profit centre, you can work out **costs** and **revenues**. This means you can set a budget for how much money you want that part of the business to **bring in** over a year, as well as how much money you want it to **cost** that year. It's that simple.

How is Hairdressing doing as a cost centre?

We're radically "trimming" costs and "restyling" price structure.

Nice.

Cost and profit centres have several **Uses**

① **Financial decision making**

1) Overall profit figures don't tell senior managers exactly **where** profits are being made. Cost and profit centres let managers **compare** costs of different parts of the business. They can try to make the less cost-efficient parts **more efficient**.

2) Managers can use **cost centres** to help them **set prices** — once they know the cost, they can set the price so that they'll make a profit.

② **Organisation and control**

1) Managers can use cost and profit centre information when they want to change the **organisation** of the business. They can focus on the **profitable** areas.

2) Managers can set **cost limits** and **profit targets** to coordinate staff and **focus** their minds on specific activities. They can link **pay** and **bonuses** to meeting profit targets and keeping costs down in each department, team or shop.

③ **Motivation**

1) Cost and profit centres with their own budgets allow **junior managers** and **employees** to control budgets.

2) Profit share schemes mean employees and managers within profitable profit centres can earn **bonus** payments — but be warned, this can backfire if profits aren't as good as expected.

Senior managers *often delegate* budget setting to junior managers — they allow them the authority to make budget decisions. P.58 has more on delegation.

Example: When British Airways came under intense pressure from budget airlines, the company realised they had to **cut costs** to compete. They calculated costs, revenues, profit and loss for each **route**. Managers **closed** the **loss-making** routes and put money toward **increasing** the services on the more **profitable** routes. The marketing department were set targets intended to motivate them and generate more customers for these routes. Company performance started to improve.

Cost and Profit Centres

Businesses *Define* cost and profit centres in *Different Ways*

Cost and profit centres can be defined by:

1) **Product**, e.g. a high street **clothing** company might monitor costs and revenues for each product, so it could work out how much profit or loss different lines of clothing contributed to the business.

2) **Factory**, e.g. **car companies** use their different factories as a cost and profit centre, so they know what percentage of costs and profits each factory represents to the business. This information is useful if the business needs to **downsize** — they can close the **least profitable** factories and keep the profitable ones going.

3) **Location**, e.g. **supermarkets** that know how much profit (as well as how much revenue) each **store** generates for the business are more informed when it comes to targeting geographic areas for future expansion. They can choose areas with **profitable** stores for expansion.

4) **Person**, e.g. businesses with a sales force will usually monitor **each sales person** as a profit centre. Sales people are very **expensive** to employ — so a business will be keen to make sure none of them are **costing** the business **more** than they generate in profit.

Cost Centres must include *Indirect Costs*

Indirect costs are **overheads** — things like senior managers' salaries, rent for a factory or shop, etc. They're the costs that a business has to pay out which aren't directly tied in to a specific product. Indirect costs are also known as **fixed costs**.

Cost and profit centres have *Advantages* and *Disadvantages*

Advantages of cost and profit centres	Disadvantages of cost and profit centres
Managers can **easily spot** the successful and unsuccessful parts of the business.	Giving junior employees responsibility for setting budgets can be **too much** for them to handle. They'll need financial **training** first.
Local managers can make decisions to **suit** their cost or profit centre. They can set prices for the **local market**.	It can be **hard** to divide a business into cost and profit centres. Sharing out the costs of **overheads** like rent is particularly tricky.
Meeting targets on a **local** level can be **more motivating** than working towards a **distant** national target.	There's **rivalry** between cost and profit centres in a business. If it goes too far, it can be a problem — branches could be more concerned with beating each other's profits than with customers.

Cost and profit centres don't suit all businesses. Owners or leaders who like to **make all the decisions** won't be happy about **delegating** budget setting. Businesses without **able junior staff** won't be able to **handle** cost and profit centres. It often isn't worth working out cost and profit centres for a business which just sells **one kind of product**.

Practice Questions

Q1 What is a cost centre?

Q2 Would the maintenance and facilities management department be a cost centre or a profit centre?

Q3 Give two reasons for using cost and profit centres.

Q4 State three ways that a business can divide its operations up into profit centres.

Q5 Give two drawbacks of using profit centres.

Exam Questions

Q1 Why might a small business owner decide not to establish cost and profit centres for their business? (6 marks)

Q2 Tanya Richards owns and manages four beauty salons, and runs each salon as a profit centre. She also has a small office where she and her assistant look after all the admin, accounting and marketing for the business.
(a) Why does Tanya run her office as a cost centre, not as a profit centre? (4 marks)
(b) To what extent will running the salons as profit centres motivate Tanya's staff? Explain your answer. (11 marks)

Need profits? Go to the local profit centre — if only it were that simple...

Cost and profit centres are especially good for businesses like banks, supermarkets and manufacturers — it makes a lot of sense to divide those businesses up into individual bank branches, individual stores and individual product lines. Don't go thinking that profit centres and cost centres are opposites — it's just that you can't measure profit for a cost centre.

Standard Costs

Standard costs are a way of budgeting for costs. These pages are for **OCR** and **Edexcel**.

Standard Costs are the costs you'd have in an Ideal World

Standard = a level of performance.

Standard Costs = the planned level of cost to achieve a certain level of performance.

Variance = the difference between the **standard cost** and the **actual cost**. This can be **favourable** (costs less than planned and so contributes more to profit) or **adverse** (costs more than planned).

Businesses **compare** their **actual costs** against **standard costs** for long term **cost-cutting**.

Standard Costs must match a Specific Product and must be Accurate

1) If a cost isn't **related** to making the product in question, it shouldn't go in the standard costing.

2) The data used must be **accurate**. The costs that are normally measured include the **labour**, **raw materials** and the **overheads** attributable to the production of **each unit** of a product.

- **Labour** is calculated based on average actual hourly rates of pay, with overtime and factors for holiday pay, sick pay, and benefits added on.

- **Equipment** is worked out as a standard hourly rate. It's calculated by dividing the daily rate for equipment hire by the predicted hourly usage, or by dividing the cost of equipment by its expected lifetime in hours.

- **Overheads** are predicted for production, distribution, marketing and admin.

Standard Costs are usually only used by Big Firms

1) The **cost** of establishing and maintaining a **standard cost procedure** is an **administrative overhead**. Normally, it's only affordable to larger manufacturing organisations producing a variety of products.

2) Large manufacturing firms need to manage their assets **efficiently**, and have **measurable standards** against which they can judge the **actual costs**.

3) Standard costs are normally run over a **short period** (monthly or even weekly) so that they can be frequently measured against actual costs and any adverse variance can be dealt with **quickly**.

4) Standard costs must be **achievable** in real world situations. If the standard cost is based on operating at 100% capacity, then any **downtime**, e.g. for equipment repairs will cause **adverse variance** from the standard costs. A standard cost based on 100% capacity isn't workable.

Managers Interpret standard costs with Ratios

1) **Efficiency ratio** = $\dfrac{\text{Standard Hours Produced}}{\text{Actual Hours Worked}} \times 100\%$

2) **Capacity ratio** = $\dfrac{\text{Actual Hours Worked}}{\text{Budgeted Hours}} \times 100\%$

3) **Production Volume ratio** = $\dfrac{\text{Standard Hours Produced}}{\text{Budgeted Hours}} \times 100\%$

standard hours produced = hours budgeted to make one unit × units actually made

Example: A firm **budgeted** for **1000 hours** for production of **100 units** but actually took **900 hours** to produce **75 units**. Each unit is allowed 10 **standard hours** (1000 hours ÷ 100 units). As 75 units were produced, total standard hours of production must be **750** (75 units x 10 standard hrs). So the **standard** hours are **750**, the **actual** hours are **900** and the **budgeted** hours are **1000**, what a mess... Now apply the formulae to make some sense of this data.

Efficiency = $\dfrac{750 \text{ hours}}{900 \text{ hours}} \times 100\% = 83\%$ ⟵ So, you could say that the firm was **less efficient** at producing these units than planned.

Capacity = $\dfrac{900 \text{ hours}}{1000 \text{ hours}} \times 100\% = 90\%$ ⟵ Not all the time available (the capacity) was utilised.

Production Volume = $\dfrac{750 \text{ hours}}{1000 \text{ hours}} \times 100\% = 75\%$ ⟵ This ratio highlights the **effectiveness** of using the budgeted hours to produce goods.

When compared to **alternative products**, a decision can be made on what to produce in what volume and at what cost.

Cost Allocation

This page is a slightly different topic — allocation of overheads to work out the total cost of a good or service.

Remember, **Costs** can be **Fixed** or **Variable**, **Direct** or **Indirect**

Type of cost:	**Fixed costs** — don't change with output.	**Variable costs** — rise and fall as output changes.
Example:	**Rent** on a factory, business **rates**, **senior managers' salaries** and cost of **new machinery**.	Hourly **wages**, **raw materials**, **packaging costs**.
Type of cost:	**Direct costs** — are linked to a good or **service**.	**Indirect costs** — can't be directly linked to one product.
Example:	The cost of **raw materials** and the hourly wages paid to **factory workers** making a product.	Wages and salaries of people **not directly involved** in making the product, business **rates** and **rent**.

Direct costs are almost always **variable**. **Indirect** costs are almost always **fixed**. Indirect costs are called overheads.

Full Costing adds direct costs to a **Percentage** of **Total Overhead**

1) **Full costing** is the **simplest** method to calculate costs.
2) The **percentage of total overheads** added on to direct costs is decided by the **finance director**. You can divide total overheads **equally** between all products, or **share them out** according to how much **revenue** each product makes.

Absorption Costing adds direct costs to a **Percentage** of **Each Overhead**

1) Absorption costing calculates total costs by **adding direct costs** to a **proportion** of **each individual overhead** — e.g. 25% of heating and lighting, 15% of admin staff salaries, 45% of factory rent.
2) The **finance department** decides how much of each **overhead** goes with each **product** — canteen costs might be divided up according to the percentage of staff working on each product, rent might be shared out according to how much floor space each product requires, and so on.
3) Absorption costing is more **accurate** than full costing but it takes **longer**.
4) It can also lead to **conflict** as managers argue over how they're going to allocate the overheads.

Marginal or **Contribution** Costing is based on **Direct Cost** and **Selling Price**

1) The **variable cost** per unit (or **direct cost** per unit) is exactly the **same**, no matter how big or small the **output**.
2) The **difference** between the **direct cost** per unit and the **selling price** of each unit makes a **contribution** towards paying for the indirect costs or **overheads**.

> **contribution = selling price** per unit – **variable costs** per unit

3) Once the overheads are covered, all contribution is **profit**. The finance department works out how many sales the business needs to make to cover the overheads and start making profit. This figure is called the **break-even output**. See p.46-47 for quite a bit more about contribution and break even.

Practice Questions

Q1 What is a standard cost?
Q2 Write down the equation for standard cost efficiency ratio.
Q3 How does absorption costing deal with overheads?
Q4 How does contribution costing deal with overheads?

Exam Questions

Q1 Explain why standard costs are only used by big firms. (8 marks)

Q2 Assess the different methods of overhead allocation that a manufacturer of TV components could use. (12 marks)

Not revising this lot could cost you...

For some reason, the OCR and Edexcel exam boards are dead keen that you know all about cost and overhead allocation, and that you can deal with standard cost calculations. This is a bit of a pain, but on the other hand, AQA bods have to learn stuff that you don't need to bother with, so it's all swings and roundabouts. Don't get the costing methods mixed up.

Company Accounts: Profit and Loss

The profit and loss account is a very useful collection of financial information.
*These pages are for **AQA** and **OCR**, but may be useful for **Edexcel** students too.*

Profit and Loss Accounts show Revenue and Expenses

1) The profit and loss account show how much money's been **coming into the company** (**revenue**) and how much has been **going out** (**expenses**).

2) Revenue is **sales income** from selling goods and services. This includes **cash payments** received and sales on **credit**.

Remember that accounting follows the matching principle — sales income is recorded when the sale's made, not when the customer pays.

3) Expenses are all the **costs** of the business. These are divided into **direct** and **indirect** costs, or **fixed** and **variable** costs.

4) Profit and loss accounts show revenue expenditure, and balance sheets show capital expenditure.

Profit = Revenue – Expenses *(and there are different categories of profit...)*

1) **Gross profit** is **revenue** minus **direct costs**. The direct cost of making and selling a product include raw materials and wages of production workers, but not wages of other staff. These direct costs are called the **cost of sales** on the profit and loss account.

2) **Net profit** is **gross profit** minus **indirect costs**. Indirect costs (**overheads**) cover wages of non-production staff, advertising, office rent, rates, interest payments and depreciation (see p.35).

3) **Operating profit** takes into account all revenues and costs from **regular trading**, but not any revenues and costs from **one-off** events. It only covers activities that are likely to be **repeated year on year**.

4) **Net profit before tax** covers **all revenues and costs**, including those from **one-off events** such as the sale or purchase of another business.

5) **Net profit after tax** is what's left after corporation tax has been paid.

6) **Retained profit** is what's left from net profit after tax, once **share dividends** have been paid to shareholders.

Maud was mainly interested in net profit.

One-off *profit is* Low Quality *— Sustained profit is* High Quality

1) Profit can be "**high quality**" or "**low quality**", depending on whether it's likely to carry on into the future.

2) Profit from **one-off events** like the sale of part of the business is considered to be **low quality**.

3) **Operating profit** is **high quality**, because it's probably going to carry on being made year on year.

4) **Shareholders** like **high quality** profit, because they want profit to continue into the future. Future profits mean future dividend payments and happy shareholders.

The Profit and Loss Account is Three accounts in One

1) The **trading account** works out **gross profit** — revenue minus direct costs.

2) The **profit and loss account** subtracts overheads (indirect costs) to work out **operating profit** and **net profit**.

3) The **appropriation account** shows what's done with profits — it's either **distributed** between shareholders, or **kept** in the business to invest in future activities. The appropriation account works out **retained profit**.

Profit and Loss Accounts calculate Profits over a period of Time

Profit and loss accounts should cover one whole accounting year. A profit and loss account that covers **less than 12 months** can be **misleading**. High Street retailers can generate **half their annual revenue** in the lead-up to **Christmas** — a profit and loss account ignoring this period won't give anything like an accurate picture of the business.

Sometimes profit and loss accounts cover a little **more** or a little **less** than a year — e.g. when a business changes its accounting year from Dec-Dec to Apr-Apr, it'll have one set of accounts that cover Dec-Apr.

Profit and loss accounts usually contain the **previous year's data** as well, for **easy comparison** to see what's changed. Some companies provide the previous five years' data as well. It's very useful to be able to spot trends in turnover, costs and profits.

Company Accounts: Profit and Loss

Here's a *Reminder* of what the *Profit and Loss Account* looks like

ABC Company Ltd
Profit and Loss Account for the year ended 30 March 2004

The title includes the period covered by the account.

This subtracts direct costs (cost of sales) from revenue generated to get gross profit.

Revenue only includes completed sales, where the goods are delivered to the customer. It makes no difference when the payment is received.

Trading Account	Revenue		£100 000
	Opening stock	£3000	
	Purchases	£42 000	
	Closing Stock	£5000	
	Cost of sales		£40 000
	Gross Profit		**£60 000**
Profit and loss Account	Wages	£15 000	
	Rent	£8000	
	Advertising	£12 000	
	Depreciation	£5000	
	Total overheads		£40 000
	Net Profit		**£20 000**
Appropriation Account	Tax		£5000
	Dividends		£7000
	Retained profit		**£8000**
	Earnings per share		**£5.80p**
	Dividend per share		**£2.70p**

Cost of sales = purchases + (opening stock − closing stock). Cost of sales only relates to sales made during this trading period. The cost of producing stock still in the warehouse doesn't count.

Gross profit = revenue − cost of sales.

This shows expenses, and subtracts expenses from gross profit to get net profit.

Depreciation is the annual drop in value of assets as they get older (see p.35).

Net profit = gross profit − overheads.

Amount paid out to shareholders.

This classifies profit according to what it's used for.

Retained profit = net profit − (tax + dividends).

Profit after tax ÷ number of shares

Total dividends ÷ number of shares

Stakeholders have an *Interest* in the *Profit and Loss Account*

1) **Managers** use the profit and loss account to judge **business performance**. They're interested in the **cost of sales** compared with **sales revenue** — this shouldn't be too high. They're also interested in how much profit was from **one-off items** — they prefer the profit to be high quality.

2) **Employees** are interested in how much **profit** the business is making, as an indicator of **job security** and potential **pay rises**. They'll be especially interested in profits if there's a **profit-related** link in their pay scheme.

3) **Shareholders** want to know the company's **turnover**, and the **operating profit**, so that they can see how the company is **performing** compared to previous years.

4) **Shareholders** also like to check **profit appropriation**. Some shareholders like to get as much **dividend** as possible for a short-term return. Some prefer to see money being **reinvested** into the business for long-term returns.

5) Limited companies and partnerships with a turnover over £15 million have to submit their accounts to the **Inland Revenue**. The tax man is interested in **net profit** before tax, because that's what a business is **taxed** on. The Inland Revenue also check through the accounts to make sure that the accounts procedure is up to standard.

Practice Questions

Q1 What is operating profit?
Q2 What is retained profit?
Q3 Define high quality profit.
Q4 Which parts of the profit and loss account are shareholders most interested in?

Exam Question

Q1 Discuss whether the profit and loss account gives a good indication of the financial wellbeing of a business. (12 marks)

Step 1: buy stuff. Step 2: sell stuff. Step 3: PROFIT...

Well, that's the simplest way of looking at business, I suppose. What the exam boards expect you to know about profit for this section is not so much how it's made, but what kind of profit it is. Profit can be gross, net, retained, operating, low quality or high quality. If you don't know what one or other of those terms mean, you need to revise these pages again.

Company Accounts: Balance Sheets

*You've come across balance sheets at AS level, but there's considerably more detail and depth for A2 level, so learn it all. These pages are for **AQA** and **OCR**.*

Balance Sheets are lists of Assets and Liabilities

1) Balance sheets are a **snapshot** of a firm's finances at a **fixed point in time**. They show the value of all the **assets** (the things that belong to the business, including cash in the bank) and all the **liabilities** (the money the business owes). They also show the value of all the **capital** in the business, and the source of that capital — they show where the money's **come from** as well as what's being **done** with it.

2) The **value** of the **assets** purchased **equals** the **amount of money** used to **buy** them. Balance sheets... **balance**.

Assets are things the Business Owns (that it's bought with capital)

1) Assets includes **machinery**, **stock**, **property**, **land**, and **cash**, as well as money owed to the business by **debtors**.

2) Assets can be classified as **fixed assets** or **current assets** — see the table below.

Fixed assets	Current assets
These are kept for **more than a year** — e.g. property, land, production equipment, desks and computers. Fixed assets are often worth **less now** than last year. This is **depreciation** — see next page.	These are likely to be exchanged for cash **within the accounting year**, before the next balance sheet is worked out. **Stock** and **debtors** are current assets.

3) Assets can also be classified as **tangible** or **intangible**.

- **Tangible assets** are **actual physical stuff** such as property, stock or machinery.
- **Intangible assets** are **non-physical things** like brands, customer goodwill, patents and licenses. It's easy to include them on the balance sheet if they have an **objective**, **quantifiable** value — if a **definite amount of money** was spent on them. For example, 3G mobile phone **licences** were bought from the government for an amount of **money**, which can go on the balance sheet. But the **brand** of a particular mobile phone company such as 3 or Vodafone can't be easily quantified. See p.39 for more on intangible assets.

Bad Debts are debts that debtors Won't Ever Pay

1) **Ideally**, every debt owed by debtors to the business would be paid. **Unfortunately**, the **real world** isn't like that. Most debts get paid eventually, but some debtors **default** on their payments — they **don't pay up**.

2) Debts which don't get paid are called "**bad debts**". These bad debts **can't** be included on the balance sheet as an **asset** — because the business isn't going to get money for them.

3) The business **writes off** these bad debts, and puts them as an **expense** on the profit and loss account. This shows that the business has **lost money**.

> It's important to be **realistic** about bad debts.
>
> The business shouldn't be **over optimistic** and report debts as **assets** when it's unlikely that they're ever going to be paid. On the other hand, they shouldn't be **too cautious** and write debts off as **bad debts** when they could make the debtors pay up.
>
> - Being **over optimistic** results in an asset valuation that's **too high**.
> - Being **over cautious** results in an asset valuation that's **too low**.

Liabilities are Debts the Business Owes (where its capital has come from)

1) **Current liabilities** are **debts** which need to be paid off within a year. They include overdrafts, taxes due to be paid, money owed to creditors and dividends due to be paid to shareholders.

2) **Long term liabilities** are debts that the business will pay off over several years, e.g. mortgages and loans.

3) All the company's **sources of capital** count as a liability, even money invested by **shareholders**. This is because if the business ceased trading, the shareholders would want their money back. The owner's equity (money they've put in) counts as a liability for a **partnership** as well.

4) **Reserves** are mostly retained profits, and also include money from any rises in asset value. Reserves count as a **liability** because they're a **source of finance**.

> **Liabilities = where the money's from.**
> **Assets = what you've done with it.**

Company Accounts: Balance Sheets

Accounts reflect *Assets* that *Depreciate* — they *Lose Value* over *Time*

1) The **drop in value** of a business asset over time is called **depreciation**.

2) Businesses **calculate depreciation** each year to make sure that an asset's **value** on the **balance sheet** is a **true reflection** of what the business would get from **selling** it. Building depreciation into each year's accounts **stops** it hitting **all at once** when the business **sells** the asset.

3) The **amount lost** through depreciation is recorded on the **profit and loss account** as an **expense**.

Use the *Straight Line* or *Declining Balance* methods to calculate *Depreciation*

1) The **straight line method** of calculating depreciation splits it equally over the life of an asset.

2) This method is quick and simple, but you need to know how long the asset **lasts** and how much it's worth when you eventually replace it (its **residual value**). This means there's a **subjective** side to working out depreciation — figuring out how long an asset will last requires some subjective **human judgement**.

3) The straight line method isn't perfect. In reality assets often lose more value early on in their life, rather than losing value steadily over a period of time.

Straight Line Method Equation: $\text{Depreciation per year} = \dfrac{\text{cost of asset} - \text{residual value}}{\text{useful life of asset}}$

Example: A piece of machinery costs **£10 000** when new. It's expected to last **8 years**. After 8 years, it's worth **£500**.

$\text{Depreciation} = \dfrac{£10\,000 - £500}{8} = £1187.50$

--- OCR --- OCR ---

4) The **declining balance method** assumes an asset depreciates by an **equal percentage** of its current worth throughout its life. This means that depreciation happens fastest in the **first year** — which is more realistic.

5) This method is more **accurate** but it's also more **complicated** and time **consuming**.

Example: An asset costs **£20 000** to buy new. It will last for **3 years**. It depreciates at **25%** per year. After **1 year**, it's worth £20 000 × 75% = **£15 000**. After **2 years**, it's worth £15 000 × 75% = **£11 250**. After **3 years**, it's worth £11 250 × 75% = **£8437.50**.

There's a subjective side to this as well — an asset that's well looked after won't depreciate as fast as one that's knocked about.

--- OCR --- OCR --- OCR ---

Practice Questions

Q1 Give two examples of fixed assets, and two examples of current assets.

Q2 Give an example of an intangible asset.

Q3 What are bad debts?

Q4 Why is share capital classified as a liability?

Q5 Why do businesses depreciate their assets each year?

Exam Questions

Q1 "It's impossible for asset valuations on the balance sheet to be 100% accurate". To what extent do you agree with this statement? (10 marks)

Q2 Rob Williams has just bought a new computer system for his office, at a cost of £2500. He intends to replace it after 4 years, when he calculates he'll be able to sell it for £500. *Answer on p.138.* How much should he depreciate the asset value of the computer system by this year? (3 marks)

Liabilities = where the money's from. Assets = what the money's paid for...

Balance sheets can seem weird — why are reserves liabilities when cash is an asset, for example. If you see it as where the money's from, and what the firm's done with it, you can see what goes where and why it balances. Valuing the assets properly is the hard part — you have to learn how to do depreciation calculations, and how to deal with bad debts.

Company Accounts: Balance Sheets

*Balance sheets arrange all the assets and liabilities in a nice table. This page is for **AQA** and **OCR**.*

Interpreting *balance sheets — Here's How It All Looks*

ABC Company Ltd
Balance Sheet as at 30 March 2004

Balance sheets show the financial state of affairs on one particular day.

Raw materials and finished products — things the business has spent money on, but not sold yet.

Value of products sold but not paid for yet. Money owed to the business.

Money owed by the business.

Money borrowed by the business.

Dividends not yet paid to shareholders.

This is the working capital available to pay for day to day spending.

Where the money comes from — loans, shares and other capital.

Premises			£100 000
Machines			£10 000
Vehicles			£15 000
Total fixed assets			£125 000
Stock		£20 000	
Debtors		£10 000	
Cash in the bank		£5000	
Total current assets		£35 000	
Creditors	(£20 000)		
Overdraft	(£2000)		
Dividends	(£10 000)		
Unpaid tax	(£1000)		
Total current liabilities		(£33 000)	
Net current assets			£2000
Assets employed			£127 000
Loan capital			£55 000
Share capital			£60 000
Reserves			£12 000
Capital employed			£127 000

Brackets mean a negative number.

Net current assets = current assets − current liabilities

Assets employed = net current assets + fixed assets

These two figures ALWAYS balance.

Balance Sheets *show the* Short Term Financial Status *of the* Company

1) The balance sheet shows you how much the business is **worth**.

2) **Working capital** (net current assets) is the amount of money the business has available in the short term. It's calculated by subtracting **current liabilities** from **current assets**. See p.38 for more on working capital.

3) **Suppliers** are particularly interested in **working capital** and **liquidity**. Suppliers can look at the balance sheet to see how liquid the firm's assets are, as well as how much working capital the firm has. The more liquid the assets, the better the firm will be at paying bills. This helps them decide whether to offer the business supplies on **credit**, and how much credit to offer.

Liquidity = how easy it is to pay debt. See p.38. The liquidity of an asset is how easy it is to turn it into cash and spend it. Cash is the most liquid asset, then debtors, stock and short term investments.

4) The balance sheet shows **sources of capital**. Ideally, **long-term loans** or **mortgages** are used to finance the purchase of fixed assets. A well managed business wouldn't borrow too much through **short-term overdrafts**, because overdrafts are an expensive way of borrowing.

By Comparing Balance Sheets *you can see* Long-Term Trends

1) Comparing this year's balance sheet to previous years' accounts lets you pick out **trends** in company finances. Looking at the "bottom line" over several years shows you how the business is **growing**.

2) A **quick increase** in **fixed assets** indicates that the company has invested in property or machinery. This means that the company is investing in a growth strategy, and may make more profit over the medium term — useful information for shareholders and potential shareholders, who want to see more profit.

3) Increases in **reserves** also suggest an increase in **profits** — good news for shareholders.

4) The balance sheet shows **trends** in how the business has **raised its capital**.   It's risky to suddenly start borrowing a lot, in case interest rates rise. A company with a high value of creditors and a relatively low value of share capital or reserves would be in trouble if the Bank of England put interest rates up.

Limitations of Accounts

*Accounts are useful, but they aren't the be-all and end-all of financial health. This page is also for **AQA** and **OCR**.*

Accounts Don't Contain anything Non-Numerical

1) **Internal strengths** such as the quality of staff, or the company's market share, don't appear on the accounts. You'd need to do a **SWOT** analysis (see p.116) to find them out.

2) **External factors** such as the **economic** or **market** environment aren't reflected in the accounts. Accounts don't tell you anything about what a **competitor** might do next, or what legislation might be passed by the government. The development of **technology**, or potential changes to the **location** of the business (e.g. a new rail link) don't appear in the accounts. You'd need to do a **PEST** analysis (see p.116) to sort out all these **external factors**.

3) Accounts only contain information about the **past** and **present**. The past isn't always a good guide to the future. Things **change**. The market environment is **uncertain**.

The Profit and Loss Account doesn't Tell All

1) The **profit and loss account** is very useful for assessing the performance of the company. It isn't the be-all and end-all, though.

2) It doesn't include any information about **external factors** such as **market demand**, which would be useful in forecasting **future turnover** and **profit**.

3) It doesn't include any information about **internal factors** such as staff morale, which would be useful in determining **productivity** and therefore **profitability**.

4) In times of **inflation**, the profit and loss account isn't so useful, because inflationary rises in price distort the true value of turnover.

5) The profit and loss account can be **deliberately distorted**, by bringing forward sales from the next trading period and including them as part of this trading period.

6) The profit and loss account can also be **window-dressed** by depreciating assets too slowly and by capitalising expenditure (see p.39).

The Balance Sheet Doesn't Tell All, either

1) The **balance sheet** is a statement about one point in the **past**, which may not help predict the **future**.

2) The balance sheet doesn't give any clues about the **market** or the **economy** that the business is trading in.

3) Balance sheets value some intangible assets (e.g. a brand recently purchased by the company), but they don't value intangible assets like **staff skill**, **staff motivation** or **management experience**.

It's best to look at the Profit and Loss Account together with the Balance Sheet

The profit and loss account and balance sheet are much stronger taken **together** than separately.

The **Directors' Report** gives more information than either, but it isn't available **outside** the company.

Practice Questions

Q1 How are assets employed calculated?

Q2 How is working capital calculated, and what does it tell a supplier about offering credit to a business?

Q3 Other than the balance sheet, describe two other sources of data that would give you a picture of a firm's financial health.

Exam Question

Q1 Analyse the value of a balance sheet to an investor considering buying shares in a football club. (12 marks)

On balance it's more than likely to come up in the exam...

It's true, examiners love this stuff. If you're doing OCR, you'll have covered some of the balance sheet gubbins in your AS exam. There's more depth and detail in the A2 exam, so make sure you look carefully at what managers can actually learn from the balance sheet, and what the limitations of the published accounts are. AQA folk have to learn the lot, anyway.

Working Capital

*Working capital is the money available to fund day-to-day expenditure. Managers must regularly plan, control and review the use of this money (cash, stock and debtors). This page is for **AQA**.*

Businesses *Need Enough Working Capital* but not too much

Working capital = **current assets** (cash, debtors and stock) – **current liabilities** (overdraft, creditors, tax)

Businesses need working capital for liquidity — liquidity is a measure of the company's ability to **pay its debt**. In addition to generating sales the business needs to **collect money** as quickly as possible from customers, so that it has enough **working capital** to pay its liabilities. See p.40, 'Ratio Analysis', for liquidity ratios.

Businesses need **just enough** working capital to pay short term debts. They shouldn't have too much working capital. **Liquid assets** like cash and debtors are great at **paying off debts**, but lousy at **earning money** for the business. To make money, the business needs **fixed assets** that work hard and make sales possible.

Factors affecting how much working capital a business needs:

1) Businesses with **high sales volume** tend to have high cost of sales, so they need more working capital.

2) The more **credit** a business offers, the more **working capital** it needs to fend off a **cash flow crisis**.

3) The longer the **cash flow cycle/operating cycle**, the more working capital is needed. E.g. supermarkets have a short operating cycle because they don't hold stocks for long, and they don't have to wait for payment on credit.

4) **Inflation** increases the costs of wages and stock, so firms need more working capital in times when inflation is high.

5) When a business **expands**, it needs more working capital to avoid **overtrading**. Overtrading means producing so much that the business can't pay its suppliers before it gets the chance to be paid by its customers.

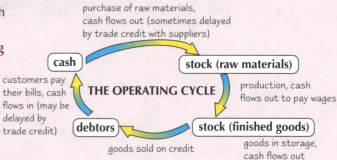

Businesses must *Control* their *Debtors*

1) A business needs to control its **debtors**, (people who owe money to the firm).

2) A company which has sold millions of pounds worth of goods over, say, a three-month period but hasn't made sure that **payment** has been received will have **no money coming in**.

3) Wages, tax, loan repayments and interest must still be paid, so it's very important to control debtors in order to remain in a position of **liquidity**. (See p.48, cash flow).

Businesses must *Control* their *Stock*

1) A business needs to control the volume of its **stock** (raw materials and unsold products) to get a level that allows the business to satisfy the demands of the market.

2) A business which holds **too little stock** will **lose sales** because it won't be able to supply enough goods to the market.

3) A business which holds **too much stock** has money in the form of stock which isn't able to **work** for the company elsewhere. Money tied up in stock could either be helping improve liquidity by paying debt and wages, or helping improve productivity by being invested in new projects.

Stock is *Valued* at *Cost* or at *Net Realisable Value*, whichever's *Lower*

1) Accounting conventions say that stock values on the balance sheet must be **realisable**. This means that the stock value must be the price which you'd actually get if you sold the stock right now in its present state.

2) This realisable price could well be **less** than the **original cost** that the business paid for the stock.

3) The rules are that the company must record the stock value as being the **lower** value of **cost** and **net realisable value**.

4) To put this into context, say a business buys **300 microprocessors** at **£30 000** (cost of £100 each) for the production of its laptop computers. Later, it **updates** the specification of the laptops and has to sell the microprocessors. In the mean time, technological advances mean that there are new, faster microchips on the market. There's little demand for the old microprocessors, and the firm can only sell the old stock for £40 each (£12 000 for the lot). The **lower value** for the stock (£12 000 rather than £30 000) is recorded in the accounts.

Window Dressing

*The apparent strength of the final published accounts can be **legally manipulated** in various ways.*
*This is called window dressing. This page is for **AQA**, although it's useful for both other exam boards.*

It's **Easy** to **Inflate** the **Value** of **Brands** and other **Intangible Assets**

1) Customers may make purchase decisions based upon a brand name. This means the **brand name** has a **value**, especially if the company is ever for sale. It's an asset of the company, but it is **intangible** — it can't be picked up or touched. Other intangible assets include **goodwill**, **patents**, **copyrights** and **trademarks** — non-physical possessions of the company which help the company make money.

2) Brands which have been **recently acquired** for **money** have to go on the balance sheet. Brands which have been in the company for a while **don't** go on the balance sheet. This is because the board of directors would decide on the valuation of these internal brands — and it would be far too easy to make up outrageous valuations.

3) Brands which have been **acquired** for money can **still** be **over-valued** by the business, by the simple tactic of not **depreciating** them enough. This is perfectly legal, if technically somewhat naughty.

Sale and Leaseback is open to **Manipulation**

1) A company may decide to **sell** its fleet of vehicles to a leasing company and then **lease** (similar to renting) the vehicles back for an agreed period of time.

2) The leasing company gains a customer and the company benefits from having a **lump sum payment** for the value of the assets sold to the leasing company.

3) This lump payment is an **income** for the company and it'll appear on the **profit and loss account** — so the **profit** will show an **increase**. This is great news if the natural level of profit is insufficient to meet company **objectives**.

"Now let us draw the curtains of sale and leaseback and close the shutters of overvalued brand assets..."

4) There'll be **reduced fixed assets** on the balance sheet and more liquid cash, so hey presto, the **liquidity** position of the company is altered.

5) This method can't be applied every year — once you've sold some assets and leased them back you can't do the same thing to the same assets the next year.

Businesses can "Capitalise Expenditure" — count Expenses as Fixed Assets

Businesses sometimes play tricks by classifying **operating expenditure** (which is an **expense** on the profit and loss account) as **capital expenditure** (a **fixed asset** on the balance sheet). Balance sheet assets look good, and can be **depreciated over several years**, which is nicer than having the expenditure hitting the profit and loss account all at once.

> **Investors** and **suppliers** use the final accounts to make **judgements** regarding a company so it's important that these people are **aware** of the methods that can be used to enhance the final figures.

Practice Questions

Q1 Why is it important to have (a) enough working capital (b) not too much working capital?

Q2 What does the term "intangible asset" mean?

Q3 What is sale and leaseback?

Q4 How does sale and leaseback affect the profit and loss account?

Exam Questions

Q1 Describe one method available to a company to affect the apparent strength of the published accounts. (2 marks)

Q2 Discuss the effect of intangible asset valuation on the liquidity of a company. (8 marks)

Trust me, I'm a Director...

To be honest, these are two separate topics, but they're both needed for the AQA exam, and they're both related to how the profit and loss account and balance sheet are used. Businesses use all sorts of tricks to make it look as if they have more in assets than they really have, or to make it look like they're making smaller losses and bigger profits than they really are.

Financial Ratios

*Ratio analysis turns final accounts into easy to understand numbers. You can use ratios to compare firms and to compare the performance of a firm from one year to the next. These pages are for **AQA**, **OCR** and **Edexcel**.*

Liquidity Ratios show How Much Money is available to Pay The Bills

1) A firm without enough **working capital** is suffering from poor **liquidity**.
   It has the assets, but it can't **use** them to **pay** for things here and now.

2) The **liquidity** of an asset is how easily it can be turned into **cash** and used to **buy** things. **Cash** is **very** liquid, **fixed assets** such as **factories** are **not liquid**, stocks and money owed by debtors are in between.

3) A business which doesn't have enough current assets to pay their liabilities when they are due is **insolvent**.
   They either have to quickly find the money to pay them, give up and **cease trading**, or go bankrupt.

4) **Working capital** and **liquidity** can be **improved** by decreasing stocks, speeding up collection of debts owed to the business, or slowing down payments to creditors (e.g. suppliers).

5) There are **two** liquidity ratios you need to know — **acid test ratio** and **current ratio**.

The Acid Test Ratio

1) The **acid test ratio** compares **current assets (excluding stock)** to current liabilities.
   It shows how much of what a business owes in the short-term is covered by its current assets.
   It doesn't include stock, because it isn't always easy to sell stock in time to pay off debts.

$$\text{Acid test ratio} = \frac{\text{Current assets} - \text{Stock}}{\text{Current liabilities}} \text{ (written as a ratio } x{:}1\text{)} \qquad \text{For example: } \frac{£30\,000}{£32\,000} = 0.9375{:}1$$

2) A ratio of 1:1 is ideal — it shows **both** amounts are the **same**. A value much **more** than this means the business has **money lying around** that they could use more profitably if they invested it elsewhere. A ratio of less than 1:1 means the business doesn't have **enough** current assets to **pay its bills.** A ratio of 0.8:1 shows a firm has only 80p of current assets for every £1 of current liabilities it owes. Not good...

The Current Ratio

1) **Current ratio** compares **current assets (including stock)** to current liabilities.
   It's also called the **working capital** ratio.

$$\text{Current ratio} = \frac{\text{Current assets}}{\text{Current liabilities}} \text{ (expressed as a ratio } x{:}1\text{)}$$

2) In reality, the business probably couldn't **sell off** all its stock. It'd also need **additional capital** to **replace** stocks — the current ratio should be **higher** than 1:1 to take account of this. 1.5:1 or 2:1 is considered ideal.

3) A value much below 1.5:1 suggests a **liquidity problem** and difficulty meeting current liabilities.
   This is called **overtrading**.

When using these liquidity ratios, managers have to be careful that a poor ratio doesn't turn into a **self-fulfilling prophecy**. For example, a current ratio of 1.4:1 suggests a liquidity problem. A manager might overreact to the problem and get the business in even more trouble. This kind of self-fulfilling prophecy is called **determinism**.

Efficiency or Performance Ratios show how Efficiently the firm is working

1) Asset Turnover Ratio = Sales Revenue ÷ Assets x 100

$$\text{Asset Turnover ratio} = \frac{\text{Sales Revenue}}{\text{Assets}} \times 100$$

1) **Fixed assets** are things like **machinery** which help the business operate efficiently, and so make lots of sales (turnover).
   A firm with a lot of fixed assets should make a lot of turnover.

2) What counts as a **good** asset turnover ratio depends on the type of business. A **discount** retailer makes a lot of sales and has low value stock, so it'd have a **high asset turnover** ratio. A **luxury** retailer such as a Rolls Royce showroom makes fewer sales, and has higher value stock, so it'd have a **lower asset turnover** ratio.

3) Managers should **compare** the asset turnover ratio to **previous operating periods**, to see if the firm is **improving** its efficiency month after month, or year after year.

4) The asset turnover ratio can be **improved** by making sure that the firm **sells everything** it makes.

5) Operating machinery to **full capacity** helps get the most sales out of your fixed assets.
   There are **problems** with this — machinery operating at its limit may break down and need **expensive** repair or **very expensive** replacement. It's better to simply **get rid** of under-used fixed assets.

Financial Ratios

2) *Stock Turnover Ratio = Cost of Sales (per year) ÷ Average Stock Held*

$$\text{Stock Turnover} = \frac{\text{Cost of Sales}}{\text{Average Stock Held}}$$

You need to know the value of sales AT COST, i.e. what they cost the firm to make. Stock is valued at cost price, so you need sales at cost price too. You'll find cost of sales on the profit and loss account and stock held is on the balance sheet.

1) This ratio tells you **how many times** a year the business **sells all its stock**. A fruit and veg stall might sell their entire stock every day, which would give a stock turnover ratio of 365. A property developer who took 4 months to do up and sell each house would have a ratio of 3. Businesses operating **JIT production** have a **very high** ratio.
2) When you analyse this ratio, you need to judge if the business has **enough stock** to **fulfil orders**, but **not too much stock** to be **efficient**. Holding twice the stock needed might not be an efficient use of funds.
3) The stock turnover ratio can be improved by **holding less stock**, or by **increasing sales**. Easier said than done...
4) **Aged stock analysis** lets managers make sure that old stock gets sold before it becomes **obsolete** and **unsaleable**. It lists all stock in **age order**, so the manager can **discount** old stock and cut down orders for slow selling stock.

3) *Debtor Days Ratio = Average Debtors ÷ Total Credit Sales × 365*

$$\text{Debtor Days} = \frac{\text{Average Debtors}}{\text{Total Credit Sales}} \times 365$$

You'll find "debtors" on the balance sheet as a current asset — it's the amount of money owed to the firm by all its debtors. You can average over two years' balance sheets to get the average debtors over the trading period.

1) Debtor Days is the number of days that the business has to **wait to be paid** for goods it supplies on credit.
2) It's best to have **low** debtor days, because it helps with **cash flow** and **working capital**. What makes a good debtor days ratio depends on the type of business. **Retailers** tend to get paid **straight away** unless they're offering credit on items such as TVs or fridges. **Medium size businesses** usually take **70-90 days** to get invoices paid.
3) You can **compare** debtor days ratios with previous months or years to look for **trends**. An **upward trend** may be because the business has offered **longer credit terms** to attract more customers. However, if it isn't monitored, the business may be heading for **cash flow problems**.
4) **Aged debtors analysis** lets managers **control debtor days**. Unpaid accounts are listed in order of how long they've been unpaid. The ones that are **most overdue** are **targeted** first for repayment.

4) *Creditor Days Ratio = Average Creditors ÷ Total Credit Purchases × 365*

OCR and Edexcel

$$\text{Creditor Days ratio} = \frac{\text{Average Creditors}}{\text{Total Credit Purchases}} \times 365$$

You'll find creditors on the balance sheet as a current liability — it's the amount of money that the business owed to all its creditors.

1) This is the number of days the firm takes to **pay** for goods it buys from **suppliers**.
2) You can establish a **trend** over a period of time and use this trend to analyse the efficiency of the firm. For instance, if the trend is upwards it may suggest the firm is getting into **difficulties paying** its suppliers. This might be OK, but if the suppliers get the hump and decide they want to be paid NOW, it's a **problem**.

OCR and Edexcel *OCR and Edexcel* *OCR and Edexcel*

Practice Questions

Q1 A firm has £40 000 assets, £10 000 of which is stock, and £28 000 liabilities. Work out current ratio and acid test.

Q2 Which would have the higher stock turnover ratio, a Porsche dealer or a shoe shop?

Exam Questions

Q1 A company is owed an average of £5000 by its trade customers and sells an average of £20 000 of goods on credit. What can you say about its debt collection using Debtor Days analysis? (6 marks)

Q2 Comment on the efficiency of a firm that has revenue of £750 000 using £2 000 000 in assets. Last year the firm had an asset turnover ratio of 25%. Is the new manager making a difference to the firm? (6 marks)

Oh look, what a lot of "lovely" ratios...

Being totally honest, these ratios are a right pain in the backside to learn. There are a lot of them, and they're practically all something divided by something else, which makes them easy to mix up. Knowing these ratios can score you good marks, so take the time to learn each one, one at a time. Don't be tempted to rush this, even though it's truly, horribly tedious.

Financial Ratios

Investment ratios show the risk of investing in a business. Profitability ratios show profit margin.
*These pages are for **AQA**, **Edexcel** and **OCR**.*

Gearing shows Where a business gets its Capital from

1) **Gearing** shows the **percentage** of a business's capital that comes from **long-term loans** (debt) rather than **share capital** or **reserves** (equity).

$$\text{Gearing} = \frac{\text{long-term loans}}{\text{capital employed}} \times 100\ \%$$

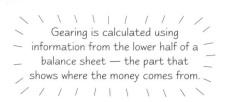
Gearing is calculated using information from the lower half of a balance sheet — the part that shows where the money comes from.

2) A gearing **above 50%** shows a business is **high-geared**, **below 50%** shows it is **low-geared**.

Gearing shows how Vulnerable a business is to Changes in Interest Rates

1) The more the business is **borrowing**, the harder they'll be hit by a rise in interest rates.

2) This is a crude **risk assessment** that an investor can use to help them decide whether to buy shares in the company. The more the firm borrows, the **more interest** it will have to pay — and this may affect **profits** and the **dividend** paid to shareholders. The more the firm borrows, the more **risk** there is that the investor won't get much dividend.

> **Example**: A firm has gearing of 11% — it's low geared.
> - This tells you that **most** long-term funds come from **shareholders**, not loans.
> - You can tell that the firm is **risk averse** — it doesn't want to run the risk of spending too much money on interest payments.
> - Because the firm doesn't have to spend its profits on interest payments, it can withstand a fall in profits more easily than a highly geared firm.

Looks quite high geared to me...

High Gearing has Risks and Rewards — for both Businesses and Investors

1) The reward of **borrowing** money for the business is extra **funds** for expansion. Ideally, the loan is invested in projects or technology, which **increase profits** by more than enough to pay off the loan repayments.

2) The **risk** to the business of borrowing money is that it might not be able to afford the repayments — it might not make enough profit to pay back the loan and interest.

3) The reward (of lending money to the business) for the **investor** is a share **dividend**, often paid out twice a year. The investor can sell their shares at a **profit** if the share price goes up.

4) The **risk** to the **investor** is that the business may **fail**. When a business goes into **liquidation**, the shareholders lose most or all of their money.

High Gearing can be Attractive — during a Growth Phase

1) A firm that's trying to become the market leader, and has growing profits along with a strong product portfolio, may decide to borrow heavily in order to **fund expansion** and gain a **competitive advantage**.

2) When interest rates are very **low**, high gearing is less risky because interest payments are lower.

3) During times of **growth**, there are more profits left after paying loan interest and repayments.

There are Various Methods of Reducing Gearing

1) Gearing can be reduced by changes to the shareholders' funds. The firm could decide to issue more shares or retain more of its profits, for example.

2) Similarly, the firm could use alternative sources of finance to reduce its loans. It may decide to borrow via a **mortgage** that offers **lower interest payments** than an overdraft or loan. It could also renegotiate its existing loans (borrow over a longer or shorter period or from a different bank).

3) Other sources of finance could also be utilised such as **leasing**, accruals and current liabilities.

Financial Ratios

Gross Profit Margin = Gross Profit ÷ Turnover × 100

1) The **gross profit margin** measures the relationship between the profits made and the amount of sales. It's expressed as a percentage, calculated by:

2) What counts as a good gross profit margin depends on the **type of business**. A business with a high asset turnover (e.g. a bakery) can afford to have low gross profit margin.

$$\text{Gross Profit Margin} = \frac{\text{Gross Profit}}{\text{Turnover}} \times 100$$

Gross profit = revenue − cost of sales.
Turnover = value of sales.

3) The ratio can be **improved** by **increasing prices** or **reducing** the direct **cost of sales**.

4) Also, a business can improve its overall gross profit margin by **stopping** selling products with a **low gross profit margin**.

Net Profit Margin = Net Profit ÷ Turnover × 100

Net profit = gross profit − indirect costs.

1) **Net profit ratio** doesn't include **overheads** (indirect costs). The ratio is again expressed as a percentage:

2) It's best to have a **high** net profit margin, although it does depend on the type of business, like the gross profit margin.

$$\text{Net Profit Margin} = \frac{\text{Net Profit}}{\text{Turnover}} \times 100$$

3) It's useful to **compare** net profit margin with gross profit margin over a **period of time**. A business with a **declining net profit margin** compared to gross profit margin is having trouble with its **overheads**.

4) Net profit margin can be improved by **raising prices** or **lowering** cost of sales or (most importantly) **overheads**.

Return on Capital Employed (ROCE) is the most Important profitability ratio

1) The **return on capital employed** (ROCE) is considered to be the best way of analysing profitability. It's expressed as a percentage, calculated by:

2) The **ROCE** tells you how much money is **made** by the business, compared to how much money's been **put into** the business.

$$\text{Return on Capital Employed} = \frac{\text{Operating Profit}}{\text{Capital Employed}} \times 100$$

The operating profit is on the profit and loss account, and the capital employed is on the balance sheet. There are several ways of calculating this ratio, but this method will get you through the exam.

3) A decent **ROCE** is about **20-30%**. It's important to compare the ROCE with the Bank of England interest rate at the time.

4) ROCE can be **improved** by **paying off debt** to reduce capital employed, or by making the business more **efficient** to **increase operating profit**.

Interest Cover Ratio = Profit ÷ Interest Paid

1) The **interest cover ratio** is a measure of ability to pay interest on loans.

2) A figure of 1 means that the firm has to use **all** of its profit to pay interest. In general, the **higher** the interest cover, the better it is for the firm.

$$\text{Interest Cover} = \frac{\text{Profit}}{\text{Interest Paid}}$$

Practice Questions

Q1 What's meant by "high gearing"?

Q2 Give two ways in which Return on Capital Employed can be improved.

Exam Questions

Q1 Evaluate the risks of investing in a business which has a high debt:equity ratio. (6 marks)

Q2 A business has sales revenue of £2 million. Its gross profit is £750 000, and its overheads are £250 000.
(a) Calculate the net profit ratio. Answer on p.138. (3 marks)
(b) How might the business improve its net profit ratio? (5 marks)

Low gearing is also helpful when driving on icy roads...

Oh joy of joys, it's more ratios. The exam boards sure know what makes A level students happy. You can probably guess what I'm going to say — learn the ratios carefully, don't get them mixed up, and be prepared to use them in the exam. Exam questions can ask straight out for specific ratio analysis, or you can get marks for choosing a good ratio yourself.

Shareholders' Ratios

*Shareholders use ratios to see how much dividend they'll get, and to see how the business is performing. Page 44 is for **AQA** and **Edexcel**. Page 45 is for **AQA**, **Edexcel** and **OCR**.*

Investors use Ratio Analysis to decide where to invest

1) **Investors** use several financial ratios when making decisions about where to invest their money. These ratios are called **shareholders' ratios**.

2) **Dividends** are paid out to shareholders once or twice a year, out of the company's profits. **Ratios** help an investor to see the **rate of return** to expect — what proportion of its earnings a company uses to pay out in dividends.

3) Investors would also expect to see the price of their shares **increase** over time. A return on investment caused by a rise in the share price is called a **capital gain**.

4) Some investors want **short-term profits** which give them a quick return through **dividends**. Shareholders' ratios are most useful for these investors.

5) Other investors want a **long-term return** through **capital gain**. They'd want the company to invest profits in growth instead of paying them out as dividends.

What it's all about...

Dividend Per Share = Total Dividend ÷ Number of Shares

1) **Dividend per share** is usually stated at the foot of the **profit and loss** appropriation account (see p.33).

2) The amount of profit set aside for dividend payment is simply divided by the number of shares issued.

$$\text{Dividend Per Share} = \frac{\text{Total Dividend}}{\text{Number of Shares Issued}}$$

3) The resulting figure is usually expressed as a number of **pence**. Say the dividend per share is 9.5p and you own 1000 shares — you'd get a dividend cheque for £95.

4) Shareholders looking for **short-term return** want the dividend per share to be as **high** as possible. Shareholders looking for **long-term return** through capital gain might be happy with a **low** dividend per share.

5) It's pretty much OK for a company with a **low share price** to have a low dividend per share — shareholders can afford to **buy more shares** to get the dividend return they want.

6) It's totally up to the **directors** how much profit they set aside for dividend payments, by the way. If the shareholders don't like it, they can vote at the AGM to sack the directors and bring in a new lot.

Dividend Yield = Dividend Per Share ÷ Price Per Share × 100

1) **Dividend yield** is a comparison between the cost of the shares and the dividend received. It's expressed as a percentage and calculated by:

$$\text{Dividend Yield} = \frac{\text{Dividend Per Share}}{\text{Price Per Share}} \times 100$$

2) Shareholders looking for **short-term return** want a **high dividend yield**.

3) Dividend yield and dividend share can both be improved by increasing the proportion of profits that are paid out as dividend.

4) Dividend yield depends on share price — which can go up and down, depending on business performance.

> **Example:** Johan buys **100 shares** at **500p** each, and the dividend per share is **15p**.
>
> $$\text{Dividend Yield} = \frac{15}{500} \times 100 = 3\%$$
>
> 3% really **isn't very good** for a short-term return. If he wants short-term profit, Johan ought to be looking at **other forms of investment** to see if he could earn more profit elsewhere — e.g. a savings account at the local bank.

Dividend Cover = Net Profit ÷ Dividend Paid Out

1) **Dividend cover** allows you to see how many times a company could pay the dividend from its profits. It's calculated by:

$$\text{Dividend Cover} = \frac{\text{Net Profit After Tax}}{\text{Total Dividends}}$$

2) So, if the dividend cover is 2 (twice) then the company is paying out **half** of its earnings as an ordinary dividend. This may well be rather **attractive** to an investor.

Limitations of Ratios

Ratio Analysis has its Limitations — just like the final accounts do

All financial **ratios** compare two figures from the **accounts**, and give you a raw **number** as an answer.

Ratios don't take account of any **non-numerical factors**, so they don't provide an absolute means of assessing a company's financial health. They have several limitations that you must able to evaluate in your exam answers:

1) **Internal strengths**, such as the quality of staff, don't appear on the accounts, so they won't come up in ratios.

2) **External factors**, such as the **economic** or **market** environment, aren't reflected in the accounts. When the market's very **competitive**, or the economy's in a **downturn**, it's OK for ratios to suffer a bit.

3) **Future changes** such as technological advances or changes in interest rates can't be predicted by the accounts, so they won't show up in the ratios.

4) Ratios only contain information about the **past** and **present**. A business which has **just started** investing for growth will have lousy ratios until the investment **pays off** — that doesn't mean it's not worth investing in.

> **Example of how ratio analysis can't predict changes in external factors**
>
> - Person A is interested in **investing** in XYZ Ltd. **Ratio analysis** indicates that XYZ is **performing strongly** and gives a **good rate of return** for the investor, so she decides to **buy 1000 shares**.
>
> - Later that day, person A talks to person B, who says **new EU health and safety legislation** will **ban XYZ** from making any more of its products from next year onwards. XYZ Ltd must now either **diversify** into another product/service or **close**.
>
> - Person A doesn't feel so clever about her investment now. XYZ Ltd will need **time** and **money** to **reinvest** in a new production line so **profits will be very scarce** for the next few months. Worse still, XYZ Ltd may decide to **close** and she'd have shares with **no value at all**. What a nightmare.

When Comparing ratios, compare Like with Like

1) It's important to **compare** today's ratios with ratios for the same business over a period of time, to spot trends. These comparisons over time need to take account of **variable factors** — things which change over time, such as **inflation**, accounting procedures, the business activities of the firm and the market environment. These things won't always stay the same over the period that you're looking at.

2) It's also useful to compare ratios with **other businesses**, either in the same industry or in different industries. It's important to **compare like with like**. Other firms may **differ** in size, objectives and product portfolio. They may do their **accounts** differently, e.g. they may have their financial year end in a different month.

Practice Questions

Q1 Why might a shareholder not automatically want as high a dividend per share as possible?

Q2 Dividend yield is a better measure of performance than dividend share. Why is this?

Q3 Give a brief outline of two non-numerical factors that should be taken into account when doing ratio analysis.

Q4 Why might comparisons of today's ratios with last year's ratios be inaccurate?

Exam Questions

Q1 Net Profit: £500 000   Profit after tax: £300 000
Dividend per share: 6p   Shares issued: 100 000
a) From the above information give the dividend cover.   (3 marks)
b) If the share price is 300p, calculate the dividend yield.   *Answers on p.138.*   (2 marks)

Q2 Outline two external factors that should be taken into account when analysing financial ratios.   (8 marks)

Q3 Ratio analysis gives information about the past.
Discuss what value ratio analysis has in predicting future performance.   (12 marks)

My analysis is that this is all rather dull...

It's not possible to make 100% solid conclusions from ratio analysis alone. You need to use other data from several sources alongside ratios. SWOT and PEST (p.116) analysis are a good starting point — they consider the market that the business is trading in. Also, bear in mind that using data from the past isn't always a great way to predict the future. Stuff changes.

Contribution and Break-Even Analysis

*These pages are for **OCR**, **AQA** and **Edexcel**.*

Break-Even *is the point where* Profit = 0 *and* Loss = 0

Definition: **Break-even** is the point where **total revenue = total costs**, so the business is making **no profit** and **no loss**. It's easy to see break even on a **graph**. Break-even graphs plot **revenue** and **total costs** against **output**. The point where revenue = total costs is the break-even point.

Example: A company has **variable costs** of **£10 per unit**, and sells each unit for **£30**. The fixed costs are **£600 000**.

Fixed costs are <u>overheads</u>, which don't vary when production is increased or decreased. <u>Variable costs</u> vary with the number of units produced. See p.31.

1) The graph shows the **variable costs** of £10 per unit as a **red line**, and the **fixed costs** of £600 000 as a horizontal **blue line**.

2) The fixed and variable costs have been added together to give **total costs**, shown as a **purple line**.

3) The revenue of £30 per unit is shown as a **green line**.

4) The point where the revenue line and the total costs line meet is the **break-even point**. It's that simple.

5) The **margin of safety** is the difference between **current output** (sales) and **break-even output**. When the firm produces 35 000 units, the margin of safety is 5000 units.

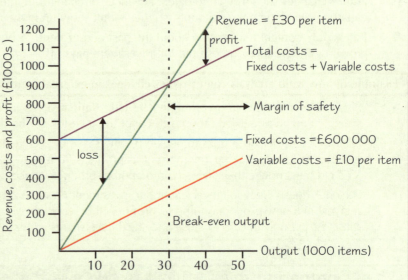

Break Even *analysis shows what happens when* Costs *and* Prices Change

Example 1: A company has **variable costs** of **£10 per unit**, and sells each unit for **£30**. The fixed costs were **£600 000**, but they're going to rise to **£700 000** because ground rents are increasing. Break-even rises to **35 000**.

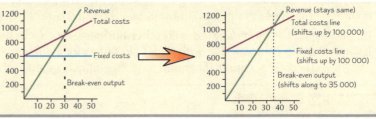

Example 2: A company has **variable costs** of **£10 per unit**, and fixed costs of **£600 000**. They're going to have to cut prices from £30 per unit to **£25 per unit**, because of increased competition. Break-even rises to **40 000**.

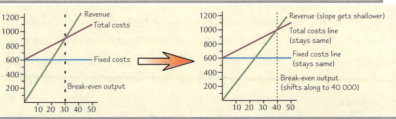

You can also Calculate Break-Even *by working out* Contribution Per Unit

1) The **contribution** that a unit makes toward the **profit** of a firm is the difference between the selling price of a product and the variable costs of making it.

> **Contribution per unit = selling price per unit – variable costs per unit**

2) Contribution is used to pay fixed costs. What's left over is profit.

3) **Break-even** is where **contribution from all sales = fixed costs**. Break-even output is fixed costs over contribution per unit:

$$\text{Break-even output} = \frac{\text{Fixed costs}}{\text{Contribution per unit}}$$

Example: A company has **variable costs** of **£10 per unit**, and sells each unit for **£30**. The fixed costs are **£600 000**.

Contribution = £20. (£30 – £10)

Break-even = 600 000 ÷ 20 = 30 000 sales

The contribution method is less fuss than the graph method, although neither method's exactly hard.

Contribution and Break-Even Analysis

Break-Even Analysis has Limitations

1) It assumes that the firm **sells everything** that it produces **without wastage**, which often isn't true.

2) It also assumes that **variable costs** vary in proportion to the level of output. Businesses can get **discounts** for **bulk purchases**, so their costs don't go up in direct proportion with output.

3) Break-even analysis is for **one product**. Most businesses sell **several products**, and a separate graph for each product would be needed to give an overall picture of the profitable output level. This would get **complicated**.

Contribution lets firms decide if it's Worthwhile to Accept Special Orders

Example: McCormack Textiles produces embroidered handbags and sells them for **£35 each**.
The variable costs of producing each handbag are **£20**. A **national retailer** asks for **8000 units** at **£25 each**.
The burning question is, should McCormack Textiles Ltd accept the order?

1) Even though the firm wouldn't make as much **profit** per item as usual, they'd still earn a **contribution** from each item. Each handbag would earn a **contribution** of **£5** (£25 price – £20 variable costs). The whole order would earn a contribution of **£40 000** (£5 × 8000).

2) McCormack Textiles Ltd would **probably** accept the order, so long as the **fixed costs** of producing the handbags don't go up. Say the firm has to rent **extra factory space** the fixed costs would go up — so long as the fixed costs go up by **less than the contribution**, it's worth taking the order.

3) **Variable costs** might go up as well. McCormack Textiles Ltd might have to pay its workers overtime, which would increase the variable costs. This would mean that the special order would make **less contribution**.

4) McCormack Textiles Ltd might decide to go ahead with the order even if it doesn't make a contribution, if they reckon that exposure to a wider market will result in **higher demand** for their handbags and more sales.

Even special one-off orders at **higher** prices than usual might not be worth accepting. An order that needs to be filled very quickly would need **extra workers**, **overtime payments** and maybe **extra factory space**. It's possible that **costs** might rise by enough to make the order not worth taking.

Contribution can help a business decide what to Make

1) The decision to **delete** a product from a company's portfolio is partly based on its **contribution** to profit and the level of **output** required to **break even**. A **high break-even output** uses lots of **resources**, which could be put to better use **elsewhere** in the company. It's better to use resources where they earn contribution.

2) Other factors such as **customer goodwill** and **employee morale** should be taken into account before deciding to delete a product. Deleting a product might turn **previously loyal** customers off the whole product portfolio.

3) A **manufacturer** which assembles components into a finished item may decide to **produce** some components itself and to **buy** others in from **outside**. The decision of which to buy and which to make is based on contribution. For each component, given the fixed and variable costs of making it and the fixed costs of buying it, you can work out break-even — the amount where the costs of buying and making would be the same.

Practice Questions

Q1 Write down the equation for calculating break even from contribution.

Q2 What happens to break even output when (a) fixed costs rise? (b) variable costs rise? (c) the selling price rises?

Q3 Give one advantage and one disadvantage of break-even analysis.

Q4 Outline the circumstances where a firm should accept a one-off order at less than the usual selling price.

Exam Question

Q1 Clough's make sieves at a variable cost of £3 per unit. Their fixed costs are £20 000 per year. They sell at £5 per unit. The Clough's factory is currently operating at 90% capacity.
(a) How many sieves would they have to sell to break even? Answer on p.138. (4 marks)
(b) Clough's get an order from a big retailer for 4000 sieves at £3.75 each. Should they take the order? (8 marks)

Well, here's my two pennies' worth...

Contribution is a very useful little thing. It comes up in pricing, it's used to work out break even, it's used to help decide whether to accept one-off orders, or whether to stop making a product. So, you ought to be able to work out contribution. Beware though, contribution calculations don't give you the final answer for special orders — there are other factors.

Cash Flow Forecasts

Cash flow forecasts predict when businesses might have money problems.
*These pages are for **AQA** and **Edexcel**.*

Cash Flow is the Movement of Cash In and Out of a business

1) The **profit and loss account** tells us what happened during the 12 month period. It records transactions that will **lead** to money **coming in** (a customer paying for an order) or **going out** (the firm paying for raw materials).

2) The **cash flow statement** tells us **when** money **arrives** at the business, or **leaves** the business.

There's a Delay between Paying for Supplies and Getting Paid for Goods

1) A firm supplying its customers with goods on credit will have to **wait** to be paid for those goods.

2) While it's waiting the firm still has to pay for **overheads** and **raw materials**, so it's paying out money every month while it waits to receive money from its debtors.

3) If the business runs out of money to pay its creditors before its debtors pay up, and can't pay its creditors, it will become **insolvent** (limited liability company) or **bankrupt** (sole trader or partnership).

4) Being able to **forecast** cash flow is vital to business survival and the decision-making process.

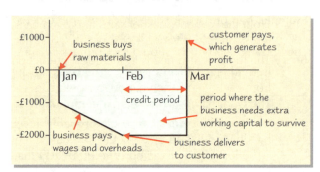

Cash Flow Forecasts Predict when cash will Come In and Go Out

1) **Cash flow forecasts** are usually done on a **monthly** basis.

2) Managers can **predict** when they'll be short of cash, and **arrange loans** or **overdrafts** in time to avoid problems.

3) Businesses show a cash flow forecast to **financial institutions** when trying to get a loan, overdraft, or mortgage. The cash flow forecast serves as **proof of ability to pay** in the future and proof that the firm is **well managed**.

4) **Venture capitalists** like to see a cash flow forecast before investing in a business.

5) **Suppliers** offering **credit** or **hire purchase** may also expect to see a cash flow statement.

6) Businesses have to predict their cash flow based on sales predictions and predictions of costs. It's generally easier to predict costs than it is to predict sales.

Here's how to Construct and Interpret a Cash Flow Forecast — *Edexcel*

Example: A new business starts up with a loan of £18 000. It sells £5000 worth of products in January, £35 000 in February, £35 000 in March and £40 000 in April. All customers are granted a **one month credit period**. Wages and rent cost £15 000 each month, and other costs are £5000 in January, £8000 in February, £2000 in March and £2000 in April.

In the exam, if you're asked to do a cash flow forecast, draw up a table like this, and fill in **revenue** and **costs** for each month from the data given. Add up the revenues to give **total cash in**, and add up the costs to give **total cash out**. Then work out the **cash flow** for each month.

This shows cash coming in from <u>sales</u> and from the initial <u>start-up loan</u>.

This shows <u>cash going out</u> to pay for the firm's <u>costs</u>.

Net cash flow = total revenue – total costs.

The <u>opening balance</u> is money in the bank at the start.

	Item	Jan	Feb	Mar	Apr
Cash in	Sales revenue		£5000	£35 000	£35 000
	Other revenue	£18 000			
	Total revenue	**£18 000**	**£5000**	**£35 000**	**£35 000**
Cash out	Wages and rent	£15 000	£15 000	£15 000	£15 000
	Other costs	£5000	£8000	£2000	£2000
	Total costs	**£20 000**	**£23 000**	**£17 000**	**£17 000**
Net monthly cash flow	**Net cash flow**	**(£2000)**	**(£18 000)**	**£18 000**	**£18 000**
	Opening balance	NIL	(£2000)	(£20 000)	(£2000)
	Closing balance	**(£2000)**	**(£20 000)**	**(£2000)**	**£16 000**

April's sales aren't included because they won't be paid for until May, by the way.

Figures in brackets are <u>negative</u>.

The business has £16 000 in the bank, but it still owes £18 000 from the <u>start up loan</u>.

<u>Closing balance = opening balance + net cash flow</u>.

The <u>closing balance</u> for <u>last month</u> is this month's opening balance.

Cash Flow Forecasts

Businesses also construct Profit and Loss Forecasts

1) A **profit and loss forecast** is a **prediction** of what the year's **profit and loss account** will look like.

2) The profit and loss forecast predicts how much the business will sell — the total **sales revenue**. Predicting sales revenue can be **tricky**, and requires good judgement and market knowledge.

3) It also predicts the **cost of sales** — the direct costs of buying the stock that the business will sell and the production labour of manufacturing the product.

4) The forecast lists all the **overheads** of running the business — rent, business rates, heating, lighting, telephone bill, wages of non-production staff, advertising costs, depreciation of assets, etc. It should be fairly **easy**, if **time consuming**, to figure these out.

5) From the revenue, cost of sales and overheads, it's easy to work out **gross** and **net profit** (gross profit = revenue – cost of sales, and net profit = gross profit – overheads, remember).

6) The forecast also needs to include a prediction of how much **tax** will be paid, which is about 25% of net profit for a limited company, and a bit less than that for a sole trader.

Cash Flow Forecasts and Profit and Loss Forecasts can't be 100% Accurate

1) Cash flow forecasts predict when the business will need a **loan** to keep it afloat. Getting this wrong can result in **insolvency** or **bankruptcy**. A forecast that's **too pessimistic** will result in the business securing **less investment** or loan capital than it could have done.

2) The **reliability** of any forecast **depends hugely** on the **quality** of the **data** used in its construction. Garbage in, garbage out. Data relating to overheads such as heating bills must be accurate.

3) Cash flow forecasts and profit and loss forecasts are based on **assumptions** about **future sales** and **future costs**, and these need to be **realistic**. Managers are often **over optimistic** about future trading.

Internal factors can change after the forecast's been made

1) **Machinery** can break down, **damaging productivity** and requiring expensive repairs.

2) Skilled **staff** may leave the company, again damaging **productivity** and **profit**.

External situations can also change after the forecast has been made

1) **Suppliers** may **increase prices**, affecting **direct costs**, and possibly affecting **pricing policy** and **sales revenue**. **Cash outflows** will definitely be altered, and **cash inflows** may be altered if the business changes its selling prices to compensate. **Profits** will be altered by this.

2) **Competitors** may **decrease prices**, which affects **demand**. **Pricing policy** may also be affected, which has knock-on effects on **cash inflow**, **sales revenue** and **profit**.

3) **Technology** may advance more rapidly than planned. This may affect **market demand** and **sales revenue**, and may require money to be spent on new product development.

4) The **economy** can change. **Interest rates** can **go up**, which would **increase costs** related to loan repayments and interest on overdrafts.

Practice Questions

Q1 Why would a firm produce a cash flow forecast when applying for credit?

Q2 How would you work out the closing balance in a cash flow forecast?

Q3 Give an example of an internal factor which could alter the cash flow forecast.

Exam Questions

Q1 "It's not worth producing a cash flow forecast or profit and loss forecast if it's going to be inaccurate." Discuss.

(10 marks)

Q2 Explain two ways in which changes in the market and the economy can affect the accuracy of a cash flow forecast.

(8 marks)

I wonder how "psychic medium" businesses do at cash flow forecasts...

Customers push for longer credit periods, suppliers push to get paid sooner, and bank managers don't like businesses to run up a massive overdraft. It's best to see the rock and the hard place coming before you get squished in between them. Unfortunately, the accuracy of cash flow predictions depends on the market, which is notoriously unpredictable.

Investment Appraisals

*Investment appraisal helps businesses decide what projects to invest in, in order to get the best, fastest, least risky return for their money. These pages are for **AQA**, **OCR** and **Edexcel**.*

Investment decisions must balance Risk and Return

1) **Investment** can mean buying shares in a business (external investment). It can also be internal investment — buying a large **asset**, spending money on **promotion**, **expanding** into an overseas market, reorganising, or developing a **new brand**. Any situation where you need to **spend money** in order to **make money** is investment.

2) Any situation where you have to spend money in order to make money has **risk**. Both external and internal investors like the risks to be low and the return (profit) to be high.

3) There are a number of **investment appraisal tools** used to gauge the **risk** and **reward** of the available projects. All of these methods are useful, but they're only as good as the **data** used to calculate them.

4) Investment appraisal methods assess how much **profit** a project is going to make, and how **fast** the money will come in. The faster money comes in, the less risk in the long run.

Payback measures the Length of Time it takes to Get Your Money Back

1) **Payback period** is the time it takes for the project to make enough money to pay back the initial investment.

2) For example, a £2 million project that has an annual profit prediction of £250,000 will reach payback in 8 years (£2 million ÷ £0.25 million = 8).

3) Managers compare this payback period with other projects and choose which project to go ahead with.

Advantages of Payback Period Calculation:	It's **easy** to **calculate** and **understand**. It's very good for **high risk** or **high tech** projects.
Disadvantages of Payback Period Calculation:	It ignores **cash flow** after payback. It ignores the **time value** of money.

Wondering what the blue cheese that's about? See next page...

Accounting Rate of Return (ARR) compares Yearly Profit with Investment

1) **Accounting rate of return** (ARR) compares the **average annual profit** with the level of investment.

2) The higher the ARR, the more **favourable** the project will appear.

3) ARR is expressed as a **percentage** and calculated by:

$$\frac{\text{Average Annual Profit}}{\text{Investment}} \times 100 = X\%$$

Example:

	Investment	Year 1	Year 2	Year 3	Year 4	Year 5
Project A	(£10M)	£4M	£5M	£6M	£7M	£5M
Project B	(£8M)	£3M	£3M	£4M	£6M	£6M

The payback period for both these projects is the same, so you need to use **Accounting rate of return**.

Project A pays back during year 3. It costs £10M, by the end of year 2 it's returned £9M and by the end of year 3 it's returned £15M. Project B also pays back its £8M investment some time in year 3.

Project A (£10M investment) has a profit of (£M) 4 + 5 + 6 + 7 + 5 = **£27M.**

Average annual profit is £27M divided by the five years = **£5.4M**

ARR = £5.4M / £10M investment x 100% = **54%**

Project B (£8M investment) has a profit of (£M) 3 + 3 + 4 + 6 + 6 = **£22M**

Average annual profit is £22M ÷ 5 years = **£4.4M**

ARR = £4.4M / £8M investment x 100% = **55%**

The managers would choose project B because it has a higher ARR, just. Just. By a whisker.

Advantages of Accounting Rate of Return:	It's **easy** to **calculate** and **understand**. It takes account of all the project's cash flows.
Disadvantages of Accounting Rate of Return:	It ignores the timing of the **cash flows**. It ignores the **time value** of money.

Investment Appraisals

The *Future Value* of cash inflow depends on *Risk* and *Opportunity Cost*

If someone offers you £100 cash in hand **now** or in one year's time, you'd do best to take it now. This is called the **time value of money**. It's the principle of money being worth less if you wait for it, because of risk and opportunity cost.

1) There's a **risk** that the person would never pay you the £100 after a year had gone by.

2) In a year's time it'd be worth less due to **inflation**. You wouldn't be able to buy as much stuff with that £100.

3) There's an **opportunity cost** — you could **invest** the money instead of **waiting** for it. A high interest account would beat the rate of inflation and give you **even more value** than the £100 in your hand today.

4) You could invest **£100** in an account giving you **6% APR interest**, and you'd get **£106** at the end of the year. If you invested **£94.34** in an account giving you 6% interest you'd get **£100** at the end of the year. So, if you assume an investment interest rate of **6%**, the value of £100 paid to you at the **end of the year** is the same as **£94.34 today**.

Amount you need to invest to get £100 at 6% interest = $100 \times \frac{100}{106}$

> A payment after a year or two, or three, is **always worth less** than the **same payment** made to you **today**.

Discounting adjusts the value of *Future Cash Inflows* to their *Present Value*

1) **Discounting** is the process of **adjusting the value of money** received in the **future** to its **present value**. It's done so that investors can **compare like with like** when they look at the cash inflows they'll receive from projects. £4 million this year **isn't the same** as £4 million in five years' time, and it's not wise to **pretend** that it is the same.

On the next page there are details of two methods of investment appraisal that use discounting.

2) **Discounting** can be seen as the **opposite** of **calculating interest**.

3) It's done by **multiplying** the amount of money by a **discount factor**. This discount factor is like the opposite of a bank interest rate. Discount factors are **always less than 1**, because the value of money in the future is always less than its value now.

4) **Discount factors** depend on what the **interest rate** is predicted to be. **High** interest rates mean that the future payments have to be **discounted a lot** to give the correct present values. This is so that the present value represents the **opportunity cost** of not investing the money in the **bank** where it'd earn a nice **high interest rate**.

5) As you might expect, when **interest rates** are predicted to be **low**, the future cash inflow needn't be discounted so much. There's less opportunity cost.

6) Discounting is also related to the **risk** element of a project. There's a **risk** that the **project won't pay out** the expected returns, because of market changes.

Year	0	1	2	3	4	5
Discount Value for 10% interest	1	0.909	0.826	0.751	0.683	0.621
Present Value of £1000	£1000	£909	£826	£751	£683	£621

Year 1 discount value = 100/110 = 0.909. Year 2 discount value = (100/110)² = 0.826. Year 3 discount value = (100/110)³ = 0.751. It's like compound interest in reverse.

Practice Questions

Q1 What does ARR take account of that payback doesn't?

Q2 Give one advantage and one disadvantage of ARR.

Q3 How does risk help to explain why the value of £1000 paid in two years' time isn't the same as £1000 paid today?

Q4 What is discounting, and what's it kind of the opposite of?

Exam Questions

Answer on p.138.

Q1 A business is investing in a new product. The initial investment is £200 000. The product will generate revenue of £100 000 per year, and costs of £60 000 per year. Calculate the average rate of return on the investment. (4 marks)

Q2 Explain why a future cash inflow must be discounted to give its present value. (5 marks)

You have to speculate if you want to accumulate...

The idea that money is worth less if you have to wait for it almost certainly seems, oh I don't know, really freaking strange. There really is good value to this "time value of money" — there's the risk involved in waiting to be paid, and there's the opportunity cost of what you could have done with the money if you had it in your hand from the start.

Investment Appraisals

*One last page of investment appraisal calculations, and then a page about why investment appraisal calculations aren't "all that and a bag o' chips" after all. These pages are for **AQA**, **OCR** and **Edexcel**.*

Discounted Cash Flow allows for Risk, Inflation and Opportunity Cost

1) **Discounted cash flow** (DCF) is an investment appraisal tool that allows for money to change value over **time**.

2) It's used to calculate the **Net Present Value** (NPV) of the cash flowing into a project. This is the amount of money they'd be worth if you had them **now**, which is **always** less than their face value.

3) The **Net Present Value** is worked out by multiplying the cash inflow by a **discount factor**. (See p.51.)

4) The **discount factor** applied is the **required rate of return** for the projects — the rate of return that the managers decide that they need to get from the project to make it worthwhile. The **discount factor** will be **supplied for you** in the exam, so you won't need to work these out — thank all that's good and chocolatey.

5) The **downsides** of DCF are that it's a bit **hard to calculate**, and that it's hard to figure out what the **discount factor** ought to be. The longer the project is set to last, the harder it is to predict the discount factor.

Example:

Apply the discount factor of **10%** to the same figures as the example on p.50.

Project A	Cash inflow	Discount Value (10%)	Present Value
Year 1	£4M	0.909	£4M × 0.909 = £3 636 000
Year 2	£5M	0.826	£5M × 0.826 = £4 130 000
Year 3	£6M	0.751	£6M × 0.751 = £4 506 000
Year 4	£7M	0.683	£7M × 0.683 = £4 781 000
Year 5	£5M	0.621	£5M × 0.621 = £3 105 000
Total Present Value of Cash Inflows			£20 158 000
Net Present Value (total minus Investment)			-£10M = **£10 158 000**

Year 1 discount value = 100/110 = 0.909
Year 2 discount value = $(100/110)^2$ = 0.826
Year 3 discount value = $(100/110)^3$ = 0.751

Remember, project A had an initial investment of £10M.

Project B	Cash inflow	Discount Value (10%)	Present Value
Year 1	£3M	0.909	£3M × 0.909 = £2 727 000
Year 2	£3M	0.826	£3M × 0.826 = £2 478 000
Year 3	£4M	0.751	£4M × 0.751 = £3 004 000
Year 4	£6M	0.683	£6M × 0.683 = £4 098 000
Year 5	£6M	0.621	£6M × 0.621 = £3 726 000
Total Present Value of Cash Inflows			£16 033 000
Net Present Value (total minus Investment)			-£8M = **£8 033 000**

Project B had an initial investment of £8M.

Internal Rate of Return (IRR) works out Several NPVs

1) **Internal Rate of Return** (IRR) is concerned with the **break even rate of return** of the project.

2) It uses **DCF** to produce **several net present values** for each project, each at **slightly different discount rates**, until they get an **NPV** of **zero.** The discount rate which gives a NPV of zero is called the **internal rate of return**.

3) Managers know that the **internal rate of return** needs to be higher than the **expected rate of interest**, otherwise they might as well put the money in the **bank** instead of investing it in the project.

4) Managers can also set their own "**criterion level discount rate**" which is their **minimum rate of return**. Projects which have an **internal rate of return** lower than this criterion level don't get the go-ahead.

5) Calculating the IRR is **really hard**, and there's a lot of repetition involved. It's best done by **computer**.

Advantages of Internal Rate of Return:	It allows you to set the **required rate of return**. It allows for the **time value of money**.
Disadvantages of Internal Rate of Return:	The calculation requires **computers**. Some managers find it **hard** to get their heads around it.

Investment Appraisals

Non-Numerical, Qualitative factors affect Investment Decisions

The investment decisions made by managers are based upon a wide range of numerical data and quantitative methods. Managers must also put the decisions into a **qualitative** context, based on internal factors and market uncertainty.

Business Objectives and Strategy Can Influence Investment Decisions

1) An investment appraisal recommended purely on financial data **may not fit in** with the **objectives** of a firm. Many businesses will only make an investment if the project will **help them achieve** their objectives.

2) For example, a business which aims to produce **low cost products** for a large mass market (e.g. teaspoons) would be unlikely to invest **as much** in **research and development** as a high-end technology business.

3) **Human resources investment** takes away from short term profit, so a firm with the objective of **maximising profit** for shareholder dividends would be unlikely to invest in staff development. On the other hand, a business which aims to produce **high quality**, high tech products would invest in **skilled staff**.

Corporate Image Can Influence Investment Decisions

1) **Good corporate image** brings **customer goodwill** and **loyalty** in the long term, and the firm may consider this more important than **short term rate of return** on investment. Investment decisions that create bad publicity and damage customer loyalty will damage the bottom line in the **long term**.

2) A firm with a green, **ecologically friendly** image would avoid investments that would damage the environment. Some firms incorporate environmental costs into their investment appraisals.

Industrial Relations can Influence Investment Decisions

1) Investments which result in a **loss of jobs** may be turned down, even if they show a good rate of return.

2) **Loss of jobs** affects **staff morale**. Cost of **redundancy payments** should be factored into the decision. Trade unions may **strike** over the job losses, which would affect **productivity**. **Corporate image** may also be damaged.

Risk is Always at Work in the Market — and Each Project Has a Risk of Failure

1) The market is an environment that has **risk** and **uncertainty** every day. **Exchange rates** may alter, **sales** may decrease/increase, **customers' tastes** may change and **competitors** may become stronger.

2) Also, **each project** has specific **risk** — a new product might not sell very well. Branching into a new market is risky and might not pay off. Every firm has a **different attitude** to **risk**.

Wrapping it all up — these Investment Decisions are Hard...

Investors have to make decisions about which firm to buy shares in. They use **ratio analysis**, **market trend analysis**, awareness of **product life cycle** and the **industry lifecycle** to arrive at their decision.

Managers of firms must also make **investment decisions** about which **projects** would be best for the future of the firm, set against the business **objectives**, **corporate image** and attitude to **risk**.

At this level you'll need to draw on all your **accumulated knowledge** of business to give the examiner some proper **critical analysis** and well thought out **evaluation**. Good analysis and evaluation will get you the **higher level marks**.

Practice Questions

Q1 What are the main advantages and disadvantages of DCF?

Q2 What's IRR stand for, and what the heck is it, anyway?

Q3 Give examples of three qualitative factors that affect investment decisions.

Exam Question

Q1 Denton Ceramics are considering investing in a new kiln. The kiln will cost £17 000, and will generate £5000 extra revenue a year for 5 years. Calculate the NPV of the project, given a discount factor of 5%. (8 marks)

Answer on p.138.

Ow, my head hurts...

These DCF calculations are slightly tricky. They'll give you the discount value, and you have to work out the discount factor for each year (it's like compound interest in reverse, you raise the ratio to the power of each year), work out the present values, add them up and take away the initial investment. At least you don't have to work out IRR calculations.

Structure of Organisations

An organisation's structure has an effect on the people in it.
*These pages are for **OCR**, and are very useful for **Edexcel**.*

Businesses can be organised in Departments

1) Departments group jobs together by **function**.

2) Organising a business in departments lends itself to a **tall** structure, with narrow **spans of control**.

3) Large businesses organised into departments can have a **long chain of command** between **directors** at the top and regular Joe and Joanne **Worker** at the bottom.

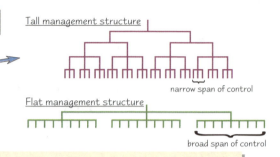

Tall management structure

narrow span of control

Flat management structure

broad span of control

A quick run down of the **big four departments**:

Finance Department — looks after the money. Prepares final accounts, and does day-to-day money management, such as paying suppliers, invoicing customers, paying employee expenses.

Marketing Department — looks after marketing strategy. Plans and delivers marketing mix for all products. Knows what's selling, why, and how to make it sell more.

Production Department — makes stuff. In manufacturing, this is everything from buying raw materials to delivering finished product. The production function can also be applied to the supply of **services**, e.g. web hosting services, editorial services, advertising design services.

Human Resources Department — makes sure the business has the right number of workers with the right skills.

Some businesses have more departments than this, e.g. R&D, customer services.

There are important Inter-Relationships between departments

The **marketing department** and **production department** have to work together — the marketing department decides what the production department should make, and what level of quality it should have.

The **finance department** decides how much money is available to all other departments. Marketing activities can't happen if the money isn't there.

Organisation by Departments (on a Systems basis) has Benefits

1) **Specialist** managers and workers can operate in their own **area of expertise**, without having to worry about anything else.

2) Organisation by departments tends to be a **rigid** structure. Everyone in the business is **familiar** with the structure. Everyone knows who his or her boss is.

3) Everyone knows what they need to do in order to be **promoted**. There's a clear **chain of promotion** within the department, for example from Assistant to Junior Executive to Senior Executive to Assistant Manager to Manager to Director.

Organisation by Departments has Disadvantages

1) Traditional organisation by departments keeps different functions **apart**. Completely different **working patterns** and **cultures** can develop in different departments — it can be like the accountants in the Finance department are on a completely **different planet** from the PR executives in the Marketing and PR department.

2) Different departments find it hard to **share ideas** with each other. It may be that only the directors and top management of different departments ever meet up. Except at the office Christmas party of course, where employees are guaranteed to meet and get off with someone from a department they've never even heard of...

3) As a business grows, **chains of command** get longer, and longer, and longer. This makes decision-making take a very **long time**. Decisions are sometimes made by someone three or four links up the chain from where the decision needs to be made.

4) Senior managers can be **remote** from the factory floor or the customer-facing part of the business, which means they can make a few daft decisions which are **inappropriate** for workers and customers.

5) As a business grows, **communication chains** get longer, and communication sometimes becomes **slow** and **inefficient**. Messages can be garbled on their way from the top to the bottom of the chain.

6) In large organisations, there's often **rivalry** between departments. The Sales and Marketing Director may want to get more money out of the Finance Director than the Production Director gets.

Structure of Organisations

Businesses can be *Organised* on a *Product* basis

1) A product-based structure allows managers to make decisions that are **relevant** to each product division.

2) Each division operates as its own **profit centre** (see p.28). This lets senior management compare the successes of each product group, which can generate **competition**.

3) Competition between sectors can be **healthy**, or it can be **negative**.

4) If each product division has its own internal structure, there may be **unnecessary duplication** — e.g. market research could be a **shared** facility between divisions.

5) Sometimes, product sectors are divided up into **small teams** working on **one specific product** each. These teams incorporate people from several business functions, and they tend to be **informally** organised.

Example: **Unilever** manufactures spreads, skincare items, tea, soups, washing powder, toothpaste, ice cream and frozen foods. It has structured its organisation into two sectors — **Food**, and **Home/Personal Care**.

Businesses can be *Organised* by *Market Segment*

Businesses can organise their **product divisions** by **type of customer** — for example a food manufacturer could have one sector devoted to microwaveable meals for busy **young professionals**, another sector devoted to **kids'** lunchbox snacks and another sector devoted to luxury foods aimed at **wannabe gourmets**.

It's easier to organise by **type of purchase** — another food manufacturer might have one sector for **take-home purchases** (e.g. family size frozen peas), one sector for **impulse buys** (e.g. ice lollies), and another sector for **catering purchases** (e.g. catering size packs of frozen chicken breasts).

Organising by *Production* means *Different Functions* work together

1) Within each **product sector**, business **functions** work **together**. Production, marketing, R&D and finance functions work together to design, make and market the products.

2) Each sector has **company objectives** to meet, related to each product within the sector, and everyone works together to meet the objectives. This gives a sense of **common purpose**, which you don't get when the finance department, marketing department and production department have their heads down to meet individual department targets.

3) Organising by production **forces** different functions and jobs within the business to **communicate** together. Different functions have to share ideas and work practices.

4) Managers in a product-organised business must be **multi-skilled**. They need to know a bit about all the areas of the business, and have a good overview of what the firm is trying to achieve.

Here we see the research and development bees in the "honeys and nectars" product sector actually coming up with radical designs for new honey.

Practice Questions

Q1 Does traditional department organisation have wide or narrow spans of control?

Q2 Give a disadvantage of organising on a systems basis (i.e. in departments).

Q3 Why would a manufacturer organise the business by product lines?

Exam Question

Q1 Discuss the ways in which the organisation of a business can affect its ability to respond to market changes.

(10 marks)

I wonder how organised your revision notes are...

These pages contain some revision from AS level, and they also cover some bits and pieces that OCR use as a kind of introduction to people and organisations. When you get a business case study in the exam, you need to be aware of the effects of the way the business is organised — in formal departments, in product divisions, in small teams or whatever.

Motivation

All businesses need their workers to be motivated so that they work as hard as they can.
*These pages are for **OCR**.*

Businesses need workers to *Work Hard* and *Work Reliably*

1) **Workers** are one of the most important **assets** of a business. Their role is to **produce** — to turn raw materials into marketable products and bring profit into the business.

2) What the **managers** of the business want is for the employees to generate as much **profit** for the business as they can.

3) It's best if this profit is **sustainable** and **high quality** (see p.32) — which means that the workers need to be able to **keep on working** at a good level of productivity. Managers want workers to be **reliable**.

Motivation is *What Makes You Work*

Motivation means anything that makes you **work harder** and **achieve more** than you might otherwise do. Obviously, businesses need to motivate their workers to keep them bringing in the bacon.

Motivation is a difficult nut to crack. Managers have to push workers to **produce** more, without pushing them so hard that they get **fed up** and **leave**. They have to motivate workers to produce **high quality** goods, at the same time as keeping **productivity** high.

1) **Ideally**, employees would **identify** with the **goals** of the business, and really want to do the job and do it well, just for the **love of the job**. But the real world isn't like that. To some workers, a job's **just a job** — they go in at 9, work, leave at 5 and don't get wildly enthused about the company mission statement, or the departmental budget.

2) Managers have to use all kinds of **tricks** to motivate employees who aren't 100% in love with their job. These include **financial incentives** like bonuses and performance related pay, and other incentives like staff parties, which try to **compensate** for the tedium of the job.

3) There are also **non-financial motivators** which try to make the job more **interesting**, such as job rotation, job enrichment and teamworking.

4) Other non-financial incentives try to make the employee feel like they **matter**, e.g. employee participation, delegation and quality circles.

5) Employees have **different personalities**, and what works to motivate one person may be useless to the person next to them. Managers have to motivate **everyone** in their team. It's best if they can tailor their motivation strategy to each employee. But this isn't always possible.

Poor Motivation creates *Big Problems* for business

1) Poor motivation can result in **low productivity**, with obvious impacts on turnover and profit.

2) Lack of motivation can result in **poor quality control**. This can damage relationships with customers.

3) Employees who aren't motivated may not bother to follow **procedures** properly. This can have serious implications for health and safety, and for quality control.

4) Poor employee morale increases **absenteeism** (sick days) and **lateness**. This costs money in **lost productivity** and in hiring **temps** or paying **overtime** to cover for absent employees.

5) **High performing employees** tend to lose morale and motivation when they feel they aren't being **recognised**, or given enough **responsibility** to make their job interesting. Their performance suffers, and they often **leave** for another job that will motivate them better. No business wants good workers to quit.

6) **Poor performing employees** who lack motivation tend to **demotivate others** — when workers see the person next to them is **lazy**, doesn't give two figs and is still in a job, they wonder why they should bother. Poor performers don't often leave because they'd find it hard to get another job. Most businesses might prefer if they did quit.

Poor Morale is *Contagious* — it *Affects Everyone*

1) A **bad atmosphere** at work makes **everyone** miserable.

2) Employee morale suffers when people at work **don't get on** with each other, or don't like the boss.

3) A **boring**, dull office environment can be **depressing**— a lick of paint and nice new curtains can go a long way.

Motivation

Motivation Theory Revisited...

Taylor and Scientific Management — people are in it for the money

1) F. W. Taylor thought that workers were motivated by **money**, but would do the bare **minimum** of work if left to their own devices.

2) Taylor did **time and motion studies**, timing work activities with a **stopwatch**. He said managers should use time and motion studies to figure out the **most efficient** way to do a job, and then make sure every single worker did it that way. This approach is called **scientific management**.

He was in favour of division of labour — breaking down work into a lot of small repetitive tasks.

3) Taylor said workers should be paid according to the **quantity** they produced, and that the most **productive** workers should get a **better rate**. He believed that these financial incentives would **motivate** workers and raise **productivity**.

Taylor's approach ignored the demotivating effect of repetitive work.

Mayo and Human Relations — people are motivated by social factors

1) **Elton Mayo** found that people achieved more when they got **positive attention**.

2) Mayo thought managers should **pay attention** to workers as individuals, and **involve** them in decision making.

3) He also thought that workers should work in teams and **socialise** together — outside of work as well as at work.

Maslow's Hierarchy Of Needs — people need basics first

Maslow said that people start by meeting the needs at the **bottom** of the pyramid. Once they've sorted out those needs, they can move on to the needs on the **next level** up.

Self Actualisation meeting potential

Businesses meet these needs by giving workers the opportunity to develop new skills and take on new responsibility.

Self Esteem — achievement

Businesses give employees responsibility for their work and offer them promotion.

Social Needs — friendship, teamwork

Team work and work social outings meet these needs.

Safety — safe work environment with job security

Health and safety policy and secure employment contracts meet these needs.

Basic Physical Needs — food, water, shelter, clothes

Businesses meet these needs by paying workers enough and providing a warm, dry work environment.

Herzberg's Hygiene and Motivating Factors — sort out a good environment first

In the 1960s, Frederick Herzberg interviewed accountants and engineers to find out what motivated and satisfied them at work. He identified two groups of factors that influenced the motivation of workers:

1) **Hygiene factors** are things like company policy and admin, **supervision**, **working conditions**, **pay**, and relations with fellow employees. They don't act as motivators, but if they **aren't good**, workers get **dissatisfied**.

2) **Motivating factors** are things like **interesting work**, personal **achievement**, **recognition** of achievement, scope for more responsibility and personal **development**. These factors **do** positively motivate workers.

Practice Questions

Q1 What is motivation?

Q2 Give three examples of problems caused by poor motivation.

Q3 Give two examples of hygiene factors, and two examples of motivating factors.

Exam Questions

Q1	Explain how a poorly performing employee can affect the morale and motivation of an entire team.	(8 marks)
Q2	Suggest how managers at a traditional production line factory might improve staff motivation.	(8 marks)

Have a cup of tea — it's good for morale...

You'll have studied motivation for AS level, but there's more detail and more depth at A level. For example, you're expected to be aware of potential problems caused by poor motivation, as well as knowing about the theories. It's important you can put motivation into context, and spot where it can be improved in any business case study that you get in the exam.

Management Styles

*There are different style of management — different ways of getting things done and different ways of dealing with people. These pages are for **OCR** and **Edexcel**. Some of it's revision of AS work, some of it's brand spanking new.*

Managers often need to be Leaders as well

1) Managers **set objectives** for their department and for the people in it.

2) Managers **organise resources** to get the job done and **achieve** their objectives.

3) Leaders **motivate** people. They **inspire** people to do things which they wouldn't do otherwise.

4) Managers who are good leaders can **persuade** people that the decisions they make and the objectives they set are the **best** ones.

There are various different Management and Leadership Styles

① **Authoritarian** or **autocratic** style — the **leader makes decisions** on his or her own. The manager identifies the objectives of the business and says how they're going to be achieved. It's useful when dealing with lots of **unskilled** workers and in **crisis management**. This method requires lots of **supervision** and monitoring — workers can't make their own decisions. An authoritarian style can **demotivate** able and intelligent workers.

② **Paternalistic** (fatherly) style is a softer form of the autocratic style. The leader makes the decisions after **consultation** with others. The leader **explains** their decisions to the workers in an attempt to **persuade** the employees that such decisions are in everyone's interest. Paternalistic managers think that getting **involved** and caring about human relations is a **positive motivator**.

③ **Democratic** style — the leader encourages the workforce to **participate** in the decision making process. Managers **discuss** issues with workers, **delegate responsibility** and **listen** to advice. Democratic leaders have to be good communicators, and their organisations have to be good at dealing with a lot of **to and fro communication**. This management style shows managers have a lot of confidence in the workforce — which leads to increased employee **motivation**. It also takes some of the **weight** of decision making off the leader.

④ **Laissez-faire** style is a weak form of leadership. **Management rarely interferes** in the running of the business and the workforce is left to get on with trying to achieve the objectives of the business with minimal input and control from the top. This **hands off** style of leadership might be appropriate for a small, highly motivated team of **able** workers. For workers who need guidance, it'd be a bit of a disaster.

Managers can Consult or Delegate

Consultation asks employees for input on decisions

1) **Consultation** means **asking** employees for their opinions before taking a decision.

2) After the consultation process, it's still the **manager** who makes the decisions. They can **ignore** employee input.

3) Consultation is a large part of the **paternalistic** leadership style.

Delegation gives employees authority to make decisions

1) Senior managers **delegate** decision-making to **junior managers**, and to employees.

2) Delegation is a large part of the **democratic** leadership style.

3) Employees need to be **capable** of making the decision. They may need extra **training** and **resources**.

Management Styles affect Communication within the Business

1) The **autocratic** style doesn't encourage communication from employees. Communication is downwards only. The autocratic style can be seen as a **barrier to communication**.

2) The **democratic** style **encourages communication** between employees and managers, and between employees on the same level. Decisions are discussed before being finalised.

Management Styles

Management is a *Balancing Act* between *"People" Needs* and *"Task" Needs*

Task needs are related to getting the **job done**. People needs are related to **morale** and **relationships**:

Examples of task needs	Examples of people needs
Meeting a **deadline**.	Feeling **appreciated** and **valued**.
Designing a **procedure** for maximum efficiency.	Feeling like **your opinion counts** in **decision making**.
Following a **procedure**.	Feeling like you **belong** in a team.
Monitoring progress towards a target.	Feeling that your effort **makes a difference** to the outcome.
Having the **physical resources** the task requires.	**Getting on** with colleagues.

1) Managers have to make sure that **task needs** and **people needs** are met.
   It's difficult to meet **both** sets of needs at the same time.
2) Task needs are best served by a **task-oriented** approach that **monitors progress** and **rewards success**.
3) People needs are best served by a **relationship-oriented** approach that makes sure everyone's feeling **comfortable** and **confident** about the work and the work environment.
4) When **people needs** aren't met, motivation and morale **suffer** — see p.56-57.

Different Situations require different Management Styles

1) Some situations need a lot of **task-oriented management**. Others need more **relationship-intensive management**.
2) **Urgent** tasks need different management and leadership from **routine** tasks. Urgent tasks may need a manager to "crack the whip" and **tell** employees what to do and when to do it.
3) A **large, unskilled** workforce suits **authoritarian** leadership, whereas a **small, educated** workforce suits a **democratic** approach much better. The more ready employees are to **take responsibility**, the less authoritarian and task-orientated the manager has to be.

Behaviour	Task/relationship orientation	What the leader does	What the employees are like
Telling staff what to do	High task/low relationship	Gives **instructions**	**Not ready** for responsibility
Persuading ("selling")	High task/high relationship	**Persuades** and **consults**	Ready for **some** responsibility
Participating	Low task/high relationship	**Shares** decision making	Ready for **more** responsibility
Delegating	Low task/low relationship	Lets **followers** decide	Ready for **full** responsibility

Delegating is "low relationship" because the leader doesn't need to get involved any more.

4) The way the organisation's been run in the **past** affects the **expectations** of the workforce, which affects how they might **respond** to leadership.
5) The **best leaders** are the ones who can **adapt** their style to suit the situation. It's hard to adapt like that, and most leaders have their own **natural style** that they're happiest with.

Practice Questions

Q1 Which leadership style is most appropriate for the following situations: a) crisis management? b) delegation?
Q2 Give two examples of people needs, and two examples of task needs.
Q3 A manager can tell staff what to do and expect complete obedience, or she can "sell" her way of doing things to them — i.e. persuade them that it's best. Which has higher relationship orientation, "telling" or "selling"?

Exam Question

Q1 Manufacturer DCP Furniture must increase productivity by 25% by next March. Manager Sam Raynes has an easy going, friendly attitude to his staff and likes to involve them in decision making. The managing director worries that Sam isn't up to it, and wants to replace him. Write a report advising the MD what to do. (12 marks)

I'm not leading you up the garden path, I promise...

The key to all this is being able to say which is more appropriate for a particular situation — in the exam, you might get a case study of two managers with different leadership styles, and be asked to assess whose ideas are best for the situation the business is in. A lot of it depends on whether the situation has more "task needs" or "people needs" — they're different.

Communication

Communication is vital in business, just to get the job done properly.
*These pages are for **AQA** and **OCR**.*

There are several **Categories** of **Communication**

1) **Formal communications** are **officially endorsed** by the business. They include corporate notice boards, company newsletters, letters from managers or the HR department.

2) **Informal communications** are unofficial, e.g. gossip, emails between employees and leaked information.

3) **Vertical communication** travels **up** and **down** the hierarchy. **Authoritarian** corporate cultures often only have downward communication — but a mixture of upward and downward communication is best.

4) **Horizontal** (**lateral**) communication occurs between staff on the **same level** within the hierarchy.

5) **Internal communication** remains within the organisation, e.g. office notice board, internal email.

6) **External communication** is aimed at **external stakeholders** such as customers, suppliers or pressure groups, e.g. websites, press releases.

Good Communication improves Business Efficiency

1) **Clear communication** reduces mistakes, saving time and money.

2) Clear, **effective communication** makes sure that all employees know what their **objectives** are.

3) **Fast, effective communication** speeds up decision-making, keeps a company ahead of competitors, and can reduce lead times for new products. This is **essential** in a fast-changing market such as IT or fashion.

Communication and Motivation are Related

1) **Poor morale** and **poor communication** go together. **Demotivated** people don't care enough to communicate. People who don't communicate feel isolated and demotivated.

2) **Demotivated** workers tend to **ignore** communication, especially if they think it might **increase their workload**.

3) **Autocratic** managers only believe in one-way communication. Not being **listened** to is **demotivating.**

4) Modern work practices such as **kaizen** (p.87) and employee empowerment require **constant communication**.

1) **Maslow** identified the **social needs** of workers as an important motivator.

2) Poor relationships with peers and managers are often caused by **poor communication**. **Herzberg** suggests hygiene factors such as relationships need satisfying **before** motivation is possible.

3) The work of **Mayo** demonstrated how employee **productivity increased** as managers took an **interest** in their employees' opinions. This required increased and improved **internal communication**.

Organisations must **Overcome** four **Barriers** that **Threaten Communication**

1) **Attitudes**	The receiver may be **distracted**. The receiver may **dislike** the sender, or feel **threatened** by the communication.
2) **Intermediaries**	The longer the **chain of communication**, the more **mangled** the message can get between sender and receiver.
3) **Language barriers**	One word can mean different things in different **cultures**. Translation can **distort meaning**. **Jargon** can be confusing.
4) **No sense of purpose**	Staff who don't understand **why** they're being told something may start **ignoring** future messages.

Giving **feedback** after communication lets the sender know that the receiver has **got the message**. This helps the sender **assess** their communication.

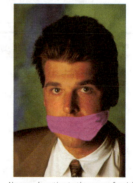

Never underestimate the power of a pink sock gag as a barrier to communication.

Noise is anything that Interferes with Communication

1) **Examples** of noise include:
2) Noise should be **minimised** wherever possible — this **reduces** the potential for messages to be **misunderstood**.

- **actual noise**, e.g. from factory **machines**.
- **technical jargon** used in specialist industries, e.g. pharmaceuticals.
- too many people trying to **talk at once** and not listening to others.
- **"junk"** communication such as **spam emails**.

Communication

ICT can Improve or Worsen Communication at work

1) **Information communication technology** (ICT) can improve communication through activities such as **email** and **intranet** sites (like a website but only accessible from computers physically linked to each other within the organisation). Benefits of these methods include the **speed** and **ease** with which messages can be sent.

2) **Databases** can be used to communicate key data to managers. They can produce instant reports which contain data such as sales revenue or productivity figures. These are called **management information systems** (MIS).

3) Care must be taken not to **swamp** managers with too much information. This is called **communication overload**. Email, in particular, proliferates like mad — emails get forwarded and copied and sent back and forth.

4) Unlike **phone** conversations, **email** doesn't have **tone of voice**. Emails can be misread as "snarky". Email isn't as **formal** as written memos and letters, so it's easier to **slip up** and write something unintentionally snotty.

Case Study — Phones4U banned internal email ← Few businesses would go this far.

Problem: Phones4U found that store managers spent so much time reading emails that they were neglecting their staff and customers. Bosses estimated that 3 hours a day were being spent on email.

Solution: The company banned email for internal communication. Head office communicated to managers and staff via the corporate intranet. Employees were encouraged to use the phone or have face-to-face meetings.

Size has an Impact on Communication

1) Effective communication is **harder** in large companies as more messages need to reach more staff. Poor communication is a key **diseconomy of scale**.

2) **Multinational** corporations have to overcome **cultural** and **language** barriers when communicating across **international borders** as well as practical constraints such as **time differences**.

3) **Rapid growth** often creates organisational structures with long **chains of command** and departments with inexperienced staff. Long chains of command with many **intermediaries** make communication difficult.

4) **Decentralisation** (sharing out authority with junior employees) makes communication chains **shorter**, which makes them more **manageable**. Managers and staff can also be **trained** in **communication skills** to help them cope.

Communication is important within Work Groups

1) Communication isn't just between head office and managers, or between managers and underlings. Employees who **work together** communicate as part of their work, and as part of their "group dynamic".

2) Verbal and non-verbal communication within a group reinforces **group norms**. Group norms are the **habits** of the group that members must **stick to** — for example "everyone takes their turn to make tea for the group".

3) The way that people **behave** within a **group** can have an effect on the **whole organisation**. A group that doesn't **get on well** together won't achieve as much as a group where people get on smoothly.

4) There are **informal groups** at work, e.g. groups of friends — as well as formal job-related groups. Employees like the **social interaction** they get from both formal and informal groups — see Mayo and Maslow (p.57).

Practice Questions

Q1 What is the difference between horizontal communication and vertical communication?

Q2 Give two examples of external communication.

Q3 How can decentralisation improve communication?

Exam Questions

Q1 Use relevant theory to explain why effective communication between managers and their employees often leads to improved staff motivation. (4 marks)

Q2 Is there a single best way for a firm to communicate with their customers? (4 marks)

Natter natter natter natter natter...

Good communication is incredibly important in business. Managers and staff have to communicate with each other to get the job done properly. There's also communication between the business and its customers and suppliers to think about. You'll have to be able to put these communication facts and ideas into context in a question you get in the exam.

Employer/Employee Relations

*Good employer/employee relations are plain good business sense. These pages are for **AQA** and **Edexcel**.*

Employers and Employees need to Cooperate with each other

1) Employers and employees **need each other**.

2) **Employers** need **hard-working staff** to contribute to the production of a good or service that can be sold for a profit.

3) **Employees** need a **secure income** to support themselves and their families.

4) However, there's scope for **conflict** between them.

5) Employers would prefer to pay **lower wages** to keep **costs** down.

6) Employees want **higher wages** to improve their **standard of living**.

The two sides must **negotiate** to reach an **acceptable compromise** on wage rates, working conditions and terms of employment. **Failure** to reach agreement could lead to a **production stoppage**, and **both parties would suffer**.

> A **successful** employer/employee relationship **maximises** the **cooperation** and **minimises** the potential for **conflict** between these two groups.

Collective Bargaining is done by Large Groups of employees

1) In most cases **individuals** don't negotiate their own rate of pay with their employer.

2) Negotiation is often done by a **trade union** or **professional association**, representing a group of employees and negotiating pay and working conditions **on their behalf**. The union **bargains collectively** for them all with their employer. Trade unions are sometimes called "**organised labour**".

3) The result is a **common pay structure**, which is often called the "**going rate**" for the job. The employer wouldn't be able to pay anyone less than this going rate without the union kicking up a stink about it.

4) Employees and unions prefer **collective bargaining**, because it strengthens their position at the bargaining table and prevents "**divide and rule**" tactics by employers.

Collective bargaining does create some **problems**, though...

1) Having a single wage rate makes it **difficult** to **reward** variations in work **effort** between staff doing jobs with a similar rate of pay. This may **reduce** the levels of **motivation** if good staff are not recognised and rewarded.

2) In some large companies, the collectively bargained rate of pay covers employees working in **different factories and offices** scattered in **different locations** across the country. This one-wage-for-all approach doesn't recognise differences between different parts of the country — e.g. cost of living, house prices, level of unemployment, or even the local wages paid by other employers. A **variation** in wage rates to take account of these factors might be more appropriate.

Bargaining can also be done by Small Groups or Individual Employees

1) In recent years there's been a shift **away** from **collective bargaining** towards **individual** and **local bargaining**.

2) **Individual bargaining** means that employers can decide to pay an employee what they think he or she is worth to the firm. This can reduce wage bills. It also provides a financial incentive to the employee.

3) **Local bargaining** is where employees at an **individual workplace** bargain collectively. It's different from national collective bargaining by a trade union.

4) **Changes in the law** have weakened the power of unions, and allowed firms to move towards local and individual bargaining. **The state sector** has phased out some collective agreements.

5) Trade Union membership has **declined** (see p.65).

Pay Settlements must balance Employer and Employee Needs

Money (and the opportunity to earn more) **motivates** employees. As well as the actual wage, the relative wage is important — relative to other possible occupations, or the same occupation in a different part of the country. When people feel underpaid, their level of motivation falls.

1) Employers see wages as a **cost of production** that must be kept down — but not so low as to **demotivate** staff.

2) Employees see wages as a form of **financial recognition**, and therefore it's a motivator. It's also the ultimate determinant of their family's **standard of living**, and so ought to be high.

Employer/Employee Relations

Short Term Contracts and Sub-contracting provide Employment Flexibility

The labour needs of factories vary **over time**. They may be working **close to full capacity** for some months and then **be less busy** a few months later. Businesses can deal with this by asking workers to work **overtime** to cover busy periods, and preventing them from working overtime during slack periods. There are other options as shown below:

Short-term contracts employ people for a short time

1) Short term contracts employ people for a **fixed period** of time (eg. 6 months) and only re-employ them at the end of that period if **they are required**.

2) This may suit the employer but it **doesn't** meet the needs of **most** employees who prefer the certainty of a **secure**, **continuous** income.

3) Workers on **temporary** (short-term) contracts face the very real possibility of no renewal of contract (with no redundancy payments) at the end of the work period. This **weakens** their **bargaining power** — they'll feel they **need** to **cooperate fully** with the employer to increase the chances of contract renewal.

4) In addition, many of these workers are employed in ways that **aren't essential** for current production so if they threaten to go on **strike**, it won't have all that much **effect** on their employer .

5) In contrast, **permanent** staff have a **contract of employment** which establishes their duties and rights. This covers the circumstances (including redundancy pay) under which the contract can be terminated and the employee made redundant.

6) It's hard to build up a relationship with short term staff, and this can make communication difficult. Workers' social needs often aren't met by temporary work.

Sub-contracting means paying other firms to do some of the work

1) Sub-contracting means **paying other firms** for particular labour skills / services that others could do better, or for **occasional work** they couldn't **justify** employing **permanent** staff.

2) Examples of services that are often contracted out are company vehicle servicing and repair, computer **maintenance** and upgrading, office cleaning and canteen catering.

3) Many contractors are **sole traders** — self employed workers. They have to **negotiate** their **own rates of pay**.

4) Subcontracting can work out **cheaper** for the employer. They get a **trained** worker without having to spend money on **training**. Plus they don't have to pay **benefits** such as pension contributions.

Practice Questions

Q1 Describe the ways in which the needs of employers and employees (a) conflict, (b) match.

Q2 Explain the term "collective bargaining" and consider its merits.

Q3 How and why does local bargaining differ from collective bargaining?

Q4 Explain the meaning of the following terms, and identify the ways that a firm might benefit from them: (a) introducing short-term contracts, (b) sub-contracting some activities.

Q5 Why are employees on short-term work contracts in a weaker bargaining position than permanent staff?

Q6 In what ways is the rate of pay a motivating factor for an employee?

Exam Question

Q1 Evaluate the advantages and disadvantages of collective bargaining to workers in a business with offices in Reading, Sunderland and Birmingham. (10 marks)

Don't even think about trying to collectively bargain with the examiners...

These pages aren't really that bad. The difference between collective and individual bargaining is fairly obvious — all you have to do is learn how collective bargaining is done, and what effects it has. Plus you have to know the ins and outs of short term contracts and subcontracting, and what the bargaining position of contractors is. So, get to learning it all.

Trade Unions

*About 7 million people in Britain belong to a trade union, which is about 25% of the total workforce. You might wonder why some people join trade unions while other people don't. These pages are for **AQA**, **OCR** and **Edexcel**.*

Trade Unions strengthen an employee's Bargaining Power

1) Trade unions act on behalf of **groups of employees** in the workforce when negotiating rates of **pay** and **working conditions** etc. with the employer.

2) By joining with others and belonging to a union an employee **strengthens** his or her **bargaining power** in a way that wouldn't be possible if he/she tried to bargain as an **individual** with the employer.

Trade Unions deal with much More than Pay Negotiations

Trade unions take action in the workplace

1) Trade unions **negotiate with employers** on behalf of their members to secure fair rates of pay and/or productivity bonuses for their work.

2) Trade unions help negotiate reasonable hours of **work**, and **paid holiday** entitlement.

3) Trade unions ask employers for **safe** and civilized **working conditions**.

4) Trade unions help their members get **job security** with protection against **mistreatment**, **discrimination** or **unfair dismissal**.

Trade unions take action at the national level

1) Trade unions **put pressure on the government** to introduce legislation that serves trade union interests.

2) The **minimum wage** was introduced in **1998** by the government after discussions with trade unions.

3) Trade unions pushed the government to make **redundancy payments** compulsory.

4) Trade unions ask for **pension protection** for those in private company pension schemes.

Trade unions take action in party politics

1) Many unions give **financial support** to the **Labour Party** because they think its policies represent their interests.

2) In the 1970s and 1980s, trade unions had a lot of power in the Labour Party. Since the **mid 1990s** they have **less power**.

Labour Party policy used to be decided by votes from members and "block votes" from unions — e.g. leaders of a trade union of 5000 people could decide to support a policy, and that policy would get all 5000 votes. In 1993, the Labour party stopped allowing union block votes, and policies were decided on a one member one vote basis.

Trade Unions are run by Local, Regional and National Officials

1) Local officials are called **shop stewards**. They're elected by employees.

2) Shop stewards represents the members on the workplace issues described above. The employer may allow shop stewards to use some time in work to carry out these union duties.

3) In **large** firms **several** shop stewards may be elected, each one representing a different group of employees. They usually come together as a **group** (**shop stewards' committee**) and negotiate with management this way.

4) When the issues are complex, shop stewards may request **help** from **regional officials**. These officials normally work **full time** for the union. They have a more detailed knowledge about employment law, bargaining procedures, economic pressures, etc.

5) The National Executive acts as the national spokesman for the union. It raises issues of concern with the **media** and **puts pressure on the government** to introduce reforms that would benefit their members.

6) The union's national executive is headed by an elected **General Secretary**.

Joint Consultation between Firm and Trade Union helps Prevent disputes

Many issues of difference between employers and trade unions **never** turn into a fully fledged **industrial dispute**. This is because the employer and the trade union reps **talk regularly** to sort things out **before** they get serious.

1) Joint consultation promotes a better **appreciation** of each other's **needs** and constraints.

2) It encourages a spirit of **co-operation** rather than confrontation.

3) Employers and union reps can **share ideas** for the benefit of everyone in the firm.

Trade Unions

There are **Different Types** of Trade Unions

Craft unions	Members of craft unions share a **common skill** but often work in **different locations**. Most of them started out as a traditional guild of craftsmen. Examples: Equity (the actors' union), the Writers' Guild of Great Britain, the PFA (Professional Footballers' Association).
Industrial unions	Members all work in the **same industry** but do a **wide range of jobs**. Their bargaining power is strong because strike action could bring production to a stop. Examples: RMT (the transport workers' union), NUM (National Union of Mineworkers).
General unions	Members range across **many different industries** in **many different occupations**. General unions tend to have a very **large number** of members. Examples: the GMB, the TGWU (Transport and General Workers Union).
White-collar unions	Members work in **administration** or **non-manual occupations**. In recent decades these unions have increased their membership, because of the growth in employment in these sectors. Examples: NUT (National Union of Teachers) and NUJ (National Union of Journalists).

Trade unions are particularly strong in **heavy industry** (e.g. mining, steelmaking) and **transport** (e.g. railways and ports). There's also strong union membership in the **public sector**, e.g. teachers, nurses and firemen.

Not all businesses **Recognise Trade Unions**

Many employers find it useful to negotiate through a trade union, so they're willing to **recognise trade unions** in the workplace.

Other employers prefer to **deal directly** with their employees. They either **don't recognise** trade unions, or **discourage** employees from joining a trade union. They consider unions to be **backward looking**, holding up innovation and improvements, and **preventing** managers from **managing effectively**.

There's been a **Decline** in **Union Membership** since the 1980s

The total number of people belonging to trade unions has **fallen** in recent years because:

1) Some industries that were **heavily unionised** have **reduced** their **output** and employment dramatically — e.g. coal mining, steelmaking, ship building.

2) Some employers, especially those in many of the newer service industries (call centres, leisure industry, retailing) have **discouraged staff from joining unions**. They prefer to discuss issues with an association made up of just their own employees.

3) **Government legislation** has **reduced** the **bargaining power** of the unions (see p.70) and so the incentive for an employee to join is lower.

Practice Questions

Q1   Why is there a need for trade unions?

Q2   What do trade unions do for their members?

Q3   Would you join a trade union if you had a job with the opportunity to do so? Explain your answer.

Q4   How are trade unions organised?

Exam Question

Q1   Imagine you are the senior manager of a medium-sized clothes retailer employing 600 people with 10 stores spread across the country. Evaluate the two possible options below.
(1) Accept union recognition and encourage your staff to join,
OR (2) Resist union recognition and discourage your staff from joining.   (8 marks)

You want a top tip — hang on, I'll have to talk to my union rep about that...

There's a fair old bit of detail on trade unions. It doesn't let up — there's more right up to page 71. But the basic facts on trade unions are here. You can be asked about the pros and cons of joining a union, and what unions do for workers. You might have to comment on union strength in a particular sector of industry, if it's relevant to a case study in the exams.

Industrial Disputes

Strikes, work to rule, overtime bans — they're all ways of putting pressure on employers.
*These pages are for **AQA**, **OCR** and **Edexcel**.*

Industrial Disputes happen when an Employer and Trade Union Can't Agree

1) Many conflicts appear on the surface to be a dispute over **wages** and **working conditions**. However, there may be **other grievances** caused by various human factors:

- **Frustration** and **alienation** caused by **lack of communication** from managers or frequent **changes** in work practices.
- **Stress** and **insecurity** caused by changing work patterns and **fears of redundancy**.

2) These feelings are difficult to express and quantify in argument — so it's often **easier** to turn the dispute into one about the more **usual workplace issues**.

3) Managers who **communicate effectively** and organise staff work responsibilities **consistently** will have a more **motivated workforce**, who'll be less likely to start a dispute.

Unions take Industrial Action — Work to Rule, Overtime Bans and Strikes

If the trade union fails to reach an agreement with the employer through negotiation, then they can apply more pressure by taking **industrial action** to reduce production. There are various tactics used, which gradually increase pressure.

Queen Victoria worked to rule, in her own way...

1) **Work to rule** — employees stick 100% to the terms of their **contract**. They only do the tasks that their contract **specifically** asks them to do. This usually **slows production**.

2) **Go slow** — employees simply work more **slowly**.

3) A **ban on overtime** — exactly what it says. Employees don't work **overtime** when they're **asked** to. They don't come in early or work late or work at weekends.

4) **Strike** — employees withdraw their labour and **don't go to work**. This might be a **one-day strike** to **warn** the employer that they're serious about the issue, or a more **prolonged** strike.

Industrial disputes have to be Resolved Eventually

A slow-down or stoppage of production means less output, sales and profit for the employer. It also means lower earnings for the employee. Because **both parties** are suffering they need to reach an agreement quickly. There's a clear incentive for both parties to return to negotiations.

In addition to the employer and employee, **other stakeholders** suffer from lost production.

1) Local businesses suffer from the **reduced spending** of those employees.

2) **Customers** can't get they goods or services they want.

3) Other firms may rely on this firm for their raw materials or components.

4) **The firm's suppliers** suffer, especially if the firm is an important customer.

Final Agreements reflect the Bargaining Strength of Both Sides

The final agreement / compromise reached reflects the relative bargaining strength of the union and the employer. This depends upon a variety of factors.

1) Whether there are **alternative** sources of **labour** and **production** (eg. other factories in this country or abroad) that the employer could use.

2) When **stocks** of **finished products** are already available, a production stoppage is not so serious. The shelves will still be stocked, and **customers** won't even notice.

3) **Public opinion** is very important. An industrial dispute might harm the business' relationship with customers. Customers may **resent** either the union, or the employer, for failing to get things sorted out.

4) The **law** may constrain the actions that the union can take to reduce production.

5) The **size** of the firm is an issue — it may have **enough resources** to **cover** the loss of production and profit.

Industrial Disputes

Employers and Unions often use Other Organisations to act as a Mediator

If the employer and union can't reach an agreement that **satisfies them both**, they might call on **another organisation** to act as **mediator** and / or **jury** to help resolve the dispute.

Industrial tribunal

This usually meets to deal with claims of **unfair dismissal** or **discrimination**. It hears the arguments of **both sides** and then announces its verdict. If it decides **against the employer** it may make them pay **compensation** to the employee.

ACAS — the Advisory, Conciliation and Arbitration Service

The Advisory, Conciliation and Arbitration Service does exactly what the name says.

1) **Conciliation** — ACAS **meets both parties** in the dispute, usually separately, and tries to develop **common ground** that they can both eventually accept.

2) **Arbitration** — It can appoint an **independent arbitrator** who considers the claims and declares what the outcome should be. If both sides agree, this outcome can be **legally binding**. There are two types of arbitration:

- **Compromise arbitration** is a result which lies somewhere between what the employer wants, and what the employee wants. It sounds good, but there's a downside — it may encourage both **union** and **employer** to adopt **extreme** first demands in order to **bias** the eventual compromise towards their position.

- **Pendulum arbitration** makes a simple choice for one or other of the competing claims — there's no compromise, and **no middle ground**. This encourages parties to adopt a more **reasonable** position to try to get the arbitrator to pick their side.

Employers and Employees can Reduce the Opportunity for conflict

1) **Single union agreement** or **single union recognition** only negotiates with one union. In one firm there may be **several unions**, each representing different employees. A large amount of management time is taken up in ensuring that any agreement with **one union** is **compatible** with the demands of all the others. The **single union agreement** avoids this because all negotiations are conducted with **just one recognised union**. This system is most likely to be introduced when a new firm is first established.

2) **No strike agreements** are where the employer provides an **independent system** for negotiating pay rises and working conditions in return for a **no-strike promise** from employees. This is more usual for some critical services such as the police force, where strikes would affect wider society.

Practice Questions

Q1 Explain why disputes may not always be about boring old pay and conditions.

Q2 List and describe the different kinds of industrial action a union might take in a dispute with an employer.

Q3 Explain who suffers in a dispute and why.

Q4 Explain the roles performed by the following: (a) industrial tribunal, (b) ACAS.

Q5 How do the following reduce the likelihood of disputes and production stoppages:
(a) Single union agreement/recognition? (b) No strike agreement?

Exam Questions

Q1 "Trade union members will lose more than they gain when they enter into a dispute with an employer."
Evaluate this claim. (8 marks)

Q2 Consider a recent industrial dispute and analyse it in terms of the following:
its causes, the tactics used by the union, the consequences for those affected,
factors influencing the relative strengths of the two sides and the final settlement. (12 marks)

You poor students don't even get paid in the first place...

Industrial disputes have to be resolved before everything goes Pete Tong. It's not in the employees' best interests to be on strike for a long time — they lose pay, and damage their job prospects by damaging the industry. It's best to get things sorted ASAP. What you need to know is how disputes affect businesses and how they get resolved — tribunals, ACAS, etc.

Employee Participation

*Remember, employees are stakeholders. If they're allowed and encouraged to participate in decisions that affect them, they are likely to be more motivated. These pages are for **AQA**, **OCR** and **Edexcel**.*

Employee Participation involves employees in Decision-Making

The work of mid 20th century **management theorists** such as Mayo, Maslow and Herzberg (see p.57) showed that **participation** could **motivate** workers. Before the 1950s, managers didn't see any need to involve employees in decision making. They believed that it was the boss's job to make decisions, and the worker's job to follow them.

Employee participation is also called **industrial democracy**. Ways businesses can **introduce participation** include:

Works councils or employee associations discuss work issues

1) Works councils are committees made up of employee representatives and employer representatives. Employee representatives are usually **elected**.
2) They **meet regularly** to discuss **general work issues** e.g. training, new technology and methods of work.
3) The sharing of ideas and information in a relatively **relaxed** atmosphere does a lot to improve **co-operation** between workers and management.
4) Where there's **no trade union presence** in a firm, works councils take care of **collective bargaining**.
5) **Quality circles** are like works councils, but they only discuss **quality** issues. They meet regularly to discuss ways of improving quality. Quality circles comprise of employees from **all levels** of the business.

Employee shareholders have more of a stake in the business

1) Employees can buy **shares** in the business. This gives them a higher **stake** in the business, and promises financial rewards in the form of dividends if the business performs well.
2) Shareholders can vote at the Annual General Meeting (AGM).
3) In practice, this one is actually more of a **financial motivator** than an instance of industrial democracy. There aren't usually enough employee shareholders to have any real influence at the AGM.

Employee directors have a seat on the board

1) Worker directors are **elected** by the employees. They serve on the **Board of Directors**.
2) **Employers** are sometimes **suspicious** of worker directors, believing that they may **spill board secrets** to the rest of the workforce.
3) **Unions** are also sometimes **suspicious** of worker directors. Unions worry that other workers will see the worker director as being on the **side of the bosses**.

Autonomous (independent) work groups give employees more control

1) Managers may **delegate** responsibility and give a team more **freedom** to **plan** and carry out their own work. This improves motivation.
2) Autonomous work groups may also be able to suggest **improvements** in **working practice**.
3) Some autonomous work groups **elect a leader**, and **appoint new staff**.
4) For this to work out, the **type** of work they're doing must be **suitable**, the group must **work well together** as a team, and they must have a good **blend** of skills.
5) Even then, it doesn't always work perfectly — some individuals may not want the **hassle** of deciding their own work plans.

Teamworking has practical Benefits and Problems

Teamworking = autonomous work groups.

Teamworking is when a business breaks down production into large chunks, each done by a **team**. In manufacturing, it's basically **cell production**, the alternative to production lines **division of labour**. Decisions are made by the team.

Benefits of teamworking:	Problems of teamworking:
It can motivate employees by making the job **less boring**.	Employees must be **multi-skilled**.
Decisions are made by **people in the team**.	Team members must **get on together**.
It can cut **management costs**, because it usually results in **delayering**.	**Experienced** middle managers are **lost**.
	Implementation is **expensive**.

Employee Participation

Employers can **Encourage Participation** and **Involvement**

Employees will participate **enthusiastically** in workplace discussion and decision-making under certain conditions.

- If they feel **valued**.
- If they feel their views are **listened to** and **taken into account** in the final decision.
- If they are treated **courteously**.

Firms can organise themselves in a way that **encourages** employees to feel respected and involved. This then leads to greater participation and commitment, which has some clear benefits for the firm.

1) Individual employees are more **highly motivated** to do their jobs well.

2) Employees might come up with good suggestions for **efficiency** improvements and **quality** improvements. This could help **improve productivity** and **product quality**.

Motivation and **Participation** go together

1) Under **Mayo's** theory of motivation, employee involvement satisfies an employee's need for **attention**.

2) Under **Maslow's** theory, employee participation and industrial democracy meet **social needs** and **self esteem** needs, and **can** go as far as meeting **self-actualisation** needs, as long as the employee feels that they can really **exercise control** over their own work and career.

3) Under **Herzberg's** theory, **hygiene factors** are met, and **dissatisfaction** factors such as poor company policy or poor working conditions are avoided or removed. Herzberg's **motivation factors** such as responsibility are increased.

Industrial Democracy has some **Problems**

In spite of the lovely **benefits** outlined above, employee participation does create some **difficulties**.

1) It's **time consuming** and takes employees away from **immediate production**. This is especially critical if decisions need to be made **quickly**.

2) When industrial democracy **doesn't** produce the result that employees are looking for, it may worsen their attitude to the company.

3) Frequent **arguments** between employees, or between employer and employee could lead to personal animosity and worsen industrial relations.

4) Some employees just want to **get on with their job**, and react **negatively** to being invited to participate as they consider this an **intrusion** on their time.

5) Industrial democracy may mean that decisions are taken by a **half-informed group** rather than by the **relevant experts**.

6) Trade unions often **oppose** works councils and quality circles because they feel that employees should be using the union for help instead.

Practice Questions

Q1 How do (a) the employer, and (b) the employee benefit from increased industrial democracy?

Q2 What do the following do: (a) works councils / employee associations? (b) joint consultation?

Q3 Why are autonomous work groups successful in some situations but not others?

Q4 How do Herzberg's hygiene factors and motivating factors relate to industrial democracy?

Exam Question

Q1 The proprietor of a chain of eight restaurants claims he has no need for participation schemes because he is "quite capable of making his own decisions". His staff are happy to get on with their jobs and do what they are told. Write a report relevant to his situation, outlining the benefits that greater employee participation might bring, AND explaining how he might go about introducing it into his business. (12 marks)

One machine, one vote...

"Industrial democracy" is a rather fancy and self-important name for the idea of having employees join in with the decision making process. The key points to learn are all on these two pages, and they're pretty much exactly the same for all three exam boards — you have to know how employee participation is done, why it's good, and what problems can arise with it.

Employment Law

Employment law regulates what employers, employees and trade unions can and can't do in their relationships with each other. These pages are for **AQA**, **OCR** and **Edexcel**.

There are **Two** main areas of **Employment Law**

1) **Collective labour law** regulates the relationship between institutions (e.g. between firms and trade unions).

2) **Individual labour law** identifies the rights of the individual employee and their obligations to the employer.

Collective Employment Law controls what **Units** can do

1) Unions can represent their members in discussions with the employer and ultimately call them out on strike, but this has to be done **within the law**.

2) During the **1980s** and **1990s**, the government passed a series of **laws** to control the way that **industrial relations** (negotiations between union and employer) were conducted.

3) At the time the government thought trade unions had **too much bargaining strength** in industrial relations. This pushed up **wage rates**, which in turn pushed up production costs and **prices**. This **wage and price inflation** made British goods **less competitive** in the global market.

4) The changes in the law reduced the bargaining power of unions. They're summarised **below**.

Employment Act 1980	Firms could **refuse to recognise** a union. Picketing was restricted to workers' **own place of work**.
Employment Act 1982	Trade unions could be sued. **Union-only clauses** were **banned**.
Trade Union Act 1984	Unions had to have a **secret ballot** before striking.
Employment Act 1988	Unions **couldn't punish** members who didn't strike.
Employment Act 1990	Employers could **sack** workers who went on **unofficial strike**. **Closed shop agreements** were **ended** — no one could be refused a job because they weren't in the right union.
Trade Union Reform and Employment Rights Act 1993	Unions had give **7 days' notice** of a strike to employers. Secret ballots had to be done by **post**.

5) There's been a move away from "**voluntarism**" where an employer and the trade union(s) representing the employees at a particular workplace come up with an agreement that only applies to that workplace — e.g. not to strike, or to inform the employer a few days before a strike. Voluntary agreements have been **replaced** by the **collective labour laws** in the table above.

Individual Labour Law controls what rights **Employees** have

1) An employee has a legal right to **fair treatment** while at work, and also while looking for employment.

2) These anti-discrimination laws **prevent** employers from **acting unfairly**, and ensure fair treatment for individuals:

Equal Pay Act (1970)	A man and woman doing the **same** or an **equivalent** job should receive the **same rate of pay**. Followed up by EU Equal Pay Directive in 1975.
Sex Discrimination Act (1975)	A person cannot be discriminated against on grounds of **gender** or **marital status** for recruitment, promotion, training or dismissal.
Race Relations Act (1976)	A person cannot be discriminated against on grounds of **colour**, **race**, **national origin**, or **ethnic origin**.
Disability Discrimination Act (1995)	The employer must make efforts to ensure that **disabled people** can be employed in that place of work (e.g installing weelchair ramps).

3) Anyone feeling **discriminated against** on the basis of sex, race or disability can go to an **industrial tribunal** (often set up by **ACAS**) to seek **compensation**. The tribunal listens to the arguments and makes a judgement.

The Data Protection Act gives **Employees** rights to privacy

Businesses hold **data** about their employees on **computer** — this includes things like their date of birth, address, and bank account details. Employees wouldn't want this information getting into the wrong hands.

The **Data Protection Act (1998)** says that anyone holding data about a person can't do anything with that data (e.g. pass it on to someone else) without the person's **consent**. Also, organisations can't pass on data if it's not **necessary**.

Employment Law

Employees' Pay and Working Conditions are protected by the Law

1) Employees have the right to have a **contract of employment** setting out the **expected tasks** of the job.

2) They have the right to **protection** from **unfair dismissal**. (See Industrial Tribunals on p.67). Employees can be sacked for gross misconduct, or for failing to carry out duties. They can be made redundant if the job doesn't exist any more. Everything else is **unfair dismissal**, which can be **costly** for a business.

3) Employees have the right to a **safe** working environment. The **Health and Safety at Work Act (1974)** states that the employer must ensure the working environment is safe. This covers a wide range of potential dangers: electrical equipment, hazardous substances and materials, moving machinery, etc. The firm can be fined if it fails to reach the minimum level required by the law. There's more about health and safety on p.96.

4) Workers have the right to a certain number of **paid holidays** per year, plus public holidays. The **European Working Time Directive** sets out the entitlement as 4 weeks' paid leave per year.

5) Employees have the right to be **paid** on or above the **national minimum wage**.

6) They have the right to **confidentiality**, and can expect that the employer keeps their personal records private.

7) Employees have the right to **paid maternity** and **paternity** leave, and the right to **job security** while on maternity leave. **Mums** get 6 months' paid leave (not on full pay), and 6 months' unpaid, plus employers have to **hire a temp** to cover for the employee. This can be **expensive** for businesses — and it can sometimes be a source of **discrimination** against women. **Dads** get two weeks' paid paternity leave.

> **In return, the employee has obligations to their employer.**
>
> These include: **attendance** for work, **punctuality**, **willingness** to do and **complete** any **reasonable work** requested, **honesty** and **courtesy** to others. Any serious breach of these could lead to the employee being **disciplined** and ultimately **dismissed**.

European Union Law has had an impact on UK Industrial Relations

Britain's membership of the **European Union** means that EU directives apply in this country. The "Social Chapter" of the Maastricht Treaty (1992) included additional labour market regulations and employee rights.

1) The **Working Time Directive** of 1998 says employees need not work for more than **48 hours per week**, unless they **choose** to.

2) EU law gives **part time** and **full time** workers the **same** employment rights.

Labour Law has an impact on the Employer in a Global Market

1) A firm interested in profit wouldn't normally offer these protections for their employees off their own bat, because they push up **production costs** and **prices**, leading to **fewer sales**.

2) To maintain a **level playing field**, the law and European directives impose these obligations on all businesses so any firm which chooses to be nice to their employees isn't penalised.

3) However, now that competition is **global**, imposing these expensive obligations on only British and European firms may put them at a disadvantage when selling into world markets.

Practice Questions

Q1 Explain the terms: (a) collective labour laws, (b) individual labour laws.

Q2 In what ways has collective employment law reduced the power of trade unions?

Q3 How is the individual protected from discrimination in the labour market?

Q4 List five rights and five obligations that an employee has.

Exam Question

Q1 "An individual firm should be left free from legal interference to negotiate pay, working rights, and obligations with its own workforce." Evaluate the arguments behind this statement. (15 marks)

Now is not the time to go on strike...

There is an awful lot of law to learn on these pages. Don't be too faint of heart, though, because it's possible to learn it all. Tackle the Employment Acts first — make sure you know what unions could do before and after the Acts. Then take your individual labour law bits one at a time — discrimination, Data Protection, then working conditions, then pay. Not so bad.

Human Resource Management (HRM)

*These pages tell you how businesses figure out their staff needs. These two pages are for **AQA and Edexcel**.*

Human Resource Management *looks after All Workers in a business*

Human resources departments are **different** from traditional **personnel departments**. Whereas personnel departments were concerned with **hiring and firing**, human resources departments **keep supporting staff** in order to keep them **contributing** to the business. Human resource management is **integrated** into the corporate planning of the business.

Workforce Planning *is a key area of Human Resource Management*

1) Human Resources plans for a firm's future staffing needs — **how many workers** will be needed and what kind of workforce will be needed — **skilled/unskilled, full-time/part-time**.

2) HRM plans how to **recruit** staff — where to advertise, how to interview etc.

3) Human Resources also decides how to treat staff while they're working for the business — how to **use their skills**, how to **retain** them, how to **train** and **reward** them, and eventually how to **terminate** their employment.

4) **Human Resources strategies** can be **short-term** (e.g. recruiting part-time staff for Christmas sales in retailing) or **long-term** (e.g. anticipating growth or a change in production techniques).

HRM departments in a business assess **demand for workers** in several ways:

1) HRM departments ask **other experienced managers** for their **opinion** and **advice**.

2) **Past statistics** (back data) are used to see if employee numbers have **risen, fallen** or **stayed the same**.

3) An increase or decrease in **demand for product** means an increase or decrease in **need for workers**.

4) Human Resources analyse the **current staff details** to see how many are likely to **leave** or **retire** in the near future.

5) The introduction of **new techniques** (automation etc.) will alter the number of workers needed.

6) HRM do an **internal stock take**. They look at all the **jobs** in the organisation — what each job entails and what sort of **qualities** and **skills** are needed. They see whether current staff **match** these requirements.

Human Resources also need to assess the potential **supply** of **new workers**:

1) They check the **level of unemployment** in the area to find out how many people are looking for work.

2) **Local infrastructure** is important — good housing, transport and schools can **tempt** people to the area.

3) HRM see how many **school and college leavers** are seeking employment locally.

4) HRM see if **competitors** are recruiting a similar workforce — if there'll be **competition** for workers.

Workforce Planning *coordinates with Corporate Planning*

1) Workforce plans have to **fit in** with the firm's other plans, and the overall **corporate plan**.

2) They must be coordinated with the **marketing plan** and the **production plan** — e.g. a plan to expand production and increase market share will require **more workers** and **new training**.

3) Changes in **production style** require **retraining, recruitment** and **redeploying** (moving workers to another job in the firm). Capital intensive production requires workers with fewer skills. Teamworking requires more skills.

Achieving Labour Targets *means Expanding or Reducing the workforce*

1) If a business thinks they need to **expand**, they have to decide whether to recruit **externally** (from outside) or **internally** (by training and promoting current employees).

2) **Reducing** the workforce is much harder than expanding the workforce.

3) The **least painful** method is through **natural wastage** — this is where staff leave of their own accord by leaving for **other work** or through **retirement**.

4) If natural wastage isn't enough a firm may offer its older workers **early retirement** — a **financial encouragement** to retire early.

5) A business may need to make some of its workers **redundant** — they have to leave as their job won't exist any more. Under the **Employment Rights Act** of 1996, workers who've been with a business for a **year** have the right to **severance pay** (the actual amount depends on the length of service and the wage at the time of redundancy). Businesses **can't re-advertise** a redundant job — redundancy means the **job doesn't exist.**

6) The **Employment Protection Act** of 1978 protects workers against **unfair dismissal**. (See p.71).

Human Resource Management (HRM)

Selection *means getting the* Right People *for the* Job

It's obviously important to get the **best** possible candidate for a job. To have the best chance of getting the best people, the HR department **analyses** the vacancy and draws up a **job description** and a **person specification**.

1) The **job description** lists the tasks and responsibilities the person appointed will be expected to carry out. It may also state the **job title**, the location, the nature of the business and other details like salary and conditions.

2) The **person specification** (or job specification) outlines the ideal profile of the person needed to match the job description. It describes their **qualifications**, experience, interests and **personality**.

Job Description

Title: Marketing Assistant
Reporting to: Marketing Manager
Role: To provide administrative support to Marketing team.
Hours: 18.5 hours Monday-Thursday
Salary £12500 pro rata
Job Duties: To provide word processing to the team, input data into databases, to assist with mailshot distribution.
Department duties: To assist with and attend marketing events as required. To provide essential holiday and sickness cover as required.

Person Specification

Qualifications: English and Maths GCSE grade C or above. Recognised Word Processing qualification.
Experience: 1 year's experience in an office environment.
Skills: Excellent organisational skills, ability to work as a member of a team, excellent communication and interpersonal skills. Knowledge of MS Word and Excel.
Personality: A sense of humour, a positive attitude.

Methods *of Selection include* Interviews *and* Tests

1) **Interviews** are the most common way of choosing candidates. Candidates can be interviewed **one to one** or by a **panel** of interviewers. Phone interviews are thought to be less effective than **face-to-face** interviews.

2) Some organisations use **assessment centres** to help them **test** candidates. Tests include **psychometric** testing which measures aspects of personality (e.g. outgoing/reserved, works best on own/works best in a group), **aptitude** tests which find out how good the candidate is at job tasks, and **group exercises** which test candidates ability to work well with others.

New Employees *need* Induction *and* Training *to show them what's what*

1) The **first day** or so on the job is usually spent learning the workings of the business, the health and safety issues and meeting key personnel. This is called **induction**.

2) Most new employees need some training — either to learn **new skills** or **improve** and **update** existing skills.

3) Training can be done **off the job** — e.g. studying part time at a local **college**, a short one or two day **course** at a business training centre or **studying at home**. Training can also be done **on the job** — i.e. in the workplace.

Practice Questions

Q1   Why must workforce planning coordinate with corporate planning?
Q2   What is redundancy?
Q3   What information would you find in a person specification?
Q4   Give three methods of selection.

Exam Question

Q1   Construct a job specification and person specification for an assistant in a high fashion retailer.   (8 marks)

It's a tough job, but someone's got to do it...

OK, people doing AQA will find part of these two pages covers the same points as you've already done in AS — you're still expected to know those bits for A2, so here they are. In your A2 exams, you can be asked all kinds of questions about what HRM is and what it does, so you need to know the basics and the details. For Edexcel people, this is all brand new.

Methods of Reward

*Most working people in the UK get paid a monthly **salary** or a weekly **wage**.*
There are other kinds of financial motivation, like commission and fringe benefits.
*These pages are for **AQA** and **Edexcel**.*

Time Based Payment *gives an* Hourly *or* Weekly Wage

1) Workers who are paid a **weekly wage** get a set rate of so many **pounds per hour**. The more hours they work the more they get paid. There's a minimum wage — in 2004 this was £4.85 per hour for adults over 22. Workers usually work a **fixed working week** of about 40 hours, and get paid more for each hour of **overtime** they work.

2) Workers who get paid a monthly **salary** get so many **thousand pounds a year**, divided into 12 monthly payments. The salary isn't directly related to the number of hours worked— salaried employees work a minimum number of hours a week, and then as many hours as it takes to get the job done.

Production Based *payment pays either a* Piece Rate *or* Commission

1) Some **production workers** are paid by **piece rate** — they get paid so many pounds or pence **per finished item**. The more the worker produces, the more they get paid.

2) Sales people are usually paid **commission** — a **percentage** of the **sales** they achieve. Most sales staff get a low **basic salary** and earn commission on top of that, but some get commission only.

3) Workers can be paid a **bonus** or a **higher rate of pay** if they achieve above a **target** rate of productivity.

Performance Based *payment gives* More *to employees who* Meet Targets

1) **Performance related pay (PRP)** gives more money to employees who meet their targets.

2) Performance related pay is linked in with employee **appraisals**. Appraisal is the process of evaluating the **development** and **performance** of an employee.

3) Appraisals can be done by **interview**, or by measuring productivity at regular intervals.

4) Some employees worry that they won't get a performance related pay rise if they don't **get on** particularly well with the manager doing the appraisal interviews.

> 1) Employee appraisal has two sides — it can look for ways to **help** an employee **improve**, or it can **judge** an employee to see if they're **good enough**.
>
> 2) Appraisal was traditionally about checking employee **skill** and **productivity**, giving **pay rises** to good employees and **pay cuts** (or the sack) to lousy ones.
>
> 3) Modern appraisal is a combination of **employee development** and reward adjustment — it's linked to **both** training and pay.
>
> 4) The type of appraisal used depends on **leadership style**. **Autocrats** favour **judgemental appraisal** and **democrats** favour **developmental appraisal**.

Businesses also Reward Employees *with other* Benefits

1) In addition to their weekly/monthly pay, employees may also get **fringe benefits**.

2) These include **staff discount** for company products (very common in retail), employer contributions to employee **pensions**, private **medical insurance**, health club membership, a company **car**, **profit sharing** schemes and options to buy **shares** in the company.

3) These are all **financial** rewards — they're things that can be objectively valued in terms of money. It'd cost the employees money to buy their own health insurance, gym membership etc.

Julia valued fringe benefits.

4) Don't forget the impact of **non-financial** rewards such as praise, training, or additional responsibility.

5) Most financial benefits are liable for income tax — they're taxed on their "cash equivalent" which is the price it'd cost to buy them. Most benefits can't be used as a tax loophole — a way of paying someone money without them paying tax on it. However, employees don't pay tax on pension scheme contributions, and share options of less than about £3000 aren't taxed either.

Methods of Reward

Training and Development is a Reward In Itself

1) Training helps the employee to be **good** at their job. It's in the interests of the employer to train the employee to be as productive as possible.

2) Training **fulfils employee needs**. It meets Mayo's attention need, Maslow's self-esteem and self-actualisation needs, and it's one of Herzberg's motivating factors.

3) **All employees** need training, not just new employees.

4) Businesses need to build training into their **workforce plan**. They must assess when employees are likely to **need** training. This could be because of **reorganising** production or making a new product which required new assembly skills.

5) There could also be a need for training to help an employee **develop**, to prevent them from getting **bored** in their job, and to allow them to take **new responsibility**.

6) Businesses should **evaluate** their training to see how it's **working** — using clear, measurable objectives. Managers should be able to compare **training costs** with the **financial gains** from improved performance.

7) Sometimes businesses might not want to be the **best** at training staff. They worry that **competitors** will "**poach**" the staff they've trained. If all businesses avoided training staff because they don't want them to be poached, there'd be **no training,** which would **severely affect the labour** market.

Employee Development aims to make employees Fulfilled and Motivated

1) Some organisations do **employee development** as well as training.

2) Whereas training focuses on skills needed for **specific job tasks**, development programmes try to help employees learn and improve **broader** skills such as people management, budget setting or customer service. Employee development helps employees take on new responsibility and **get ahead** in the organisation — so it can be quite highly motivating.

3) The idea is that the organisation will benefit from a more broadly skilled, **fulfilled** and **motivated** employee.

Reward Schemes must fit the organisation's HRM Style

There are two schools of thought in human resource management — hard HRM and soft HRM.

Hard HRM	Soft HRM
1) Employees are a resource just like any other.	1) Employees are the **most important** resource.
2) Employees are hired and fired on a **short-term basis**.	2) Employees are managed on a **long-term basis**
3) Motivation is largely through pay.	3) Motivation is through **empowerment** and **development**.
4) Managers tend to be **Theory X** managers.	4) Managers tend to be **Theory Y** managers.
5) Appraisals are **judgemental**.	5) Appraisals are **developmental**.
6) Training is only done to meet **production** needs.	6) Training is done to meet **development** needs.

Practice Questions

Q1 Give three examples of fringe benefits.

Q2 Give two characteristics of hard HRM and two of soft HRM.

Exam Question

Q1 There is a shortage of postmen in London. The Royal Mail could resolve this shortage in two ways. It could increase the pay for all postmen across the whole country or it could restrict wage rises so that they apply to London staff only. Evaluate the impact of these choices on each of the following:
a) Royal Mail (production costs, recruitment, motivation, etc). (6 marks)
b) Employees of Royal Mail (postmen and others). (6 marks)

Pay a basic wage of peanuts and give bananas as bonuses, get motivated monkeys...

There's quite a lot more detail on reward schemes in A2 Business Studies compared to AS. You're expected to know how payment and reward tie in with appraisal and employee management. They're particularly keen on getting you to say how HRM fits in with the activities and objectives of a business — why they might want to train staff, why they might not, etc.

Measuring Labour Effectiveness

*A business needs to measure the effectiveness of every resource used, including the workforce. Managers can use qualitative data and numerical ratios to assess the **efficiency** and **competitiveness** of a workforce. For **AQA** and **OCR**.*

Labour Productivity measures How Much each Employee Produces

$$\text{Labour Productivity} = \frac{\text{Output per period}}{\text{Number of employees}}$$

Example: A factory has 30 workers per shift working 3 shifts per day to produce 9000 DVD players per week.
Productivity = 9000 ÷ 90 workers = **100** DVD players per worker per week.

The **higher** the labour productivity, the **better** the workforce is performing. As labour productivity **increases**, labour costs per unit **fall**. This is important in **labour intensive** firms, where labour costs are a high proportion of total costs.

Ways to improve labour productivity

1) Labour productivity can be improved by **improving worker motivation** (see p.56-57).

2) Training can make workers more productive.

3) Labour productivity can also be improved by changing to **more efficient** methods of production (p.79) — e.g. changing from job to batch production or from batch to flow production. These gains need to be balanced against the **costs** of changing production method, and the **reduced production flexibility**.

4) Improvements can be had by **rewarding** increased productivity. Paying workers using a **piece-rate** system encourages staff to produce more. Managers should take care that **quality** doesn't suffer in the process.

1) Increasing labour productivity means **redundancies** and **job losses** unless sales increase. Businesses need to **plan** for the consequences of improved productivity to avoid upsetting staff.

2) Businesses should **monitor** their labour productivity over time. When they're setting targets, they should compare their productivity to **competitors' productivity** through **benchmarking** (p.87).

3) Businesses must **balance** productivity against issues such as product **quality** and long-term worker **motivation**.

Absenteeism measures the Proportion of Time employees are Off Work

1) Absenteeism is measured as a percentage. Obviously, **low** is best.

2) Figures need to be analysed in the **context** of each industry. For example, **police** officers might have

$$\text{Absenteeism} = \frac{\text{Number of staff days lost}}{\text{Number of days}} \times 100$$

higher than average figures because of the dangers and stresses of the job, while **sales** people paid on commission have **lower** rates because time off work can reduce their pay.

3) **Causes** of absenteeism include poor **working conditions**, poor **relationships** with managers and other staff, **stress** or **disillusionment** with the job, and poor **motivation**.

4) Absenteeism **increases costs**. It results in **lost opportunities**, e.g. sales enquiries left unanswered. There's also a cost of additional **wages** to cover for the absent employee — this is often expensive **overtime** pay.

5) Absenteeism increases if employees believe the firm **accepts** it as unavoidable. Some businesses require employees to fill in a **self-certification form** if they take any time off sick. Some require a **doctor's note** for anything over 7 days in a row off sick. **HR** or line managers may **interview** absent employees on their return to work to find out why they've been absent, and to let them know that their absenteeism has been noted.

6) There are several ways a firm might **reduce absenteeism**, depending upon what's causing it.

Method	How it works
Job enrichment	Employees with satisfying, challenging jobs **enjoy work** more than those with boring jobs, so they're less likely to miss work.
Improved relationships	Making employees feel **valued** will encourage them to be more **loyal** to their employers and reduce absenteeism rates.
Improved conditions	Good working conditions reduce **work-related illness** and **injury** — e.g. ergonomically designed workstations reduce RSI.
Flexi-time	This stops many employees missing work due to **family commitments** or **medical appointments**.

Measuring Labour Effectiveness

Labour Turnover *measures the* Proportion *of* Staff *who* Leave *each year*

$$\text{Labour Turnover} = \frac{\text{Number of staff leaving}}{\text{Average number of staff employed}} \times 100$$

Work out the part timers as if they were fractions of a full time employee. Two people who each work half a week = one person working a whole week.

Example: A business has 100 full time staff and 100 part-time staff who each work 50% of a normal week. Over a year 10 full time and 10 part-time staff leave.

Average staff = 100 + (100 × 0.5) = **150**. **Average leaving** = 10 + (10 × 0.5) = **15**, so **labour turnover** = 15÷150 = **10%**.

1) The **higher** the figure the larger the proportion of workers leaving the firm each year.

2) **External causes** of high labour turnover include changes in regional **unemployment** levels, and the growth of other local firms using staff with **similar skills**.

3) **Internal causes** of high labour turnover include poor motivation of staff, low wages, and a lack of opportunities for promotion. Staff will **join other firms** to increase their pay and job responsibilities.

4) A **poor recruitment** process which selects lousy candidates will also increase labour turnover.

5) Increased **delegation**, **job enrichment**, higher **wages** and better **training** can reduce employee turnover.

6) Businesses need **some** labour turnover to bring new ideas in. Labour turnover of 0 means no one **ever** leaves.

Benefits of high staff turnover	Disadvantages of high staff turnover
Constant stream of **new ideas** through new staff.	Lack of **loyal** and **experienced** staff who know the business.
Firm can recruit staff who've **already been trained** by competitors — saves money.	Firm **loses** staff it has **trained**, often to direct competitors.
If sales fall, firm can reduce workforce through **natural wastage** rather than costly redundancy.	**Training costs money** and **productivity drops** while new staff get trained.
Enthusiasm of new staff influences other workers.	**Recruitment** costs are high.

Health & Safety *measures* Time Lost *through* Accidents *at work*

1) Low numbers are **best**.

2) A work environment that's perceived as **dangerous** will damage employee **morale**. A high rate of absence due to work related injuries and illness causes bad publicity. Employees may seek **compensation** for accidents at work.

$$\text{Health \& Safety} = \frac{\text{Number of staff days lost through work accidents}}{\text{Number of working days}} \times 100$$

3) Many accidents at work are **avoidable**, so businesses can take action to make the workplace safer.

4) Some industries are more prone than others to accidents so firms should **benchmark** within their own industry.

5) Managers should compare this measure to calculations in **previous years** and also to the **absenteeism measure**.

Practice Questions

Q1 Define labour turnover.

Q2 State two possible causes of a high labour absenteeism measure.

Q3 What's the formula firms use to measure labour productivity?

Q4 State two benefits and two drawbacks of a high labour turnover percentage.

Exam Questions

Q1 Why should a major employer such as the NHS be concerned about differing absenteeism percentages in different hospitals, and what action might they take? (10 marks)

Q2 What problems might arise when changing the method of production to improve labour productivity? (6 marks)

How about a nice apple turnover... and custard...

Managers need to choose the right measures to focus on. For each one, there are good points and bad points of it being high, and good points and bad points of it being low. Remember that when you revise these measures — for the best marks, you need to put the facts into the context of the business. Focusing on absenteeism will suit some firms, but not others.

Production Planning

*Operations management is all about **planning** and **monitoring** business operations to
make sure they are as **efficient** as possible. These two introductory pages are for **OCR only**.*

Operations Management *is about* Planning *for* Efficiency *and* Quality

1)   Businesses aim to produce the **right quality** of goods and services.

2)   They aim to produce goods as **quickly as** possible.

3)   They aim to produce goods as **cheaply** as possible.

*It's pretty clear that you can't <u>have your cake
and eat it too</u> — you can't have top quality,
lowest costs and quickest production all at the
same time. <u>Something's gotta give</u>.*

Operations managers decide:

1)   **Where** to produce — what **location** is best from the point of view of
physical resources, human resources, customers etc. (see p80-81).

2)   What the **scale of production** should be — how to achieve **economies of
scale** and avoid diseconomies of scale, how **big** each plant should be, etc.

3)   **How** to manufacture the product — what methods to use, how to organise
production (production line, cell production, etc).

4)   Where to buy **supplies** from — which suppliers offer best quality, best
price, best terms and conditions, etc.

Look at it. 200 tonnes of finest yellow sand.

Shame the client wanted white sand, isn't it?

In a nutshell: ➡

> Operations management is about **managing** a business to produce **quality** goods
> and services with **low costs** per unit, at the **right time** to meet customer needs.

Planning *of* Production Operations *is linked to* Business Objectives

A corporate objective for **growth** must be followed up by **increased production**.

A corporate objective of **increasing market share** may mean **increased production**,
or it may mean **changing production** in order to manufacture a new product.

Operations Management *is linked to other* Functions *and* Departments

1)   Operations management has to work with **other functions** of the business.

2)   The **finance** department decides **how much money** can be spent on equipment and wages.

3)   The **marketing** department tells the operations managers what customers want, and what they're willing to
pay for it. Marketing will also say when the goods need to be produced to hit the market at the right time.

4)   **Human resources management** are in charge of managing employees. They need to know how many
employees are needed, what skills they need, and whether they'll need training.

5)   These relationships go **both ways**. The marketing department can ask the production department to
produce a large amount, and the production department has to say if it's possible or not.

Example: The operations department want to bring in a **new production method**,
        using **expensive** new machinery that gets the job done in **half** the time.

1)   This impacts on the **finance** department, who'll want to know if it's justifiable to spend lots of money on new
equipment. They'll want to do **investment analysis** to see if the increased productivity is **worth the cost**.

2)   This also impacts on the **marketing** department — the cost might push production costs up so much that
the finance department want to raise the **selling price** of the product. This will impact on **demand**.

3)   The **human resources** department are also affected. They'll want to know what **training** the
production employees will need in order to use the new equipment effectively. If the new
machinery really gets the job done in half the time, fewer staff may be needed — it's up to the
human resources department to manage any **redundancies** and **redeployments**.

Production Planning

Operations Planning *involves choosing production* Style

Job production	Production of **one-off items** by **skilled workers**.
Flow production	Mass production on a **continuous production line** with **division of labour**.
Batch production	Production of **small batches** of **identical items**.
Cell production	Production divided into **sets of tasks**, each set completed by a **work group**.
Lean production	Streamlined production with **waste at a minimum**.

1) Changing from job to batch or flow production improves **efficiency**. The cost per unit is much lower, and it's also possible to produce much **more** in the same amount of time.

2) On the other hand, flow production is an **inflexible** process, so the ability to tailor products to specific customer needs is lost. A niche manufacturer with close relationships with its customers might think twice before moving away from job production.

3) Flow production can be switched to **cell production**. In cell production, each team is responsible for one unit of work, which increases motivation and engagement with the work. Cell production involves **self checking** for quality, and quality can **improve** if workers are sufficiently motivated. Changing to cell production requires **training** so that workers are **multi-skilled** enough to tackle all the tasks within their work group.

4) Other lean production techniques such as kaizen and just-in-time require changes in organisation style — a more **democratic management style** is appropriate, to encourage a strong sense of cooperation between everyone in the firm. Employees need **training** to become multi-skilled, so that production can be **flexible**.

Operations Planning *involves choosing production* Size

Economies of scale — things that mean that as firms **increase output**, the **costs** per unit go down.
1) Large businesses can afford to buy better machinery and technology.
2) Large businesses can employ specialists such as market researchers, designers, etc.
3) Large businesses can negotiate **discounts** from suppliers for buying in bulk.
4) They can borrow money more easily than small businesses.
5) Large businesses have a greater ability to bear **risk** than small businesses.

Diseconomies of scale — things that make **unit costs of production rise** as output rises.
1) Diseconomies of scale happen because large firms are **harder to manage** than small firms.
2) It's hard to **coordinate** activities and objectives between **departments** in a large business.
3) **Communication** is harder in a large business where there are **long chains of command**.
4) It can be hard to **motivate** employees in a large businesses. In a **small** business, managers are in **regular contact** with staff, and it's easier for everyone to feel like they **belong** and that they're working towards the same aims.

A business needs to get **output** to levels where **economies of scale** make **unit costs** as **low** as possible — without letting it get to the point where **diseconomies of scale** start pushing unit costs up again.

Practice Questions

Q1 What are the aims of operations management?
Q2 What must a business do before switching to cell production from flow production?
Q3 Give an example of an economy of scale.

Exam Question

Q1 Analyse the pros and cons to a food manufacturer of operating flow production on a large scale. (8 marks)

It's not just surgeons who have to plan operations...

Some of this is revision of AS material, granted. But the OCR board are dead keen on getting you to know what's what — what operations planning involves, why it's important to choose the right style of production, and why it's important to choose the right size of production. Get this stuff straight before you get into the harder material later in the section.

Location

*A fundamental decision for any business organisation is where to locate its factory, distribution centre or admin HQ.
Lots of factors come into consideration. These pages are for **AQA** and **OCR**, and they're useful for Edexcel, too.*

Location Decisions are based on Quantitative Cost-Benefit Analysis

1) When deciding where to locate, businesses analyse the potential impact on **costs** and **revenues**. Businesses use **quantitative analysis** techniques such as **break-even analysis** and **investment appraisal analysis** to assess this.

2) Businesses calculate how many sales they'll need to break even at each location. Where the costs of operating from a location are high (e.g. because of high labour costs or high ground rents), the break even output will be higher. It's preferable to locate where break-even output is low. See p.46-47 for more on break-even.

3) Location or relocation of a business is a big **investment**. Businesses do **investment appraisal analysis** to calculate the **payback period**, **accounting rate of return** and **internal rate of return**. See p.50-52 for more on this.

Quantitative Factors affect choice of Location

Location decisions depend on distribution and supply costs

1) **Manufacturing** businesses which provide **bulky finished products** should be located near to their **customers** to cut down on distribution costs. Bulky products made from **lightweight** components are called "**bulk increasing**" commodities.

2) Other products need **bulky raw materials** to make a **lightweight end product** — these are "**bulk decreasing**" commodities. They need to be located near the source of **raw materials** to keep transport costs down.

3) A good **transport infrastructure** cuts distribution costs.

4) **Services** don't have large distribution costs. Decisions on where to locate services are based mainly on other criteria.

> E.g. <u>beer</u> — made of <u>water</u> (available anywhere), plus hops and barley (<u>low in bulk</u> compared to the <u>finished</u> product). Breweries tend to be located near <u>consumers</u> and <u>transport infrastructure</u>, not near hop or barley fields.

> E.g. the <u>steel</u> industry in South Wales. The three basic ingredients are <u>iron ore</u> (imported to local ports), <u>coal</u> and <u>limestone</u> (both from South Wales). The product is rolled steel, which is less bulky and can be transported by <u>rail</u>.

Location decisions depend on the availability and cost of resources

1) There must be a **good supply** of labour resources in the area where a business will be located.

2) The labour force must also be **suitable** — e.g. they might need to be literate, they might need special skills such as IT, technical knowledge of machinery, etc.

3) The area might need **local training facilities** for staff e.g. a college or university.

4) The area needs **facilities** such as affordable housing, suitable schooling, medical facilities, retail and leisure outlets to provide a good **quality of living** for staff.

5) Businesses can afford to pay workers less in areas where the **cost of living** is lower. To take full advantage of this, businesses need to locate overseas where labour costs are far lower than in the UK — see p.82.

6) Businesses also need the right land resources. There may be a requirement for room for **future expansion**.

7) The **cost** of **land** and **property** for factories and business premises varies significantly from area to area — land in the London area is far more expensive than land in mid Wales, for example.

8) **International** location decisions must take account of variations in the cost of water and **electricity**.

Location decisions depend on the market

1) Some businesses such as **retailers** need to locate **near to customers**, in order to catch the passing trade.

2) Businesses prefer to be based in locations which will **maximise their revenue**.

A good location needs an efficient and appropriate infrastructure

1) Business organisations benefit from access to **motorways**, fast **rail** links, **sea ports** and **airports**.

2) Transport infrastructure is needed for the **import** of **raw materials**, the **distribution** of **finished products**, and for **staff** to get to work.

3) Businesses also need **support services**. Most business organisations need some form of **commercial** support such as **banking**, **insurance** and **marketing** agencies.

4) Often there's a need for **technical** support such as engineering services and **IT** assistance.

Location

Some Locations benefit from Government Incentives

Successive governments have attempted to attract business organisations to areas with high **unemployment**.

They use both "**carrots**" and "**sticks**" to encourage businesses to locate in deprived areas. An example of a "**carrot**" would be a **grant** given to a business locating in an area of high unemployment. An example of a "**stick**" would be **refusing planning permission** to build a factory in an area where there are already lots of jobs.

1) Since the 1970s, the UK government has set up **Development Agencies** for Scotland, Wales, Northern Ireland and the English regions, to coordinate and encourage development. These development agencies get money from **central government** to spend on attracting businesses to their area.

2) They can provide **financial assistance** to business through grants, loans and equity (share) investment. They also provide **financial guidance** and **management support**.

3) They can also help businesses find the right sort of **property** to locate in.

1) The UK government has also set up **Enterprise Zones** to attract new business. They offer **tax breaks**, and reduce the amount of paperwork that businesses have to complete. Enterprise zones last for 10 years.

2) Within Enterprise Zones, there's financial assistance with **property** — businesses don't have to pay the full rate of tax for capital expenditure on buildings, and they don't have to pay the full **rates** (tax on business premises).

3) **Planning rules** and other regulations are made **simpler**, and **government paperwork** is processed more **quickly**.

There are also Qualitative Factors involved in Choosing a Location

1) Entrepreneurs might choose to start a business near where they **live** — e.g. Dyson is based in Wiltshire, near the owner and inventor's home.

2) Some places have a **good image** which suits the image of the product. High fashion works better in New York, London and Paris than in Scunthorpe or Workington — New York, London and Paris already have a fashion image.

> All these factors rarely, if ever, combine in one place to create an **ideal** location. It's more likely that the decision of where to locate a business is based on a **compromise** between different factors.

Businesses may have to Relocate — move facilities somewhere else

1) Established businesses sometimes have to up sticks and **move**. This may be because the firm has **grown too large** for its premises, or because **government incentives** have been withdrawn, or because taxes have risen.

2) Some organisations have "**industrial inertia**"— this means they **should** relocate but they fail to do so.

3) Deciding where to relocate is similar to deciding where to locate, with some added problems:

- Production is likely to be reduced during the move — there may be **downtime**.
- **Staff** may not **want** to move. They may need to be **paid** to relocate, especially if they have dependent family.
- Notifying **suppliers** and **customers** costs money. Updating **headed notepaper** and **brochures** costs money.

Practice Questions

Q1 Identify and briefly explain three factors which affect location cost.

Q2 What are Enterprise Zones?

Q3 What factors can cause problems for a firm wishing to relocate?

Exam Question

Q1 One of the major decisions of a business organisations is where to locate a new factory.
What factors would be taken into consideration in the decision procedure? (10 marks)

Phil and Kirsty can't help you now...

You're going to have to learn the factors which affect business location, no "maybe"s about it. If this comes up in the exam (more than likely) you'll probably get a case study with some facts and figures about a business, and you'll be asked to say why the business chose to locate where it did. Or you might have to write a report recommending a location for a business.

Locating Abroad

Businesses may decide to locate production abroad. These pages are for **AQA** *and* **Edexcel***.*

Multinationals *locate in* Several Countries

Multinational corporations (**MNC**s for short) are large manufacturing and trading organisations with their **headquarters** in one country and bases in other countries. MNCs tend to locate their **headquarters** in a more economically developed country (**MEDC**) and their **manufacturing** plants in less economically developed countries (**LEDCs**).

Locating **Abroad** *can* **Reduce Costs** *— and incur some new costs*

Advantages of locating abroad

1) MNCs locate production facilities in countries with **low labour costs**. LEDCs such as Bangladesh, Vietnam and Malaysia have a large supply of low cost unskilled and semi-skilled labour. Many manufacturers of electrical goods, clothing etc. have located production facilities in these countries.

2) The cost of **land** and **buildings** is also significantly lower in LEDCs.

3) LEDCs tend to have much **looser employment laws** than the UK — e.g. there's often no minimum holiday requirement and far fewer health and safety regulations. This reduces the cost of **production**.

4) Often, host countries have **lower tax** rates. A lower tax bill is appealing to any business.

5) Locating in several countries **weakens trade union** power — a business with factories in just **one country** is vulnerable to **trade union action**. A business with factories in **several countries** won't have to stop production altogether if a union in one country goes on strike.

Disadvantages of locating abroad

1) Of course, relocating abroad **incurs costs** of its own. **Equipment** may have to be moved abroad — which is very **expensive**. It's best if equipment can be **sourced locally**.

2) Moving UK production abroad means making all your UK production workers **redundant**, which costs money.

3) Businesses can end up chasing low labour costs from one country to another. For example, Nike had shoe factories in **South Korea** in the late 1980s. They moved a lot of these to **China** and **Indonesia** in the mid 1990s, and they're now getting their shoes assembled in **Vietnam**.

4) Executives have to **travel** abroad between all the different sites, but this cost is relatively **low** and can be reduced by use of ICT such as email, telephone conferencing and videoconferencing.

It's better from this point of view to make goods for the UK market in the UK, goods for the US market in the US, goods for Japan in Japan, etc.

5) **Exchange rates** affect the cost of business. By producing in the same market where goods are sold, businesses get around the problem of exchange rates going up and down.

Case Study — Dyson in Malaysia

Background: The vacuum cleaner and washing machine manufacturer Dyson was originally set up in the UK. Their HQ and manufacturing facilities were both located in Malmesbury, in Wiltshire, southern England.

Relocation: Production of vacuum cleaners was moved to Malaysia in 2002, with the loss of 800 jobs in Malmesbury, Wiltshire. Production of washing machines went to Malaysia in 2003, with the loss of 65 more jobs.

Benefits of location in Malaysia: Production costs would be 30% lower in Malaysia than the UK. At the time of the relocation, Malaysian workers were paid one third of the wages of UK workers. At the time of the relocation, office space in Malaysia cost one third of the rental cost of office space in the UK.

Disadvantages of location in the UK: Apart from the high cost of production in the UK, the local government had refused planning permission for enlargement of the vacuum cleaner production factory in Malmesbury.

Jobs in UK: Research and development and head office jobs remained in Malmesbury. The company's owner, James Dyson, claimed that moving production to Malaysia enabled the company to enlarge R&D facilities in Malmesbury, creating more skilled jobs in Wiltshire.

Locating **Abroad** *can help businesses to* **Grow**

1) MNCs can take advantage of **new markets** in the host country. This is particularly beneficial when the home market is **saturated**.

2) By operating on a **worldwide scale**, firms can grow **very large**, and gain the benefits of **economies of scale**.

Locating Abroad

Host Countries offer Incentives to tempt businesses to locate there

Governments of host countries are keen for foreign companies to locate facilities there. Multinationals bring **jobs**, which boosts the host nation's economy.

Governments of host countries are often willing to **pay incentives** to foreign companies — sometimes over 50% of the cost of a production facility. They see it as **investment** in the economy.

Locating Abroad can get around Trade Barriers

1) MNCs who want to trade in foreign countries with **high trade tariffs** need to **locate there** to get round the tariffs. **China** has barriers to trade which mean it's difficult and expensive to export to China unless you have a base in China.

Trade tariff = customs duty. It's a tax you have to pay when importing goods.

2) The **European Union** is a common trading market. There are no trade tariffs on trade **between** EU member states, but companies based outside the EU have to pay a tariff on imports into the EU. It makes sense for companies **based outside** the EU to set up facilities **within** the EU. This allows them to sell to EU countries **without** paying a tariff, which makes their goods much more competitive.

Case Study — Toyota and Nissan car plants in the UK

Background:	**Japanese** car manufacturers **Toyota** and **Nissan** both wanted a foothold in Europe to get around **EU trade barriers**.
Why the UK:	The UK has less red tape than the rest of Europe. It's easier to dismiss workers, for example. The UK government offered **incentives**. Nissan and Toyota had **strong market share** in the UK.
Toyota:	Toyota located a factory in Derbyshire in 1989, production started in 1992. The site had space to expand, a supply of skilled **workers**, and good **road** and **rail** links for bringing in parts and distributing finished cars.
Nissan:	In 1984 Nissan located a factory in **Sunderland**. Production started in 1986. Sunderland had a supply of skilled workers, and good **road** and **rail** links, plus a nearby port.

Multinational involvement has Pros and Cons for Customers and Workers

	Advantages of multinational involvement	Disadvantages of multinational involvement
Workers	MNCs provide **employment**. Workers learn new **skills**.	**Working conditions** may be **poor**, with long hours and low health and safety standards. MNCs introduce their own managers, so little opportunity for **promotion**.
Consumers	MNCs offer **cheap prices** for UK consumer. **Host country** consumers have more money.	Goods may be of **lower quality**. Goods produced may not meet **host country needs**.
Host state	**Employment** and **national wealth** increase. MNCs bring **technology** and **investment**.	Most profit goes **overseas**. MNCs often **outcompete** local business.

Practice Questions

Q1 What is a multinational?

Q2 Give three examples of costs that can be reduced by locating abroad.

Q3 Why might a host government offer to pay incentives to a multinational?

Exam Questions

Q1 Catterick Cookwares are considering relocating production to Eastern Europe. Examine the factors they would take into account when making this decision. (10 marks)

Q2 Describe the advantages and disadvantages of a multinational manufacturing business setting up in an LEDC to the potential employees and to the host government. (8 marks)

If only I could relocate to the Bahamas — that'd suit me...

Although the Edexcel syllabus only gives a specific mention to the problems associated with multinational corporations, Edexcel students will probably find it useful to have a gander at p.80-81 — it'll help you understand the reasons why companies locate abroad. It's important to revise the effects on customers and workers — you can get asked about that.

Productive Efficiency

*These two pages are for **OCR**. There's some revision from AS level, but you're expected to know more detail for A2.*

Productive Efficiency *is* How Good *a firm is at turning* Inputs *into* Outputs

Productive efficiency is usually measured as **cost per unit**.
The more **efficient** the business, the more output it gets
for the same input, and the **lower** the **cost per unit**.

Productive efficiency doesn't take **quality** or **selling price** into account.

Input	process →	Output

Firms *measure* Labour Productivity *and* Capital Productivity

Output is measured as monetary value of goods produced.

$$\text{Labour productivity} = \frac{\text{Output per year}}{\text{Number of employees}}$$

$$\text{Capital productivity} = \frac{\text{Output per year}}{\text{Capital employed}}$$

Labour productivity doesn't always relate **directly** to competitiveness, or costs per unit. A business with
high labour productivity might pay its workers **high wages**, which would increase its **production costs**.

Businesses *can* Improve *their* Productive Efficiency

Businesses can cut production costs

1) The **cost of materials** can be reduced, to reduce the total cost per unit.

2) The **cost of employee wages** can also be reduced.

This can reduce quality, which has a negative effect on sales.

This can reduce motivation, which lowers labour productivity.

Businesses can change production method

1) Changing from **job** to **batch** production or from
batch to **flow** production increases efficiency.

2) Increasing the **scale** of production improves efficiency, because of **economies of scale**.

3) Switching to **lean production** improves productive efficiency. Lean production
reduces waste to a minimum and it can also **motivate** employees to achieve more.

Businesses can change the way the workforce is managed

1) **Motivation** gets employees to work harder, and **reduces absenteeism**. See the AS book, and p56-57 of this book.

2) Employees must be **trained** in the **skills** they need to do their jobs **productively** and **efficiently**.

3) **Multi-skilled** employees with broad training can be moved to **different**
tasks to respond to increases in demand, and can cover for **absences**.

Training also improves motivation.

Businesses can invest in equipment

1) Employees may need **new equipment** to help them produce more,
e.g. robotic equipment is used in modern car factories.

2) The **cost** of investing in new machinery may be prohibitive.

Work Study can show where productive efficiency can be improved

1) **Work Study** has two parts, Method Study and Work Measurement.

2) **Method Study** examines a task and finds the most **efficient** method to use. It can
cover worker motivation and ergonomic design as well as basic production methods.

3) **Work Measurement** times standard tasks. It's used for **setting targets**.

4) Work Study is useful in finding out **where** and **how** a task can be done **more efficiently**.

Work measurement is also called time and motion study.

There are Human Resource Issues *with attempts to* Improve Productivity

Attempts to improve productivity can be perceived by staff as a way to
wring the last drop of work out of them without **paying** them any more.

Staff may also worry that an improvement in productivity may result in **redundancies** — if everyone's working
harder, there may not be enough work to go around. The introduction of new labour saving equipment such as
robots is likely to bring redundancies, although **remaining staff** will probably be **better trained** and **better paid**.

Productive Efficiency

Capacity is Maximum Output with the Resources Currently Available

Capacity depends on:

- the **number of employees** and how skilled they are.
- the **technology** the business has — what **machinery** they have, what state it's in, what kind of computer system they have, etc.
- the kind of production **process** the business uses.

Capacity Utilisation is How Much Capacity is being Used

$$\text{Capacity Utilisation} = \frac{\text{Output}}{\text{Capacity}} \times 100\%$$

For example: a hotel with half its rooms booked out has a capacity utilisation of 50%. A clothing factory with output of 70 000 shirts per month and a maximum capacity of 100 000 shirts is running at 70% capacity utilisation.

Ensuring High Capacity Utilisation improves Productive Efficiency

Low capacity utilisation is inefficient

1) Low capacity utilisation is called **under utilisation**.
2) It's **inefficient** because the business isn't getting use out of machines and facilities it's **already paid for**.
3) The **fixed cost** of the firm's assets is spread over **less output** — which means that **unit costs go up**. This reduces profit margins, and makes the product **less profitable**.

Undercapacity — it's kinda echoey in here.

100% capacity utilisation has drawbacks

1) The business **won't** have the **flexibility** to increase production, e.g. for a one-off order.
2) There's no **downtime** — machines are on **all the time**. If a machine has a problem, it'll cause delays and bottlenecks as work piles up waiting for the problem to be fixed. There's no time for equipment maintenance, which can reduce the life of machinery.
3) There's no **margin of error**. Everything has to be perfect first time, which causes **stress** to managers and staff. **Mistakes** are more likely when everyone's working flat out.
4) The business can't **temporarily increase output** for seasonal demand or one-off orders.
5) If output is greater than demand, there'll be **surplus stock** hanging about waiting to be sold. It's not good to have valuable **working capital** tied up in stock.

Therefore, businesses should plan production levels to achieve **almost** full capacity utilisation.

Practice Questions

Q1 Why is cost per unit not the be-all and end-all of operations management?

Q2 Give four examples of things a business can do to improve productive efficiency.

Q3 A ceramics factory could produce 40 000 plates a month at maximum capacity. It's currently producing 34 000 plates a month. What's the capacity utilisation percentage?

Q4 What are the negative impacts of operating too far under capacity?

Exam Questions

Q1 Analyse the factors that could affect the cost of producing one unit of a product. (8 marks)

Q2 A manufacturer of towels is operating at 98% capacity. Examine the potential impacts of reducing capacity utilisation to 85%. (10 marks)

Bring on the robots, I say...

Capacity utilisation is one of those things that businesses have to get "just right" — not using enough capacity is inefficient, but using too much is inflexible, and likely to result in mistakes, knackered machinery and knackered workers. The OCR board expect you to know more detail about productive efficiency for A2 level than AS, so don't skimp on learning this lot.

Stock Control and Quality Control

*These pages are for **OCR**.*

It's **Costly** to hold lots of **Stock**

The value of stock a business is holding is recorded on the profit and loss account (see p32-33).

1) **Storage costs** are the most **obvious cost** of holding stock. Storage costs include rent for the warehouse and also the non-obvious costs of heating, lighting, refrigeration, security etc. Don't forget those.

2) **Wastage costs** are the costs of **throwing away** useless stock. The longer a business holds stock, the more likely it is to create waste. Stocks get **physically damaged** as time goes on, and they can also go **out of fashion**.

3) **Opportunity cost** is the cost of **investing** money in stock instead of **something else**. Capital tied up in stock is **unproductive** and could be used more productively elsewhere, such as financing a marketing campaign.

Stock Control aims to keep levels of stock **Just Right**

1) Most businesses try to reduce the level of stocks they're holding. The **maximum** level of stock a business wants to hold depends on the size of their warehouses, and also on **opportunity cost**.

2) A business needs a **minimum** level of stock so that it **won't run out** of raw materials or finished goods — if it ran out, production would grind to a halt, or customers would be turned **away**. This minimum stock level is called **buffer stock**.

3) The **amount** of **buffer stock** needed depends on the warehouse **space** available, the kind of product (**perishable**, or something which keeps), the **rate** at which stocks are used up, and the **lead time**.

4) The **lead time** is the time it takes for goods to **arrive** after ordering them from the supplier. The **longer** the lead time, the **more buffer stocks** you need to hold — if customer demand suddenly went up, you wouldn't want to wait a long time for stocks to arrive from the supplier. A **short lead time** means you can have **small** buffer stocks and top them up as and when you need to.

Stock Control Charts help control **Stock Management**

Stock control charts allow managers to **analyse** and **control** stock over a period of time — as shown below. Have a good look at the diagram. It'll make stock control easier to understand.

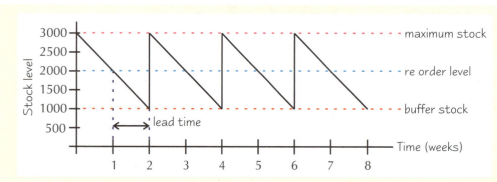

1) The **buffer stock level** is **1000 units**. The **lead time** is 1 week, and the business goes through **1000 units** each week. That means they have to **re-order** stock when they've got **2000** units left — just so they don't go below their buffer stock level. 2000 units is the **re-order level**.

2) The firm re-orders **2000 units** each time. This takes them back to their **maximum stock level** of 3000 units.

Just-In-Time (JIT) Production keeps stock levels **Very Low**

1) **Just-in-time** production aims to have as **little stock** as possible. Ideally, all raw materials come in one door, are made into products and go straight out another door — all **just in time** for delivery to customers.

2) JIT is based on very efficient stock control. **Kanban** is the JIT system of triggering **repeat orders**. When staff reach coloured kanban cards towards the end of a batch of components, they order more straight away. The **supply** of raw materials is **linked directly** to the **demand** for raw materials, and there's no need for lots of stock.

3) JIT has **advantages** — **storage costs** are reduced and **working capital control** is improved. There's **less waste** because there's less out-of-date stock lying around.

4) There are **disadvantages** — no stock means customers can't be supplied during **production strikes**. Businesses using JIT can't respond to **sudden rises** in **demand**. Suppliers have to be **reliable** because there isn't much stock of raw materials to keep production going.

Stock Control and Quality Control

Remember, Quality Control and Quality Assurance are Different Things

Quality Control	Quality Assurance
Assumes that errors are **unavoidable**.	Assumes that errors are **avoidable**.
Detects errors and **puts them right**.	**Prevents errors** and aims to get it **right first time**.
Quality control inspectors check other people's work, and are responsible for quality.	**Employees** check their own work. **Workers** are **responsible** for passing on good quality work to the next stage of the production process.

Total Quality Management assures Commitment To Quality

1) **Total Quality Management** (TQM) means the **whole workforce** has to be committed to quality improvements. The idea is to **build quality** in every department and not let quality get squeezed out. It's QA on wheels.

2) With TQM, every employee has to try to **satisfy customers** — both **external** customers that the business sells things to, and **internal** customers within the business.

3) It takes **time** to introduce TQM. Employees can be **demotivated** — TQM can seem like a lot of extra work. Workers need **training** to not see quality as someone else's problem. **Rewards** for quality can be motivating.

Kaizen is Japanese for Continuous Improvement

1) The **kaizen** approach means that employees should be **improving** their work slightly **all the time**, instead of making one-off improvements when management tell them to.

2) For kaizen to work, employees at the bottom of the hierarchy have to be given some control over **decision-making** so that they can actually **implement** quality improvements.

Benchmarking Learns from Other Businesses

1) Benchmarking studies **other businesses** with excellent **quality standards**, and aims to **adopt** their **methods**.

2) It's very simple to see that a competitor has done something to improve quality, but it's not at all easy to figure out what that something is. **Competitors** are unlikely to **share** important information.

3) **Working practices** can't always be transferred between different **corporate cultures**.

4) Businesses can **benchmark internally**, by studying similar activities in different departments.

Quality Circles are Groups of Employees who work on quality issues

1) **Quality circles** meet a couple of times a month to discuss quality.

2) They include employees from **various departments** and **all levels** of the organisation.

3) Quality circles aim to **identify** and **solve** specific quality problems that arise.

4) Quality circles can be very effective because they use the knowledge and experience of factory floor staff.

Practice Questions

Q1 How do (a) lead time, and (b) buffer stock differ between a traditional firm and a firm doing JIT production?

Q2 What is the central idea of Total Quality Management?

Q3 Why is benchmarking often not straightforward?

Exam Questions

Q1 A consultant advises a furniture store to reduce its levels of stock. Explain why this advice is given. (8 marks)

Q2 Gerald and Foster manufacture parts for aeroplanes. The MD is concerned about quality after complaints from customers. Discuss the possible implications for Gerald and Foster of implementing TQM. (10 marks)

Time to relax and take stock...

Right, it's generally bad to have too much stock, and it's bad to have too little stock. Like so many things in business, the trick is to get it just right — to give yourself enough flexibility so that you never run out of stock, but not to tie up all your money in stock on the shelves which might go out of fashion before it's ever sold. It's a toughie, and that's for sure.

Research and Development

*Businesses need to do technical research before launching new products. These pages are for **AQA**, **OCR** and **Edexcel**.*

Research and Development comes up with New ideas, products, and processes

1) Research and Development (R&D) does **technical research** to come up with new products and production processes. The idea is to increase productive efficiency or to increase sales.

2) R&D has to turn raw ideas into **actual products**, or **actual new processes**. This can take a long time.

3) R&D is **related** to market research, but they're not the same. Market research **discovers** consumers' wants and R&D comes up with new products to **meet** customer wants.

Research and Development is Costly, but Essential

1) Research and Development is a very **costly** process.

2) It's also a **risky** process — it's estimated that in the **pharmaceutical** industry, only **one in twelve** new drugs **researched** are actually **developed** as having a commercial potential.

3) Some organisations choose not to have a specific R&D department, but instead to **adapt** and **modify** new products brought out by their **rivals**. This may be because the business is risk averse, or because its shareholders prefer profits to be paid as dividends in the short term rather than invested for the long term.

4) However, market leaders normally invest in R&D. The most successful businesses have a **large portfolio** of products, **balanced** between **innovative new products** and proven older products (see product portfolio analysis, p17).

5) The ability to launch a new product in the market is of great value. A business can charge a high price for its innovative product (this is called market skimming), and the product can achieve a sound **market image**, before competitors enter the market with **similar products** at **competitive prices**. The Sony Walkman is a great example of this.

6) Some industries are particularly **fast moving**, and need to **constantly** develop new products — e.g. the pharmaceutical industry, the microchip industry and the mobile telecommunications industry.

New Product Development (NPD) has Six Stages from Idea to Launch

1) Idea

The business comes up with **new ideas**, explores and **develops existing ideas** or **modifies competitors' ideas**. New ideas can come from **brainstorming** in a group, from **employee suggestions** or from **R&D department meetings**. New ideas are also discovered through **market research** finding out what consumers want, or from customers submitting requests to a business. Businesses can also use **already patented ideas**, for a fee.

2) Analysis and Screening

The business wants to see if the product can be produced and sold at a **profit**. All aspects of the idea are investigated — whether there's a **potential market** for it or not based on market research, whether the **technology** and **resources** exist to develop it, whether a **competitor** has an existing patent on a similar idea. At this stage, a **prototype** may be made to see what the product will be like.

3) Development

The **R&D department** develop a **working prototype**. They test it **scientifically**, and tweak the design to make the **functional** design (how it works) and **aesthetic** design (how it looks, feels — or smells and tastes if it's a food) as good as possible. This is the real "meat" of research and development.

4) Value Analysis

The business tries to make the product good **value** for money. They look at the economy of **making**, **warehousing** and **distributing** the product to make sure the whole process will be **efficient** and value for money — for the **business**, and for the **consumer**.

5) Test Marketing ← *This is where the marketing department gets involved again.*

The business sometimes sells the new product in a **limited geographical area**, and then analyses **consumer feedback** on the product, price and packaging. This allows **modifications** to be made before a wider launch.

6) Launch

All systems are go. A successful launch requires **enough stock** of the product to be distributed across the market, and it also needs an effective **advertising and promotion campaign** in place to **inform** and **persuade** retailers and consumers to buy the product.

Research and Development

Value Analysis finds out if the product adds enough Value to Justify its Costs

1) **Value analysis** looks at factors which affect "**value added**" — how much the customer is prepared to **pay** for the product compared to how much it cost to **make** the product.

2) Businesses do value analysis to assess how well the product does its **job**, whether consumers like the way it **looks**, and whether they'd be prepared to pay a little more for it.

3) Value analysis investigates all the **costs of production** to see whether they could be reduced. For example, maybe cheaper materials could be used, or maybe cheaper processes could be used.

4) Value analysis has been blamed for reduction in **quality** — cheaper materials and cheaper labour often end up with a **tatty product**.

"But could we have used cheaper bottle tops?"
This is the question that kept Anton up at night.

Time Based Competition means R&D should be as Fast as possible

1) The pressure of **intense international competition** means that larger, multinational businesses feel they need to come up with new, better products, **all the time**. Businesses need to pursue **new product R&D** to maintain or increase their global market share.

2) This increasing pressure has shifted the emphasis in product development from **price** and **quality** (**value analysis**) to **time based competition** — where the aim is to be the **fastest**.

3) The **demands** of the market **change rapidly**, and manufacturers are under pressure to **react rapidly** to meet these changing demands. New product development is squeezed into as short a time as possible, production is squeezed into as short a time as possible, to get the product out onto the consumer market as quickly as possible.

4) **Technology** also **changes rapidly**, so manufacturers are under pressure to develop products which are more modern and technologically advanced all the time.

5) Critics of this **time based competitiveness** complain that the **quality** of many products has been **lowered** in the quest to cut costs and production time.

6) It can be argued that **too many** new products **bewilder** the consumer. Some market research reports that consumers are **confused** and **irritated** by the sheer amount of choice in consumer markets such as chocolate snack bars, shampoo and mobile phones.

> **Example: Computer hardware and software**
> In **personal computer hardware**, as soon as one manufacturer has come out with a **new product** such as a teeny 1" hard drive or a superfast processor, other manufacturers have to get similar products onto the market **immediately**.
>
> Computer **software** is often released before it's **really 100% ready**, and the software producer supplements the release with "**patches**" which fix any problems with the original release. This is because of the **intense time pressure**.

Practice Questions

Q1 What's meant by "research and development"?

Q2 Give two reasons why R&D is risky.

Q3 What is time-based competition?

Q4 What is value analysis?

Exam Question

> Q1 Explain why it is important to invest in research and development. (10 marks)

They could be researching a new, tougher exam — just you watch out...

Hey, all those amazing new products have to come from somewhere. Just think, there are research and development eggheads beavering away even now, as we speak, to come up with something utterly amazing that we'll all rush out to buy. Of course, it could turn out to be yet another shampoo for colour treated hair, or yet another web publishing tool.

Critical Path Analysis

*Critical Path Analysis is used to find the most cost-effective way of doing a complex project. For **AQA**, **OCR** and **Edexcel**.*

Critical Path Analysis works out the Quickest Way to Finish a Set Of Tasks

Critical Path Analysis (CPA) identifies the most **efficient** and **cost effective** way of completing a complex project — i.e. a project made up of a series of activities.

1) The various activities which together will make up the project are **identified**, and the **order** or **sequence** of these activities are identified.

2) The **duration** or how long each activity will take is **estimated**.

3) These factors are then arranged as a **network** or graph, showing the whole project from start to finish, and showing which tasks happen at the same time.

For large, complicated projects made up of tens of steps, computer programs are used to construct the network.

Task C and task D can be done at the same time.

4) The **shortest time** required to get from start to finish is identified. The sequence of tasks which have to be done one after another with **no gaps in between**, to get the project done as fast as possible, is called the **Critical Path**. Activities on the critical path are called **critical activities** — if they're delayed, the **whole project** is delayed.

Critical Paths include Earliest Start Times and Latest Finishing Times

1) **EST = earliest start time**, in number of days since the start of the project. An activity can't start until the activity before it has been completed — e.g. you can't ice a cake before it's baked. EST is worked out by **adding** the **duration** of a task to the **EST** of the **previous task**.

2) **LFT = latest finishing time**, in days since the start of the project. This is the **latest** time by which the activity can be completed without **holding up** the **next activity**. It's calculated by **subtracting** the **duration** of the task from the **LFT** of the **next task** — you have to work out the LFTs by **working backwards** from the **end** of the project.

3) **Float time** is the amount of **spare time** available for a task.

Total float time is the amount of spare time between the time an activity takes, and the time it must be completed by.

LFT (this activity) – **Duration** (this activity) – **EST** (this activity) = **Float time**

Example: 12 days LFT – 7 days duration – 3 days start time = **2 days float time**.

Note: activities on the <u>Critical Path</u> don't have any <u>float time</u>.

Free float is the difference between the time a task takes and the time where the **next task** has to start.

EST (of the **next** activity) – **Duration** of task – **EST** (of **this** activity) = **Free float**.

4) **LFT** and **EST** are written on the right hand half of each node. The number on the left hand side is just the number of the node — the nodes are numbered left to right.

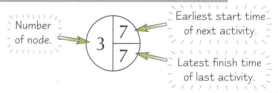

Number of node.

Earliest start time of next activity.

Latest finish time of last activity.

Here's an Example of Critical Path Analysis

1) A project is made up of **eight separate tasks** A to H. Task **A** takes **4 days**, **B** takes **7 days** and **C** (which can be done as the **same time as B**) takes **9 days**, **D** takes **6 days** and task **E** (can be done at the same time as D) takes **5 days**. Tasks F (5 days) and G (7 days) must be finished before task H starts, and task F can be started at the same time as task A. Task **H** takes **3 days**. The network looks like this:

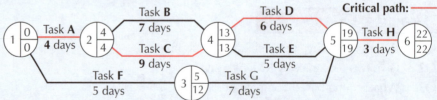

2) The **critical path** is task **A** followed by task **C**, then task **D, then** task **H**. Adding up the durations of these tasks tells you the project takes **22 days** in total. The EST and LFT of task H in the final node are both 22 days.

3) You can work out the **ESTs** of all the tasks by working **forwards** from the start of the project, and then work out the **LFTs** of the tasks by working backwards from the end of the project.

4) In each nodes on the critical path, the EST equals the LFT. Node 3 is off the critical path, and the EST and LFT are different — the EST of task G is 5 days after the start of the project and the LFT of task F is worked out by subtracting the duration of task G from the LFT of task G (19 days – 7 days = 12 days).

5) **Task B** has a **float time** of **2 days** and **task E** which runs alongside **task D** has a **float time** of **1 day**.

Critical Path Analysis

Critical Path Analysis has several Advantages

1) CPA identifies the **critical activities** (activities on the critical path), which need to be supervised closely, to make sure they meet their deadlines.

2) Labour resources can be transferred from activities with **float time** to **critical activities**, to make sure that deadlines are met.

3) CPA allows managers to operate **Just-In-Time** production. **Resources** such as raw materials, labour and equipment can be employed right at the **earliest start time**, instead of hanging around waiting to be needed. This saves on the **storage costs** and opportunity costs of stock holding, and **improves liquidity**.

4) Critical path analysis helps firms forecast their **cash flow** — it gives definite earliest start times when cash will need to be spent on raw materials, which allows the firm to predict its liquidity.

5) Critical path analysis finds the shortest time possible for completing a complex project. This can give a competitive advantage. It's an important element of **time-based management**.

6) It's an excellent **visual aid** to communications, because it shows at a glance which steps take place at the **same time**, and which have any **float time**.

7) Critical path analysis forces managers to think about the activities involved in the project. Without the systematic approach of critical path analysis, something might be forgotten.

8) CPA can be used to review progress on individual tasks. If there are changes and modifications to the progress of the project, the critical path can be **updated** as the project goes on.

Critical Path Analysis has Disadvantages as well

1) Critical path analysis relies on **estimates** of how long each task will take. If these aren't accurate, the whole analysis will be inaccurate.

2) Unless **critical activities** are identified and supervised closely, there'll be **delays** to the whole project. Critical path analysis puts **pressure** on managers to **manage effectively** and **meet deadlines**.

3) Managers must make changes to the CPA once they know that delays are likely. Otherwise, it'll be inaccurate.

4) Constructing the CPA will require a significant amount of **planning** and **time**.

5) Critical path analysis sets **tight deadlines**, especially for critical activities. It's tempting for employees to **cut corners** in the rush to meet deadlines. **Quality** can suffer.

6) Critical path analysis can't tell you anything about **costs** — or anything about **how good** the project is.

Practice Questions

Q1 What do the initials EST and LST mean?
Q2 Explain the term "total float time".
Q3 What is meant by the expression "critical path"?
Q4 Give two advantages to managers of using critical path analysis.

Exam Questions

Q1 A project is analysed and six separate activities are identified. Activity A must be done first, and it has an estimated duration of 8 days. Activities B, C and D can take place at the same time — B takes 4 days, C 6 days and D 4 days. E is a separate activity and will take 7 days. F and G can take place at the same time — F taking 3 days and G five days.

Answer on p.138.

(a) construct a critical path analysis from this data. (5 marks)
(b) Mark in the critical path and state the minimum number of days the project will take to complete. (2 marks)
(c) what are the float times at B and F. (2 marks)

Q2 What is the purpose of a critical path analysis? Provide and explain three advantages and three disadvantages of employing such a technique. (14 marks)

What did the critical path say — "get your badly dressed self off my gravel"...

To be honest, this is hard to learn from scratch. Once you've got a diagram to show the order of tasks in a project, and which ones can be done simultaneously, you can figure out where in the project there's spare time. Remember that you work out EST by working forwards from the start date, and you work out LFT by going backwards from the end date.

Controlling Operations

*IT is used to plan and control operations. IT makes decision making easier and speeds up communication. Hooray for computers. These pages are for **AQA**, **OCR** and **Edexcel**.*

IT is used to **Control Operations**

IT (Information Technology) has dramatically changed the way that businesses are run. It is now used in most parts of a business, but especially in the following areas:

1) **Production**
2) **Communication**
3) **Finance**
4) **Employment** and **Location**

> **Information management** is **vital** to good decision making and operational control.
>
> As IT is used more and more in business, the amount of **information available** to managers increases. It's important to **manage** this information so that managers get the information they **need**, no more, no less. **Successful** organisations keep **up-to-date** with changing information.

IT helps make **Production** more **Efficient**

1) **Computer-aided design** (CAD) uses computers to design new products, or make alterations to existing products. CAD produces 3D mockups on screen — managers don't have to wait for a **prototype** to be built before they know what the product will look like.

2) **Computer-aided manufacture** (CAM) uses computers to produce a product, usually involving **robots** or computer numerically controlled machines (CNC). CAM is often combined with the CAD process — products are designed on computer, and the design data fed straight into the production machine. This is called **CAD/CAM**.

--- *AQA & OCR* --- --- *AQA & OCR* ---

3) Computers make **stock control** easier. Holding stock information in a database makes it much easier to monitor when new stocks are required. In retailing this is often combined with Electronic Point of Sale (EPOS) systems that rely on barcodes to record which products are being purchased by customers. This means stocks can be re-ordered automatically.

4) **Purchasing** over the Internet allows businesses to see at a glance which suppliers have the best prices. This cuts costs and speeds up purchasing.

IT helps make **Communication Faster** and more **Effective**

Communication now happens very **quickly** thanks to IT. Information can be passed **between departments**, between businesses, and between businesses and their **customers** using fax, email and Internet.

1) Email is a fast and efficient method of communicating, both internally and externally.

2) The **Internet** allows businesses to reach a **larger customer base**, and do business **24 hours a day**. Customers can check a business' **webpage** for information rather than phoning a helpline or sending a letter in the post.

IT helps make **Finance** departments more **Efficient**

1) **IT** helps with **budgetary control**. Once budgets have been set the finance department can easily compare current expenditure levels with original budgets using **spreadsheets**.

2) **Forecasting and Planning**. Large amounts of **data** can be held on computer, to make forecasting easier. Computers are also used to **model** complex planning tools such as Internal Rate of Return.

3) Spreadsheets allow managers to investigate "what if?" scenarios. They can see the impact of **potential changes** in expenditure or sales at the proverbial **touch of a button**.

IT has had an impact on **Location** and **Employment**

1) More workers are able to **work from home** using email to communicate with the office. This is called **teleworking**. Teleworkers are still able to communicate with their colleagues, but can work more **flexible hours**. The employer doesn't have to **pay** for teleworkers' heating, lighting or health and safety.

2) Many businesses are now able to locate in cheaper areas because they can **use technology** to **communicate** with **customers**, e.g. call centre staff can bring up a customer's whole history on the computer screen, rather than looking through paper files, or dealing with the customer face-to-face.

--- *AQA & OCR* --- --- *AQA & OCR* ---

Controlling Operations

Gantt Charts help Control Operations
OCR & Edexcel

1) A business must make sure to carry out marketing, production and sales processes in the correct order. After all, you wouldn't try to wrap a chocolate bar before it had been produced.

2) Gantt charts have horizontal bars which represent the duration of each individual task in a complex operation. The tasks are arranged to show which can be done at the same time. It's a similar tool to network analysis.

Example: This simple Gantt chart shows the things that a business must do before it is able to open a new shop.

Task	Week 1	2	3	4	5	6	7	8	9	10	11	12	13	14	15	16	17	18	19	20
Market research	■	■	■																	
Analysis of research				■																
Obtaining premises					■	■	■													
Planning permission							■	■	■											
Shopfitting										■	■	■	■	■	■	■	■	■	■	
Recruiting workers						■	■	■	■											
Training workers										■	■	■								
Grand opening																				■

1) The **length** of each bar represents the **time** that a task takes.

2) The chart helps to schedule the events. Some tasks can take place simultaneously, while other tasks are dependent upon another task getting finished first.

3) So... in this example the firm can begin to **start shopfitting** in **week 10** once planning permission has been granted to use the premises as a shop. Shopfitting takes 9 weeks, therefore the chart shows that the new shop can't open until **week 20**.

There are Several Advantages to using Gantt Charts

1) They show at a glance whether a project, or production line is **on schedule**.
2) If it's falling behind, more resources can be allocated. This means operations can be **controlled** more efficiently.
3) The graphical format is **less complex** than **critical path analysis** which could be used as an alternative.

Practice Questions

Q1 State one reason why a business might use CAD when designing a new product.

Q2 Why do most large retailers now use EPOS systems?

Q3 What does the length of a horizontal bar on a Gantt chart show?

Q4 What is a teleworker, and why might workers be more motivated if they are given the opportunity to become a teleworker?

Exam Questions

Q1 Discuss the implications on the stakeholders of a business that has decided to close its UK customer call centre and replace it with one in India. (12 marks)

Q2 Evaluate the effect of the internet upon high street retailers. (8 marks)

Q3 "The introduction of an Electronic Point of Sale (EPOS) system will mean that never again will customers be faced with an empty shelf". Discuss the extent to which you agree with this statement. (12 marks)

I still say "bring on the robots"...

I wonder how operations control was handled before there were computers — there must have been an awful lot of paper flying around the office. For OCR and AQA you're expected to know about all the uses of IT in operations on p.92 — and there are a lot of them. Edexcel people only have to know about CAD and CAM, and Gantt charts.

External Constraints on Production

*External factors have an effect on businesses (e.g. laws, availability of resources, market size). Businesses also have an effect on their external environment and they need to be aware of this and control it, e.g. producing waste, using energy and causing pollution. These pages are for **OCR**, but they're relevant for **Edexcel** as well.*

There are **External Constraints** on **Production**

Whenever a business is producing it will face constraints which it **can't control**, because they're **external** — outside the business. These might include:

1) **Market size**. There's no point in producing 1000 units if you know that last year there were only 300 sold in the whole of the market.

2) **Supply chain**. A business must be aware of what its **suppliers** are capable of supplying them with. There's no point in filling 2000 bottles with cola if your supplier can only provide you with 1000 bottle tops.

3) **Competition**. No business operates in isolation — everyone's got competitors, and each business must keep an eye on what the competition is doing. Competitor actions may affect the **number of units** that need to be produced, or **what product** needs to be produced.

4) **The Law**. Some aspects of production are controlled by law. There's much more about this on p.96-97.

5) **Public Relations**. Businesses try to avoid doing things that'll give them a **bad press**. Environmental damage, ethical problems such as the use of child labour or testing on animals can give a business a bad name.

What do you mean, we can't produce a billion units of deadly radioactive lemonade in a year? How about a million — the production line would handle a million units, right?

"Green" stuff and external constraints are linked. The way the business affects the environment has an effect on how people <u>see</u> the business — and on the <u>laws</u> that are passed to impact on the business' activities.

Resource Management means trying to use resources in the **Best Way**

Obviously, it makes **financial sense** to avoid wasting resources. Not using what you've paid for really wrecks those precious **cost-per-unit** ratios.

In the longer term, it makes sense to use resources **sustainably**. Completely **running out** of a resource would be bad news. Also, as resources **run low**, their **price rises** (supply and price are linked, remember), increasing **costs**.

For example, as **oil supplies** start to dip, the **price of oil** will **go up**, and it'll keep going up. Producing goods made from crude oil, such as **plastics**, will become more **expensive**. **Electricity** that's generated by burning oil will get more expensive, which will **increase production costs** for pretty much everything.

...unless someone comes up with a better way of making electricity from renewable resources like wind and solar power, or a better way of using nuclear power.

Resource Management involves **Environmental Issues**

1) Most people just think of environmental issues as **pollution**. Environmental issues also cover things like use of **natural resources**. From a green point of view it's best to use sustainable natural resources, and sustainable sources of electricity.

2) Environmental costs can cause **bad publicity** for a business. Bad publicity can impact on sales, so it's worthwhile to avoid causing environmental problems in the first place.

3) It's become common for businesses to do **green audits**. These are reviews of the environmental effects of the firm's activities. There's more about environmental audits on p.110-111.

4) Green audits assess whether the firm is meeting **legal requirements** for environmental protection, and whether it's meeting its own green targets for things like carbon dioxide emissions, amount of cardboard recycled, amount of waste discharged into waterways, etc.

5) Businesses need to consider the **responsibilities** they have towards the environment and the **improvements** they can make to reduce damage to the environment.

There are **Community Issues** in **Production**

NIMBY stands for Not In My Back Yard. NIMBYism has become much more common as local communities recognise they can wield a hefty influence if they act together. Communities who object to a new production development often form a **pressure group** to represent their views. For example, the owners of **Coventry airport** have not yet been allowed to build a new passenger terminal building because the local community **protested** about the increased **traffic** and **pollution** they believe it will create.

External Constraints on Production

There are Ethical Factors in Production

1) A business looking to **reduce its costs** as much as possible would use the **cheapest labour** possible, and make sure that its employees worked the **longest hours** possible, with the **least** possible **health and safety** protection and employment **rights**. Moving production facilities to some LEDCs can achieve this.

2) However, this style of "sweat-shop" production is **frowned on** by some people because it's thought that it doesn't give workers **basic human rights**. Workers in this system can't get trained or educated, and don't have free time.

3) The same goes for **child labour**, which is fairly common in some poorer countries. Many people think that children have the right to play and have an education, instead of working long hours. Customers may **boycott** products made using child labour, so it's often worthwhile for a business to avoid child labour, and **publicise** the fact that they're avoiding it.

4) There's a growing trend towards **fair trade production** in some **foodstuffs**. Fair trade means that producers are paid a good price for their crops, whatever the market price is. Currently, fair trade goods are a **niche market**.

5) Ethical considerations aren't limited to production in LEDCs. Switching to **24 hour production** could be seen as forcing workers to accept non-family friendly **night shifts**.

Good Waste Management can increase Efficiency and Profits

Effective **resource management** will involve good **waste management**. It's in the interests of a business to minimise waste, since **more waste** means **more costs per unit**. These costs can take a number of forms:

1) **Financial costs.** The most **obvious** cost involved in throwing away resources is the money that's been spent on **purchasing** them. Ensuring that the production process **makes the most** of every raw material that is used will mean that the costs are minimised.

2) **Opportunity costs.** The money that has paid for the wasted materials could have been used **elsewhere** in the business.

3) **Social costs.** Waste has to be handled and managed and this imposes costs on **society**. For example, waste that's disposed of in **landfill sites** may be an **eyesore** to the local community.

4) **Environmental costs.** These include **air pollution** from incinerating waste, **water pollution** from discharging it into rivers and **groundwater pollution** from burying it.

Lean production techniques aim to reduce waste to an absolute bare minimum — mainly in order to reduce **opportunity costs** and increase **productive efficiency**. The benefits to **society** and the **environment** are a happy knock-on effect.

Practice Questions

Q1 Name one external factor that might affect how much a business produces, and explain how it might affect production.

Q2 Explain why a business might want to reduce the amount of pollution that it emits.

Q3 Explain how the NIMBY syndrome might affect a business.

Q4 Give an example of an ethical factor affecting production.

Q5 Give three examples of the costs of waste.

Exam Questions

Q1 A business is considering the introduction of a new shift pattern, which will allow it to run the production line for 24 hours a day. Discuss the issues that the business should address before deciding whether or not to go ahead. (14 marks)

Q2 "Effective waste management is as important to a business as effective human resource management". Evaluate this statement, using examples to justify your views. (16 marks)

Waste not, want not...

Waste management isn't only about pollution. There are also opportunity costs — it makes business sense to reduce waste. Production decisions are affected by what competitors are doing, what customers are doing and what suppliers are doing. Operations management can do a lot to earn goodwill or wreck goodwill, which affects sales.

Production and the Law

*There are a number of laws that affect the production of goods, and so any business that's involved in production must be aware of their implications. These pages are for **OCR**, and the health and safety stuff is useful for **Edexcel**.*

The **Law** protects **Workers** while they **Manufacture** Goods

The Health and Safety at Work Act (1974), updated in 1996.

1) The main focus of this law is to **prevent accidents**, and it requires employers to provide safe working conditions. This may require the provision of **safety clothing** and **equipment** for workers.

2) In addition, businesses that employ **more than five people** must have a **written** health and safety policy **on display**, and a copy of the Health and Safety at Work Act on display.

3) This law protects not just employees but also **visitors** to a workplace — e.g. customers in a shop, or trade sales reps visiting a factory.

Working Time Regulations (1998)

1) This is a directive from the **European Union**.

2) It says that workers can't be forced to work more than an average of **48 hours a week**. However, workers can **volunteer** to work more than this if they **choose** to do so.

3) This directive also gives workers the right to **appropriate breaks** whilst at work.

Other Safety Regulations

1) Most safety regulations have been developed from the Health and Safety at Work Act.

2) The **Reporting of Injuries, Diseases and Dangerous Occurrences Regulations (1995)** or **RIDDOR** say that businesses must **report** certain accidents.

3) The **Control of Substances Hazardous to Health Regulations (2002)**, or **COSHH**, protects employees who work with hazardous substances.

Vicarious Liability means it's all the *Employer's Responsibility*

1) In addition to the above laws, workers are protected by the legal notion of **vicarious liability**. This means that an **employer** will normally be **liable** for any act committed by an employee in the normal course of their job.

2) The idea of vicarious liability has **serious implications** for businesses. Imagine a situation where a lorry driver has loaded his vehicle incorrectly. When on the road the load comes loose, and causes an accident. The **employer** will be responsible for paying **compensation** to any people injured as a result of the accident.

The **Law** protects the **Community** and the **Environment**

1) Industries which release waste into the **water** or **land** are regulated by the **Environment Agency**. Businesses have to change their production processes to reduce pollution, or risk heavy fines.

2) Light industry processes which only release pollution into the **air** are regulated by **local authorities**. Businesses must get **authorisation** from the local council before carrying out processes which create **smoke** or make **noise**. **Environmental health** officers can force factories to **stop making noise** at night, if the noise is disturbing **local residents**.

3) Here are some examples of specific laws:

- The EU directive on **Waste Electrical and Electronic Equipment (WEEE)** forces businesses to increase **recycling** of waste electrical and electronic equipment, much of which previously ended up in landfill sites. From August 2005, manufacturers have increased responsibility for ensuring that goods such as computers, TVs and VCRS are recycled once they've come to the end of their useful life.

- **The Landfill Tax** was introduced in 1996 as a punitive tax to **reduce the amount of waste** being dumped into **landfill** sites.

- The **EU Packaging Waste Directive** forces businesses to increase the recycling of packaging. There are targets for the % of wood, paper, glass and plastic that must be recycled.

Production and the Law

The Law protects Customers and Consumers

The Trade Descriptions Act (1968)

This law ensures that businesses don't **mislead** consumers with **false descriptions** on **packaging** or **advertising materials**.

The Sale of Goods Act (1979)

1) This Act sets out the main **rights** of customers when making a purchase.
2) It's been updated by the **Sale and Supply of Goods Act (1994)**, and the **Sale and Supply of Goods to Consumers Regulations (2002)**. Together, these laws mean that goods must be **fit for their purpose** and of **satisfactory quality**.

The Consumer Protection Act (1987)

1) This act says that **new consumer goods** must be **safe**.
2) Along with this law, there are **regulations** governing things like **furniture fire safety** — all new products made after the regulations came into effect have to conform to the regulations. Manufacturers had to **change the materials** they used for sofa and chair cushions, and this incurred costs.

The Food Safety Act (1990)

1) Under this Act producers must ensure that foodstuffs are **not harmful**.
2) If any **part** of a batch of food is considered unfit for human consumption, then the whole lot is unfit, and it all has to be **destroyed**. This has serious implications for cost and revenue.
3) Foods must also not be **labelled** in a **misleading** way. The **Food Labelling Regulations** of 1996 say:
   - Food must labelled with a **descriptive name** and a list of **ingredients**.
   - Labels can only claim "low in fat" or "high in vitamins" if the food meets **set standards**.
   - Claims such as "**prevents cancer**" or "**cures measles**" are **not allowed**.
   - Food labels must also have a **Best Before** or **Use By** date, and should say how to store the food.
4) The Act also requires that workers **handling food** should be trained in **basic food hygiene**.

New Laws incur Costs to Manufacturers

When each new law is introduced, manufacturers may have to **change** their **production processes** to comply, or face hefty fines. Changing production processes costs money, as there may be **reduced productivity** during changeover. New processes may not be as **efficient**. New materials required by law may be **more expensive**.

Practice Questions

Q1 Which Act of Parliament ensures that workers are provided with necessary safety equipment?

Q2 Give two examples of European Directives that affect manufacturers.

Q3 Name the government agency that is responsible for overseeing many of the European directives regarding pollution.

Q4 Explain how vicarious liability may affect a business.

Exam Questions

Q1 Discuss how the Health and Safety at Work Act may be beneficial to a manufacturing business. (10 marks)

Q2 "It is time that manufacturers of equipment such as fridges and computers took responsibility for the disposal of these items". Discuss the extent to which you agree or disagree with this statement. (10 marks)

I fought the law and the law took my profits and stopped me from trading...

It'd be great if businesses automatically did "the right thing", but unfortunately they don't. You'll always have some businesses who try to get away with endangering employees, cheating customers and selling dangerous tat. The law's there to make sure that every single business obeys the rules, or faces the costs. The law hits 'em in the pocket, where it hurts.

SECTION FOUR — OPERATIONS MANAGEMENT

Economic Growth

Economic growth affects businesses and governments.
P.98 is for AQA and OCR, and p.99 is for AQA, OCR and Edexcel.

GDP (Gross Domestic Product) indicates the Size of a Nation's Economy

GDP is the **total market value** of **goods** and **services** produced **by** a nation **within** that nation during a period of time.

GDP = total **consumer spending** + business **investment**
+ **government spending** + the value of **exports** − the value of **imports**.

The UK is the world's fourth largest economy (after the USA, Japan and Germany) and the second largest economy in the European Union.

GDP is calculated in **real terms**, i.e. by ignoring **inflation**.

Economic Growth is the Increase in Size of a nation's Economy

1) Economic growth is an **increase** in the nation's production of **goods** and **services**.

2) It's measured as the **rate of increase in GDP** (Gross Domestic Product).

3) Economic growth means the same thing as "an increase in **economic activity**" — growth means there's **more demand** in the economy and **more output** to meet that demand.

The rate of growth for the UK is estimated to be 2.5% per year.

Economic Growth is determined by Resources and Productivity

1) The **growth potential** of an economy depends on the **amount** and **quality** of economic **resources** available — e.g. labour and fixed assets.

Quantity and quality of labour	**Quantity** of labour depends on **population size**, and on its **gender** and **age** composition. The **quality** of labour is the level of **education and training** that workers have reached. **High quality** of labour enables an economy to **grow faster**.
Investment	**Investment** increases the amount of **productive assets** (machinery etc used for production). For **growth** to happen, the **level of investment** in productive assets has to be greater than the amount of **depreciation** (the amount by which machines wear out) during the year.

2) It also depends on their **productivity** — how hard the nation works.

3) **Governments** can encourage **short term** growth by cutting taxes and interest rates (see p.100-101). This encourages businesses to borrow money and invest it in production. It also encourages consumers to borrow money and spend it on goods, which increases demand in the economy.

4) These days, economists tend to think it's better to **encourage steady growth** by "supply-side policies" which encourage **investment**, training and **employment**. These increase the **quality of labour**.

Economic Growth has Mainly Positive Effects for business and government

Economic **growth** means an increase in **national income**, which is good news.

Individual Businesses

1) **Growth** in GDP means **higher revenues** and higher **profitability** for **businesses**.

2) Economic growth gives the potential for **economies of scale**.

3) Sustained growth increases **confidence** and helps businesses **plan** for the future.

4) Fast growth may cause **shortages** of raw materials and skilled labour.

Governments

1) **Higher revenue** encourages investment in new projects, which creates jobs. This is good for the government — there's less need to pay welfare benefits.

2) Growth also enables the government to earn **increased revenues** through **taxes**.

3) Very high rates of growth are usually followed by recession. Governments try to avoid this boom-and-bust situation by keeping growth at a sustainable level.

It appears someone's gone a bit wild with the fertiliser.

The Environment

1) High levels of economic activity may deplete **non-renewable resources**.

2) Increased economic activity may also cause increased **pollution**.

Economic Growth

The **Business Cycle** is a regular pattern of **Growth** and **Recession**

1) In a **recovery** or upswing, **production increases**, and **employment** increases. People have more money to spend.

2) In a **boom**, production levels are high. As production reaches **maximum capacity**, there are **shortages**, and price increases. Shortages of skilled labour mean **wages rise**.

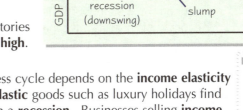

3) In a **recession** incomes start to go down, and **demand** goes down. Business **confidence** is reduced.

4) In a **slump**, production is at a **low**. Businesses close factories and there are a lot of **redundancies**. **Unemployment** is **high**. A lot of businesses become **insolvent** or **bankrupt**.

Income elasticity of demand = extent that demand depends on customer income.

5) The extent to which a business is **affected** by the business cycle depends on the **income elasticity of demand** of its products. Businesses selling **income elastic** goods such as luxury holidays find that demand shoots **up** in a **recovery**, and dives **down** in a **recession**. Businesses selling **income inelastic** goods such as staple foods **aren't affected** all that much by the business cycle.

Businesses deal with **Changes** in **Economic Activity Locally** and **Globally**

1) During **booms**, businesses can **raise prices**. This increases profitability, and it slows down demand a bit. Businesses may have to increase prices to cover their own costs if there are wage rises due to shortages of labour.

2) In a long lasting boom, businesses **invest** in **production** facilities to increase capacity. They may come out with **new products** to take advantage of increased consumer income.

3) During **recessions**, businesses can make workers **redundant** to **save wage costs** and **increase capacity utilisation**. They may also **subcontract** to other businesses in order to increase capacity utilisation.

4) During a **local recession**, businesses can **market** their goods elsewhere in the country — a local shop could go mail-order. In a **national recession**, businesses can **market** their products **overseas**.

5) When the national recession or slump lasts a long time, businesses have to **relocate** abroad.

6) In general, **global upswings** provide growth opportunities for **everyone**, and **global recessions** are bad for **everyone**.

Supply and **Demand** can **Vary Seasonally**

1) As well as cyclical variations in demand caused by the business cycle, there are **yearly variations** in **demand** and **supply**. This is called **seasonality**.

2) **Weather** and **holidays** such as Christmas produce variations in **demand**. For example, **Christmas** creates high demand for **toys**. Hot weather creates demand for ice lollies, paddling pools and air conditioning units.

3) They can also cause variations in **supply** — there are more strawberries available in summer, for example.

4) It's impossible to avoid seasonality. Businesses must have **strategies** to deal with it. After Christmas, demand for retail goods drops, so shops **cut prices** (the **January sales**) to artificially boost demand, and get rid of stock.

5) Food producers can cope with seasonality in supply by **preserving food** — e.g. by canning or freeze-drying.

Practice Questions

Q1 Give two examples of factors which encourage economic growth.

Q2 What are the effects of economic growth on governments?

Q3 What strategy might a business use to cope with seasonality in the supply of milk?

Exam Question

Q1 Discuss the negative effects to a business of rapid economic growth. (12 marks)

It'd sound more fun if they called it the "business rollercoaster"...

Growth in the national economy is a good thing for business, and for society in general. The problems come when growth is too fast — production can't keep up, and a pleasant period of growth swings round into an unpleasant recession. Learn the whys and wherefores of the business cycle, and learn a couple of things that businesses do to cope with the cycle.

Economic Variables

*Interest rates, inflation, exchange rates and tax all affect business strategy. These pages are for **AQA**, **OCR** and **Edexcel**.*

OCR & AQA

Inflation *is an* Increase *in the* Price *of* Goods *and* Services

The main measure of inflation in the UK is the **Retail Price Index** (RPI) — it lists the prices of hundreds of goods and services which the average household would buy.

It's the duty of the **Bank of England** to keep the inflation rate within a target range set by the Government.

OCR only

1) High inflation can be caused by **too much demand** in the economy — more than the economy can supply. This is called **demand-pull** inflation. Excess demand when the economy is near its full capacity is called **overheating**.

2) Rises in inflation can be caused by **rising costs** pushing up **prices** — this is called **cost-push** inflation. **Wage rises** can cause prices to go up — especially if productivity isn't rising, because firms have to put prices up to **cover** increasing wage costs.

3) **Expectations** of inflation can make inflation worse. A business which expects its **suppliers** to put their prices up will put its **own** prices up to cover increased costs. Employees' expectations of rising prices makes them demand **higher wages**, so prices go up. This is the **wage-price spiral** — it's a big cause of cost-push inflation.

4) **Deflation** is the **opposite** of inflation — it's when prices keep going down. It happens when there's **excess supply**, or very **high unemployment**. It's **rare** these days.

OCR only

Inflation *affects* Consumer Spending *and* Business Strategy

1) When inflation is high, **spending goes up temporarily** — people **rush to buy more** before prices go up even more. If wages don't go up in line with inflation, spending goes down as people can afford less.

2) It's easier to **plan** when inflation is low. Stable prices mean businesses can make **accurate sales forecasts**.

3) **Cost-push** inflation makes **profit margins** go **down** if businesses decide not to put up their prices.

4) **Demand-pull** inflation can actually make **profit margins** go **up**. Businesses operating at or near full capacity can put up prices in response to **high demand** without their **costs** going up by as much. Businesses may decide to **expand** during demand-pull inflation, to take advantage of increased demand.

5) When inflation in the UK is high, it makes UK **exports** expensive abroad. UK businesses become **less competitive**. When inflation in the UK is low, UK businesses have a competitive advantage.

OCR & AQA

Interest *is the* Price Paid *for* Borrowing Money

1) Interest rates show the **cost of borrowing**.

2) A **fall** in the interest rate makes businesses **increase** their level of activity, because it's **cheaper** for them to borrow money to invest in the business.

3) A **rise** in the interest rate makes businesses **decrease** their activity, because it's **more expensive** for them to borrow money to invest.

4) Interest rates also affect **consumer spending**. High interest rates mean **less disposable income**. People with existing **borrowing** like **mortgages** have to pay more money back in **interest**, and consumers **save more money** because they get a better rate of return on it. When people have less disposable income, market **demand** goes down.

5) The effect that interest rates have on demand depends on the **product**. Products that require **borrowing** (e.g. cars, houses, new kitchens and high-end consumer electronics) are more sensitive to interest rate changes. When interest rates go up significantly, businesses change strategy to diversify away from these products and into cheaper goods.

6) Businesses compare UK interest rates to interest rates **abroad**. When the UK interest rate is higher, or more volatile than abroad, businesses are likely to invest in **foreign countries** with low, stable interest rates, as it's **cheaper** to borrow money to invest in expansion.

7) Remember **Internal Rate of Return** from p.52 — it's an investment appraisal technique that works out the required rate of return from a project so that it beats investing money in the bank. Clearly, the higher the interest rate, the better the project must be predicted to do before the business will go ahead with it. Again, high interest rates mean **less investment**, fewer **new projects** and less **expansion**.

Economic Variables

Exchange Rate is the Value of One Currency in terms of Another Currency

1) Exchange rates affect the amount of **foreign trade**.

- When the exchange rate is **high** (e.g. more euros to the pound), UK **exports** are relatively **expensive** in Europe and **imports** into the UK are relatively **cheap** for Brits. A **strong pound** is **bad** for UK exporters because their goods aren't competitively priced abroad.

- When the exchange rate is **low**, UK **exports** are relatively **cheap** for foreigners and **imports** into the UK are relatively **expensive** for Brits.

2) A **strong pound** and **cheaper imports** mean **lower costs** for UK businesses importing raw materials from abroad, but they're bad news for UK manufacturers who export goods abroad.

3) When a rise in the value of the pound is predicted, a business might decide to move its **production** abroad. The business can also consider **importing** the **raw material** from abroad.

4) **Cheaper exports** should lead to increased **demand** and therefore higher **output**.

Exchange Rate Fluctuations create Uncertainty

1) For example, a UK manufacturer agrees a contract to sell to the USA, and agrees to be paid in **US dollars**. After the deal is made, the pound rises in value against the dollar. The dollar payment in the contract is now worth **fewer pounds** than before, so the UK manufacturer makes **less profit** from the contract than predicted.

2) Let's say that the UK manufacturer insists on being paid in **pounds**. When the pound rises in value, the goods are more expensive in dollar terms for the US firm. They put the **selling price** up to compensate. The increase in price reduces **demand** for the goods, and there may be **less revenue** than predicted.

Some manufacturers based in the UK and **exporting to the EU** are considering **relocating** to **Euro zone** countries, so that their costs are in Euros — the same currency their customers pay in. They may also decide to pay UK suppliers in Euros, again to keep costs in the same currency that their customers pay them. See p.106 for more on the Euro.

——— OCR & AQA ——— OCR & AQA ———

See p.108 for more about government taxation policy.

Taxation Rates affect Economic Activity

1) **Individuals** are taxed on their **income**. Businesses are taxed on their **profits** — sole traders and partnerships pay **income tax**, and companies pay **corporation tax**. These taxes are **direct taxes**.

2) There are also **indirect taxes on spending**, e.g. VAT, taxes on pollution, tax on tobacco and tax on alcohol.

3) **High** tax rates **discourage** individuals from **spending**, and businesses from **expanding**. Increasing **income tax reduces spending power**, **cuts demand** and **lowers economic activity**.

4) The effect of a tax cut or tax rise depends on the **income elasticity** of the good or service. Rises in income tax hit **luxury goods** (e.g. luxury new kitchen appliances) harder than **staple goods** (e.g. petrol or bread).

Practice Questions

Q1 What is inflation?

Q2 How does a rise in interest rate affect: a) business activity, and b) consumer spending?

Q3 What is the effect on consumer demand of an increase in the basic rate of income tax?

Exam Questions

Q1 Explain why high UK interest rates cause problems for a business producing expensive audio equipment. (8 marks)

Q2 Discuss the strategies that a manufacturing business can employ to respond to a rise in the value of the pound compared to the US dollar and the Euro. (14 marks)

Your interest in this may well be flagging by now...

You need to know that bit more detail for these things at A2 level than you do at AS. For example, it's not enough to say "inflation causes demand to fall" — you have to consider how high inflation is, what's causing it and the inflation rate in other countries. With exchange rates, you have to worry about rate fluctuations as well as whether the rate is high or low.

OCR & AQA (side margins)

Economic Variables

*P.102 is for **AQA** and **OCR**. P.103 is for **AQA**, **OCR** and **Edexcel**.*

The **Labour Market** *is a key external influence*

Labour is obviously a very important **resource** needed for the production of output. Labour **costs** the business money in the form of **wages**.

The **demand** for labour is the firm's **willingness to employ labour** (at a particular wage).

1) An increase in wages will increase the **cost of production**. This in turn will raise the **prices** of products, which will reduce the **demand** for those goods. As demand for goods falls, demand for labour will decrease.

2) Also, the demand for labour will **fall** when labour can be substituted by a **cheaper alternative** i.e. capital expenditure on machinery.

The **supply** of labour is the employees' **willingness to work** (at a particular wage).

1) As wages rise, the **supply** of labour **rises** — higher wages **attract workers** from other industries and those who are currently unemployed.

2) As wages **fall**, the supply of labour goes down, because people aren't willing to work for peanuts.

Chipmunks won't work for less than two peanuts per hour these days.

Unemployment *is measured by the number of* **People Seeking Work**

1) Unemployment is measured by the number of jobless people who are a) **available** for work, and b) **actively seeking jobs**.

2) In the UK unemployment has twice surged above 10% of the labour force in the last 20 years. Unemployment peaked in 1993 and has fallen steadily ever since.

3) There are different **types** of unemployment.

Structural unemployment is due to changes in the structure of the economy, e.g. a **decline** in a **major industry** such as coal mining. Structural unemployment is often concentrated in particular regions of the country.
Frictional unemployment is temporary, caused by the delay between **losing** one job and **getting** another.
Cyclical unemployment is due to the **downturn** in the business cycle, i.e. a lack of **demand** for labour.
Seasonal unemployment is due to the **season**, e.g. ice cream sellers in the winter.

4) High unemployment can affect **sales**. Producers of **luxury** goods are badly affected by **cyclical** unemployment. Businesses producing **essentials** aren't affected all that much.

5) **Structural** unemployment affects **local** businesses — unemployed people in the area have little money to spend.

6) When unemployment is **high**, businesses can hire staff easily. There's a good **supply** of labour, so businesses won't have to pay **high wages**. People in work will be extra **productive** to protect their job.

7) If unemployment is **structural** or **regional**, it's not all that easy to hire staff. Unemployed workers often aren't in the **right place** or the **right industry** for the jobs that are out there. They need **training**.

For a long time, there was an inverse relationship between inflation and unemployment — when one was high, the other was low. This was because policies designed to reduce inflation lowered demand, so output fell and workers were laid off. Policies to reduce unemployment increased demand, which fuelled inflation. More recently, supply-side policies (see p.98) have been successful in keeping both low.

Low Unemployment *is linked to* **Skills Shortages**

1) As well as a labour surplus or shortage, you can also have a **skills surplus** or **shortage**.

2) There are **shortages** of skilled labour in many industries.

3) Skills shortages are solved by **training**, but training is **expensive**. Governments can help by providing **training schemes** and pushing colleges to offer **vocational** (job-related) courses and qualifications. Businesses who invest in training can find that competitors **poach** employees once they're trained.

4) Businesses can get round skills shortages by investing in labour saving **machinery** — in other words, switching from labour intensive production to **capital intensive** production.

5) Businesses can also get round skills shortages by **relocating production** or service provision **abroad** where there are plenty of skilled workers.

Skills shortages are bad news for most businesses, but good news for recruitment consultants.

Capital intensive = tends to use machinery rather than human labour. Remember, machinery is a capital asset.

Economic Variables

The *Different Economic Variables* are all *Linked*

1) As business activity increases, the level of **employment** and **inflation** increases as well. So, changing the **interest rate** is the main weapon governments use to control inflation and unemployment.

2) **Interest rates**, **exchange rates** and **inflation** are all linked by the following mechanism. Read carefully, because it's slightly tricky:

> • **Higher interest rates** attract capital from **overseas investors**, who want good return on their investment.
> • This inflow of money increases the **demand for sterling**, and causes the **exchange rate** to **rise**. The exchange rate is the **price of pounds sterling** in terms of another currency, remember. When the demand for something rises, the price rises as well — that's how markets work.
> • As the exchange rate rises, **imports** become **cheaper**. Prices drop — in other words the **inflation rate falls**.

3) When interest rates rise, borrowing becomes **expensive**. Businesses cut down on **expansion** plans. People **reduce** their **spending**. Both of these actions result in **lower demand**, which **reduces inflation**. So, higher interest rates today mean lower inflation in the near future and vice versa.

4) However, when inflation falls due to **lack of demand**, businesses have to **downsize** and lay off staff. Policies to **reduce unemployment** increase **demand**, which fuels inflation. It's generally difficult for governments to keep inflation and unemployment down at the same time.

Businesses need to *Predict* the *Economic Variables*

Businesses with the best idea about where the economic situation is **going** are in the best position to make **plans** for the future. Businesses need to **analyse** the **current economic situation** so that they can make **predictions** about the future.

Example: Imagine that **demand** is very **high**, the current **inflation** rate is **high**, and the **interest rates** are low.

1) Comparing this situation with the recent past, it'd be reasonable to reckon that the **interest rates** will **rise soon**.

2) The management would be **unwise** to expand their capacity — even though today's demand is high. The **future high interest rates** would lead to **lower demand**.

3) Therefore, the business would be better off to supply current demand by **temporarily outsourcing production**.

Fluctuating variables make prediction difficult. There's uncertainty in the national economy and the global economy — governments like to keep things stable so that businesses can make better decisions about future strategy.

Future *Technological Change* is another key *External Influence*

1) **Technological advances** are a huge **external influence** on business. There's more about technology and production on p.92 — check it out.

2) Technology can be both an **opportunity** and a **threat**. For example, new computerised production methods increase productivity, which is a clear opportunity for growth and cost cutting. They also require quick capital investment — businesses have to invest in the new methods or they'll get left behind by their rivals.

3) Technological advances are very **difficult to predict**. New stuff gets invented all the time.

Practice Questions

Q1 What is the effect of a wage cut on the supply of labour?

Q2 What is structural unemployment?

Q3 How might a business respond to a skills shortage?

Q4 Increasing demand reduces unemployment, but what does it do to inflation?

Exam Question

Q1 Imagine that the interest rate has recently gone up from 5.5% to 6%. Clearly illustrate the effect of this change on:
   a) Exchange Rate b) Employment c) Inflation. (6 marks)

All too much like hard work if you ask me...

If you're not wildly interested in economics (and if you're not doing Economics A-level, then you're likely not madly into it) then a second double page spread about economic variables probably seems cruel. The basics of this are already covered in AS level, so some of this isn't brand new to your eyes. Learn it all anyway, because you've probably forgotten half of it.

International Markets

*International **opportunities** and **constraints** affect business strategy.*
*Page 104 is for **AQA** and **Edexcel**. Page 105 is for **Edexcel** only.*

Foreign markets present **Opportunities** and **Threats**

1) Selling to a much **larger market** is a huge opportunity to **increase sales revenue** and grow your business. The world's your oyster, as the saying goes.

2) Selling to a larger market allows businesses to have **economies of scale**.

3) A business that has access to **many markets** has a lower risk of bankruptcy. Not all markets go down at the same time. In fact, a business may see **growth** in one market, and **recession** in another market at the same time. This helps the business **weather** the ups and downs of the business cycle.

4) Trading in international markets also presents a **threat**. Foreign businesses may be able to **undercut** domestic businesses on the domestic market and abroad.

Businesses **Trading Abroad** need to be **Internationally Competitive**

1) **International competitiveness** means the ability to **compete** with businesses **abroad**.

2) Businesses need to be competitive in terms of **price**. They need **efficient production** systems and a productive workforce to keep **costs** and prices down.

3) They also need to compete in terms of **quality**. High quality products can sell at a premium price. Sony, Philips, Porsche and BMW are examples of international businesses who compete successfully with low-cost rivals.

4) Businesses need a good **public image** and **customer goodwill**. For example, the international oil giant BP tries to project an environmentally friendly image by publicising its research into sustainable energy.

5) Businesses trading abroad must **market** their products and services effectively to compete with foreign rivals. Huge global businesses such as **Coca Cola** and **General Motors** market their goods very successfully, and they are particularly good at getting into **new markets** all over the world.

6) **Governments** have a role in international competitiveness. Governments can create an economic environment that's **favourable** to businesses. A **stable economy** and a **well educated workforce** make it easier for businesses to be competitive right across the world.

Businesses must **Adapt** their **Marketing Strategy** when **Selling Abroad**

1) Overseas markets may have **different tastes**, and want slightly different products. The firm must decide whether to make the product **different** for different markets, or whether to keep it the **same**. **Tailoring** the product is good for **sales**, but raises **unit costs**. **Coca Cola** is an example of a manufacturer who tailor their product to different tastes — a can of Coke in Argentina tastes different from a can of Coke in Britain.

2) **Established brand names** might be **rude** or **funny** words in the language of the target market. Also, a **logo** or an image used in **advertising** might have a **negative meaning** in the local culture.

3) When exporting, it's hard to get into all the local **distribution** channels, so exporting firms usually use an agent in the target country to handle distribution. The agent can get the product into wholesalers and retailers.

Multinationals have manufacturing bases in **Several Countries**

Multinational corporations (**MNCs**) are large businesses with production and distribution facilities in more than one country. A firm can't be called an MNC if it just engages in overseas trade or as a contractor to foreign firms. It has to send abroad a **package** of capital, technology, managerial talent, and marketing skills to carry out production in foreign countries. Examples include General Motors, Ford, Shell, Nike and Coca Cola.

There are pros and cons of multinational involvement for consumers, workers and the host state. There's more about this on p.82-83. To summarise:

- Multinationals provide **employment** and **training**, which is good for **workers** and the **host government**.

- On the other hand, **working conditions** are often **poor**, and there's not much opportunity for **promotion** because the multinational usually brings in senior managers from the home country.

- Multinationals offer **cheap prices** for consumers in the home country, but the goods may be of **low quality**.

- They bring **wealth** and investment, but most profits go to the **home country**, and don't stay in the host country.

International Markets

Businesses **Enter International Markets** by four main methods

Exporting — make the goods in your home country, and ship 'em abroad

1) Exporting is the **traditional** and simplest method of reaching foreign markets.

2) There's no need to invest in **foreign production facilities**. Risks are limited and profits can be reaped early.

3) However... **transport costs** can be a problem.

4) **Manufacturing labour** might actually be **cheaper** in the country where you're selling your exported goods.

Licensing — allowing a foreign firm to make the goods

1) **Licensing** is when one firm allows another firm in a foreign country to use its **intellectual property** (e.g. trademarks, patents and production techniques) in return for a fee.

2) The licensor (the business allowing their patent or trademark to be used) can earn a **large return on investment** (ROI) because the actual investment is **minimal**.

3) However... the **licensee** has the rights of **production** and **distribution**, so the licensor may lose potential returns from manufacturing and marketing activities. The licensor might be better off to keep making their product themselves, and **export** it to foreign markets.

Joint Venture — do things together with a foreign firm

1) A **joint venture** is a contract between two or more firms to start a new project together. A UK firm might set up a joint venture with a Japanese firm to sell in Japan.

2) The main objectives of foreign market entry through a joint venture are **risk and reward** sharing, **technology** sharing and joint **product development**.

Foreign Direct Investment —buying or setting up a firm in a host country

1) The firm making the investment is called the **parent firm**.

2) Foreign direct investment is a **high-risk**, **high-reward** entry mode. The level of investment required is very high and it takes a while for profits to be realised. This requires the parent firm to have enormous **financial muscle** and plenty of **expertise** in its business.

3) The **parent firm** will also have to adhere to all **government regulations** in the **host country**.

Which **market entry strategy** to choose depends on **market circumstances** and on the opportunities and challenges presented by the target country:

1) A high level of **competition** in the **domestic market** may lead to price wars, which make survival difficult. In this situation, a firm may decide to **export** the product to gain access to a **larger market**.

2) When there's a large supply of **cheap labour** in the host country, it makes sense to locate production there.

3) A **joint venture** is preferable when there's a big **difference** between the cultures of the two countries. The business from the target country can help the other business **understand** the market.

4) Where the target country's **government** has imposed **restrictions** on the import of goods (e.g. trade tariffs), a UK business might either set up **facilities** in the target country, or enter into a **joint venture**.

Practice Questions

Q1 Give an example of a strategy to maintain international competitiveness.

Q2 Give two reasons why businesses adapt their marketing strategy to suit a foreign market.

Q3 Define the term MNC.

Q4 What do the following terms mean: a) Joint venture, b) Licensing, c) Foreign Direct Investment?

Exam Question

Q1 "In a global economy, it does not matter if a computer producer decides to have its factory in Silicon Valley or in Nigeria." Do you agree? Give three reasons for your answer. (8 marks)

The world's your oyster — except if you're a pearl, the oyster's your world...

There's a story that the General Motors Nova doesn't sell in Spain because "no va" means "doesn't go" in Spanish. Actually, that one's an urban legend. The story about the Mitsubishi Pajero isn't. Anyhow, the message here is that businesses adapt their strategy for the overseas market, and they have to choose the right method of entry.

The European Union

*The EU is a union of 25 independent countries, with a population of over 450 million — bigger than the US and Japan put together. Ten new countries joined in 2004, and more have applied to join. It's a big deal. For **AQA** and **Edexcel**.*

The EU is a **Single Market** — **Trade** between member states is **Easy**

1) There aren't **trade barriers** between EU member states — this is called the Single Market. Businesses don't pay **tax** when they **import** goods from other EU countries. The EU provides easy export opportunities for UK firms.

2) The EU has **customs union**, which means the **same customs duties** apply to all goods entering the area irrespective of which country they come from, and which country they're going to.

3) The Single Market **smooths out price differences** between member states. **Producers** can look for the **highest selling price** within the EU, and consumers can look for the **lowest purchase price** within the EU. When the price in part of the EU is high, producers flood that area with their product, driving down prices. Low prices attract more buyers to the market, pushing prices up.

4) There's freedom of movement of all "factors of production" within the EU. That covers **raw materials**, **finished goods** and **workers**. EU citizens can work in any country of the EU.

5) A common **EU competition law** controls anti-competitive activities — e.g. setting up a **monopoly**.

6) There are **common policies** on **product regulation** as well.

The **Growth** of the **EU** has increased **Business Opportunities**

1) Whenever the EU expands, the **size of the market** available to an EU based producer increases. Businesses can enjoy **increased sales** and take advantage of **economies of scale**.

2) The EU collectively has **more political whack** than its member states. For example, the EU can negotiate any trade dispute with the USA on equal terms. This increases competitiveness.

3) **Production costs** are **low** in the **new EU countries** that joined in 2004 such as Poland, Hungary and Slovakia. Businesses can locate production facilities there to increase their competitiveness.

Increased Competition in the EU can be a Threat

1) The expansion of the EU also brings **businesses** from **new member states** into the market.

2) There's **increased competition** in industries where new member states such as Hungary and Poland have an advantage — e.g. **manufacturing** and **agriculture**. This threatens UK manufacturers and farmers. Polish farmers can produce food more **cheaply**.

3) **High tech** UK businesses keep their **competitive advantage**.

4) Increased competition may also hurt **inefficient** producers in the new member states, who were previously serving protected national markets.

The **Euro** is the **Common Currency** of **Most** EU countries

1) The euro became the **common currency** of 11 EU member states in **1999**. They completely changed over from their old currencies in **2002**. These countries are commonly called the **euro zone**. Changing to the euro was the final stage in the plan for **European Monetary Union** (EMU).

2) All these euro zone countries have the **same interest rate**, and the **same exchange rate** with **other currencies**. This means euro zone businesses can sell stuff to each other without the **hassle** and **uncertainty** of constantly changing exchange rates.

3) **Changing money** on the foreign exchange market **costs money**. The common currency **reduces transaction costs** between businesses in different euro zone countries.

4) It's also easy to **check prices** between euro zone countries.

5) The **UK** isn't in the euro zone, so UK businesses exporting abroad face the **uncertainty** of fluctuating exchange rates. When the **pound rises in value** against the euro, UK exporters **lose** international competitiveness because their goods become more **expensive** for euro zone countries.

6) Many UK businesses trading in the euro zone **price** and **trade** in the euro to make things easier. UK **banks** offer **euro accounts**, but there's a charge for them, so they may not be **cost effective** for businesses who mainly trade in the UK.

The European Union

It's **Difficult** for businesses to come up with **Pan-European Strategy**

1) It's easy for businesses to think of EU as a big single market, with same rules and regulations throughout. In reality, it's tricky to come up with a **pan-European strategy** — one that works all over Europe.

2) There are still **cultural differences** between countries, and lots of **different languages**, so EU businesses need to market products in different ways to suit **different countries**.

3) Having to do lots of marketing campaigns for one product **reduces economies of scale**.

4) There are also still **legal** differences between EU countries.

EU Institutions pass **Laws** which affect **Business**

EU laws are divided into **four main categories**:

1) **Regulations** are **binding laws** that apply to **all** EU citizens as soon as they're passed.

2) **Directives** tell **member state** governments to **pass a law** that meets a specific objective — e.g. reducing working time to 48 hours per week, reducing pollution. It's up to member state governments how to word the law. Some member governments make **strict** laws in response to EU directives, while others are more slack.

Most EU laws are directives.

3) **Decisions** are **binding laws** that apply to a **specific country** or a **specific business**.

4) **Recommendations** aren't really laws at all, because they're **not legally binding**.

The European Commission and the Council of Ministers decide on policies and laws

1) The **European Commission** puts forward new laws. The EU Commission is **appointed**, not elected.

2) The Council of Ministers **decides** whether or not to bring in **new laws** suggested by the Commission. It's made up of **government ministers** from **each member state**.

There's one commissioner from each member state.

The European Parliament gives its opinion on new laws

1) The European Parliament is **directly elected**, so it gives some democratic legitimacy to European law.

2) However, it's the Council of Ministers who have the final decision on laws, not the European Parliament.

The European Central Bank (ECB) controls the euro

1) The **ECB** decides monetary policy (interest rate) in the euro zone.

2) Only the euro zone countries have a say in the running of the bank.

The European Court of Justice interprets EU law

1) The European Court of Justice makes sure that **EU law** is applied in line with the **Treaty of Rome** — the treaty that says how the EU must be run.

2) It also sorts out disputes between member states.

3) The decisions of the court take precedence over the laws of each member state.

Practice Questions

Q1 Give an example of a benefit to business of the EU Single Market.

Q2 Give one benefit to business if the UK adopted the euro.

Q3 What is an EU directive?

Exam Questions

Q1 Analyse the ways in which a Welsh toy manufacturer would be affected if the UK decided to adopt the euro. (10 marks)

Q2 "The bureaucrats in Brussels can't change the way I run my business"
Do you accept this statement? Justify your answer. (6 Marks)

450 million people — that's a lot, boss...

The EU is a big deal for businesses — as the Single Market grows, there's more opportunity for easy importing and exporting. The EU is also another source of laws and regulations that businesses have to follow. Whether you're generally pro-Europe or anti-Europe doesn't change the fact that you need to revise both these pages to be prepared for the exam.

Government Policy

Government policy alters economic variables to change the level of economic activity.
*These pages are for **AQA** and **OCR**.*

Monetary Policy *controls the* Interest Rate

Monetary policy means **tweaking the interest rate** in order to control **inflation** and **exchange rates**.
The main objectives of a country's monetary policy should be:

1) Controlling **inflation**.
2) Controlling the overall rate of **economic growth**.
3) Managing the level of **unemployment**.
4) Influencing **foreign exchange rates**.

Even though the Bank of England sets interest rates independently, the Bank of England Monetary Policy Committee should bear the government's fiscal policy in mind when it makes its decisions. The Treasury has a non-voting representative at MPC meetings, who keeps the MPC up to date on fiscal policy decisions.

Fiscal Policy *changes* Taxes *and* Spending *to* Heat *or* Cool *the Economy*

1) **Fiscal policy** does **two** things — it sets **tax rates**, and it sets the amount of **government spending**.

2) **Raising taxes** cools the economy down, and cutting taxes heats it up —
low rates of tax give businesses more profit, and **encourage business activity**.

- It's fairly easy to predict the effects of a change in **direct taxation**. Raising **income tax** reduces consumer spending, and reduces business output.
- **Indirect taxation** is slightly harder to predict. Increases in **VAT** cut consumer spending, but also **raise inflation**.

3) **Government spending** on social services, health, education etc., also heats up the economy.

- Changing government expenditure on **welfare benefits** has a **quick** impact on the economy, because poorer people who receive benefits will change their spending habits straight away.
- Government spending on **infrastructure** such as roads has a **slower** effect on the economy.

4) **Fiscal policy** is really about the **balance** between tax and spending.
The Chancellor of the Exchequer decides what the balance is going to be in the yearly Budget.

Fiscal Policy	How it's done	The effect it has
Expansionary fiscal policy	Cutting taxes and/or Raising spending	Government **borrowing increases** (or government **surplus decreases**)
Contractionary fiscal policy	Raising taxes and/or Cutting spending	Government **borrowing decreases** (or government **surplus increases**)

5) In times of **high unemployment** and economic slowdown the government may **borrow** money to spend, to **increase demand** for goods and services. This is **expansionary** fiscal policy.

6) The government may spend **less** than its revenue when high demand has pushed production to its limits, and threatens to bring on excessive inflation. This is **contractionary** fiscal policy.

Intervention *vs* Laissez-Faire *— whether governments* Interfere *in the economy*

1) The idea of **laissez-faire** says **governments shouldn't interfere** in the economy. The idea of **interventionism** says they **should** get involved. *Laissez-faire is French for "leave alone".*

2) Governments **intervene** by charging taxes, passing laws which affect business, providing public services, taking part in the economy as a consumer, and providing subsidies. Some governments intervene more than others.

3) Governments that take a **laissez-faire** approach **dismantle** existing regulations that **constrain** business, abolish wage controls and **reduce taxation rates**.

4) The argument for **laissez-faire** is that **intervention raises costs** and makes business less **efficient** and less **profitable**. Allowing businesses to cut wages makes them more **competitive**. Supporters of laissez-faire say that it encourages individuals to be **responsible** instead of relying on the state.

5) **Interventionists** say governments must step in to ensure **fair competition**. Also, a totally **free**, totally **profit driven** market does things which create **social** and **environmental** costs.
See p.112 for more on market failure and government intervention.

Government Policy

Nationalisation is Government Ownership and Control of Businesses

1) **Nationalisation** means taking businesses into **government ownership**. Supporters of nationalisation say it protects loss-making businesses, reduces expenditure on competition, and produces the goods society needs.

2) However, nationalisation **almost always fails**, because it ends up with a **legally protected monopoly**. Lack of competition often makes for inefficiency and poor quality. Nationalised industries often don't make much profit.

Privatisation is when State Owned Business are sold to Private Investors

1) In the 1980s and 1990s lots of state owned companies were sold off into the private sector. Examples include **British Telecom**, **British Gas**, **British Steel**, the **water** companies and the **electricity** distribution companies.

2) The government sold off these businesses to private investors to improve their **efficiency**, and to make a **profit**.

Benefits of privatisation	Drawbacks of privatisation
Privatisation **promotes competition**, which **increases efficiency**, and offers **better quality** products at **lower prices**.	**Some** privatised companies have **raised prices** and **cut quality** to **exploit** consumers — especially if they're effectively a **monopoly**.
The **government** has made a big **profit** from privatisation. This has helped the government to **cut taxes** and **reduce its borrowing**, which in turn **encourages business activity**.	Privatised companies tend to have **lots of shareholders** — often **private citizens** holding just a few shares. Shareholders tend to look for **quick profit** at the expense of **long term strategy**.

This profit is one-off profit — the privatisation can't be repeated.

3) Some industries are **natural monopolies**, for example, you wouldn't have several sets of rail tracks from one city to another. When privatising a natural monopoly like the **railways**, the government needs to build in regulations to prevent the new owners from exploiting their position and raising prices or cutting quality.

Case study: Railtrack

Privatisation: The UK government privatised the railways, and placed them under control of Railtrack. Railtrack was effectively a monopoly, with train operating companies as its customers.

Regulation: The Government set up the Office of the Rail Regulator (ORR) to keep an eye on Railtrack. The ORR had to make sure that Railtrack did not allow its commercial interest to get in the way of public standards and safety.

Political Changes Affect Business

Domestic political changes affect business, because they usually result in a change to **economic policy**.

Political change **abroad** can also affect business. For example, when the old Soviet Union and Eastern Bloc collapsed in the early 1990s, the economies of **Eastern Europe** opened up to trade with the West. This presented opportunities and threats to UK businesses.

Practice Questions

Q1 What are the two component parts of fiscal policy?

Q2 Explain two ways in which governments intervene in the economy.

Q3 Why do some privatised industries need to be regulated?

Exam Questions

Q1	Outline the effects of contractionary fiscal policy on businesses.	(6 marks)
Q2	Describe the arguments for and against government intervention in the economy.	(8 marks)
Q3	"Privatisation must create competition." Discuss.	(12 marks)

I thought we elected governments to think about all this for us...

All the stuff on these pages affects everyone in some way — tax rates affect everyone, and government spending affects everyone too. Political parties fight elections on this sort of thing. Of course, that doesn't mean that you wouldn't rather be doing something else than revising this. Sure, I sympathise. But I can't make it go away. You'll have to learn it some time...

Social and Environmental Influences

*Society and environmental concerns affect business. These pages are for **AQA**, **OCR** and **Edexcel**.*

Social Responsibility *means being responsible towards the* Whole of Society

1) Corporate social responsibility is the **voluntary** role of business in looking after **society** and the environment.

2) Businesses have special responsibility to their **stakeholders** — everyone who's affected by the business, e.g. **employees**, **suppliers**, **creditors**, **customers**, **shareholders** and local **communities**.

Employees

1) Every firm has **legal responsibilities** to its staff. ⬅ *Examples — providing a safe work environment, not discriminating based on race or gender, giving lunch breaks and paid holiday. See p.71.*

2) Firms have a responsibility to **train** employees.

3) Firms can **choose** to give their employees a better deal than the bare legal minimum. Firms that operate internationally can **choose** to give workers abroad similar rights to workers in the UK.

Suppliers

1) It's not in a firm's best interest to treat their **suppliers** badly. For good results, be **honest** and **pay** on time.

2) Firms can build **long-term relationships** with suppliers — e.g. by offering **long-term exclusive supply contracts** and placing **regular orders**. A good loyal relationship makes it more likely that the supplier will pull all the stops out to deliver **fast service** when it's really needed.

3) There's also a responsibility to the rest of **society** to choose suppliers who don't **exploit** their workers or **pollute** excessively. Firms may not see this as worthwhile, **unless** customers care enough to **boycott** the product.

Customers

1) Firms who treat their **customers** well can build up **customer goodwill**. Good customer service, good quality products and reasonable prices all encourage **customer loyalty** and **repeat business**.

2) Customers are more and more willing to **complain** when firms don't treat them well. Customers can even **campaign against** firms who disappoint, and **persuade** other people **not to buy** their goods and services.

Local Community

1) Firms can be responsible to the local community by keeping **jobs secure**, and using **local suppliers**.

2) They can also avoid **noise pollution**, **air pollution** and excess **traffic** on local roads.

3) Businesses can **earn goodwill** by making **charity** donations or **sponsoring** schools, leisure centres, parks etc.

Some people think that firms should only be responsible to their **shareholders** and no one else.

Business Ethics *help businesses make* Socially Responsible Decisions

1) Ethics means a shared set of attitudes and morals. Business ethics is about doing the "**right thing**". Not everyone **agrees** on what's ethical and what's not. For example, most people agree that child labour is unethical, but opinions differ on whether it's unethical to sell cigarettes even though they cause cancer.

2) Until recently, business ethics was considered almost a contradiction in terms — why would businesses choose to be "**nice**". Of course, there's a benefit in being "**nice**" to **stakeholders**. Taking an ethical stance **attracts customers** who **approve** of the decision. An ethical approach can be a **unique selling point**, particularly in retail (e.g. Body Shop toiletries, Fairtrade coffee, etc). Ethics can be **good PR**.

3) The **corporate culture** (see p.124) of a business affects its ethics. For example, in an environment that is heavily oriented to meeting sales targets, sales staff may be tempted to act unethically to get more commission. It's up to management to set **ethical guidelines** to make sure staff don't act dishonestly.

4) When introducing a **new ethical policy**, senior management have to set out **firm guidelines**, and make ethical policy part of **training** for new and established employees. In a business environment with a high degree of **delegation**, it can be **difficult** for senior management to push through a new ethical policy. Junior managers and employees who are used to managing their own work may **resent** being told what to do.

- Businesses may be tempted to **exploit** their workers, particularly in countries with weak labour laws. Many businesses have a **policy** against "sweat-shop" labour or child labour. Examples are IKEA and Levi Strauss.

- Businesses may be tempted to **charge high prices** for important goods such as medicines. For example, drug companies agreed to lower prices of anti-HIV drugs in South Africa, but only after legal and social pressure.

- The **Fairtrade** movement aims to get businesses to pay suppliers in LEDCs a fair price for goods. The Co-op has taken an ethical stance on fairtrade — all its own brand chocolate is fairtrade.

Social and Environmental Influences

Social Audits account for Social and Ethical performance

1) A social audit assesses the **social impact** and **ethical behaviour** of a business in relation to its aims and those of its stakeholders. So, before performing a social audit, a business has to come up with **clear social objectives**.

2) The actual audit is done by an **independent external organisation**, just like a financial audit. They look at various **indicators** of performance, and they check up on what actually goes on inside the business.

3) The results of the audit are fed into the business's **strategic review** and planning processes, so that the business can make changes to improve social performance.

Mm, tell me about the performance indicators.

Sociable auditing.

Environmental Issues create Costs and Opportunities

1) Businesses pollute the environment through **production** processes, through **traffic pollution** caused by **transporting** raw materials and finished goods, through **dumping waste** in waterways and seas, and through **burying** or **burning waste**. **Packaging** creates a large amount of **landfill** waste.

2) Businesses also damage the environment through unsustainable resource management — e.g. cutting down rainforest for mining developments, building on greenfield sites.

3) The **Environment Act (1995)** set up the **Environment Agency**, which coordinates pollution control. Businesses can't release pollution into waterways or land without a **permit** from the Environment Agency. There are also a lot of EU directives relating to pollution.

4) Most environmental costs are **external costs**, i.e. they affect society, not the business itself. External costs include health issues caused by air pollution, the greenhouse effect and acid rain.

5) The government **fines** businesses who pollute more than a certain level. Pollution control is also done by **taxation**. This means that pollution has **internal financial costs.**

6) There are business opportunities as well. Increased awareness of green issues creates **demand** for **environmentally friendly** products. For example, organic products command **higher prices**.

7) Because of increased awareness of environmental issues, and increased legislation about environmental issues, there's **demand for support services** to manage environmental control — e.g. consultancy and equipment.

Environmental Auditing shows how a firm is affecting the Environment

1) An environmental audit is a review of the **environmental effects** of the firm's activities. It assesses whether the firm is meeting legal environmental protection requirements, and whether it's meeting it's own **targets**. Environmental audits show businesses where they need to **change** their **waste management** practices.

2) For example, one of the environmental costs of business activity is the **greenhouse effect**. A business which has decided to **reduce** the amount of **greenhouse gases** emitted into the atmosphere would set a clear **objective** for reducing emissions, and **check their progress** towards this objective through an **environmental audit**.

Practice Questions

Q1 What are the responsibilities of a business towards its suppliers?
Q2 How can a business create goodwill in the local community?
Q3 What are business ethics?
Q4 What is a social audit?
Q5 Give an example of an opportunity created by environmentalism.

Exam Question

Q1 Evaluate the following statement: "Profit should be a higher priority than social responsibility for businesses". (9 marks)

All of a sudden, it's all fwuffy wuv...

Being all caring and sharing wouldn't seem to come naturally to businesses. It's a hard knock life, after all. A dog eat dog world, if you like. So, for a business to act ethically, there must be something in it for them. Learn the reasons why businesses might choose to act ethically, and learn how businesses check they're meeting social and green standards.

Market Failure

*Here are two one-page topics to round off this section. This page is for **OCR** and **Edexcel**.*

Market Failure is when Free Market supply and demand Don't Apply

Free markets are supposed to **allocate resources** efficiently by the mechanism of supply and demand. Ideally, where there's a **demand** for a good, there'll be a **supply** to meet it — and supply and demand determine the **price** of the good.

Market failure occurs when free markets **don't** deliver an ideal **allocation of resources**, so supply doesn't meet demand. This can be when the good or service **can't** be provided by a free market of private suppliers because it's **impossible** to keep **non-buyers** from consuming it. It can also be when a monopoly charges **prices** which are too high.

Market Failure can have several Causes

Monopolies:
Market dominance by monopolies can lead to **under-production** of goods and services and **higher prices**.

Externalities:
1) An externality is when the **outcome** of an economic action **isn't felt** by the person or business **responsible** — i.e. when the **social** costs and benefits don't match the **financial** costs and benefits.

2) For example, cancer is a **negative externality** caused by the consumption of tobacco. The government penalises tobacco manufacturers for this negative externality by charging higher tax rates on the sale of tobacco.

3) There are also **positive externalities**. For example, education and training benefit all of society. When a business invests in training, other businesses can benefit by employing the trained staff.

Public goods:
1) The goods and services that are provided by the government for the benefit of **society as a whole** are called public goods. The police service, roads and national defence are examples of public goods.

2) They aren't provided by a **free market** because it's **difficult** to keep **non-buyers** from consuming them — e.g. **everyone** would get the benefit of a private police service which arrested criminals, even people who **didn't subscribe** to the service.

3) They're also **not used up** by consumers — one person benefiting from the police service doesn't stop someone else benefiting from the police service. It's impossible to sell public goods to several individuals one at a time, so the private sector doesn't usually touch them.

Merit goods and **demerit goods**:
1) **Merit goods** or services are those which the government thinks people **wouldn't use enough** of if the price was set by a totally **free market**. Health and education are merit goods.

2) **Demerit goods** are those which the government thinks people **would use too much** of if the price was set by a totally **free market**. Alcohol and cigarettes are demerit goods.

3) Merit goods and demerit goods are related to something called **imperfect information** — this is where the market doesn't provide all the information the consumer needs to make the "right" choice about the product.

Labour market failure:
Structural unemployment is a kind of market failure. Redundant workers have **skills** which aren't needed by employers, and they **don't** have the skills which are needed. Labour **resources** therefore sit **idle**.

Governments Intervene to Prevent Market Failure

1) The government uses **fiscal policy** to alter the level of **demand** for different products.

   - **Indirect taxes** increase the prices of **demerit goods**, and goods/services with negative **externalities**. For example, **cigarettes** are taxed to reduce demand. **Pollution taxes** correct for a negative externality.

   - **Subsidies** to consumers are used to reduce the prices of **merit goods** — e.g. most NHS services are free.

2) **Monopolies** are **regulated**. The Competition Commission prevents firms from becoming monopolies.

3) The government directly **provides public goods**.

4) The government intervenes to provide **better information** — e.g. compulsory labelling on cigarette packaging with health warnings to help the public make **informed choices**.

5) Governments have policies to **introduce competition** into markets — e.g. de-regulation of bus services.

Pressure Groups

*This page is for **AQA** and **Edexcel**.*

Pressure Groups *try to* Influence *government policies and business decisions*

1) The aim of all pressure groups is to influence the people who have the power to make decisions.

2) There are **environmental** pressure groups such as Greenpeace and Friends of the Earth, **consumer** pressure groups such as the Consumer's Association, **animal welfare** pressure groups such as the RSPCA and BUAV, **human rights** pressure groups such as Amnesty and Liberty, **business interest** pressure groups such as the CBI (Confederation of British Industry) — and all **trade unions** are pressure groups as well.

3) Pressure groups use different methods to influence business policy:

The CBI lobby the government to make laws more favourable to businesses.

Lobbying	Pressure groups discuss issues with **business decision makers** and **political decision makers**, to try to **influence** their thinking.
Direct action	Pressure groups organise **direct protests** against specific businesses (e.g. **boycotts** of Nestlé products, **blockades** of Shell petrol stations).
Publicity	Pressure groups try to make the **public** more **aware** of the issues. Consumers may **choose not to buy** a product which they think causes **social** or **environmental problems**.
Petitions	Petitions (lists of signatures) **prove** that people **agree** with the point of view of the pressure group.
Legal Action	Pressure groups can fight the firm through the **courts**, if they believe that the business is acting **illegally**.

Lobbying Politicians *takes time*

1) The aim of lobbying is to get politicians to word policies and laws the way you'd like them to be. It takes time for a pressure group to **win politicians around** to their point of view.

2) The first step for any pressure group is to put forward their issues and concerns to the lawmakers. Pressure groups do this by **writing letters** and holding **meetings**, and providing analysis and information.

3) Politicians are more likely to change the law if the think the new law will have **public support**, so it's important for pressure groups to do **publicity** campaigning at the **same time** as lobbying.

Direct Action *against* Businesses *can be* Very Powerful

1) Businesses hate **negative publicity**. Direct protests by pressure groups bring unwanted publicity for the businesses, which may result in lower sales, or loss of reputation.

2) Direct action can take the form of a **picketing** protest outside a factory or shop, an **organised boycott** of a product, or even illegal **violent direct action** such as damage to property.

3) Businesses weigh up the **costs** and **benefits** of giving in to direct action. They're more likely to give in when there's **widespread public support** for the pressure group, where the market is **competitive** enough that a boycott would hurt, and where their **public image** is seriously damaged by the protest.

Practice Questions

Q1 What are merit goods and demerit goods?

Q2 What can governments do to deal with externalities?

Q3 Why do pressure groups lobby politicians?

Q4 Give an example of legal direct action.

Exam Questions

Q1 Analyse the government's policy to tax tobacco products, in terms of market failure and action to prevent it. (9 marks)

Q2 Evaluate the methods that Greenpeace might use to stop supermarkets selling GM products. (12 marks)

This market gets an F...

When I go to the supermarket, and they're all out of tomato soup, is that market failure I wonder? Well, no, not really — market failure is when the private market as a whole can't make supply and demand match up. Learn the different types of market failure, and what governments do to sort it out. The pressure group topic is a bit more straightforward, luckily.

Business Plans

*This section looks at how businesses make decisions and the methods they use to help analyse and evaluate their options with a view to future planning. These pages are for **AQA**, **OCR** and **Edexcel**.*

Business Planning shows Where a business Is, and where it's Going

1) Planning forces managers to take a good hard look at their **current situation** — both **within** the business, and **externally**, in the market and the economy. This is called a **situational audit**.

2) Plans also force managers to look towards the future and work towards defined goals.

3) Without plans, it's easy to get **lazy** and **drift along** doing the same old routine.

4) Plans can go **out of date**, especially if the business **environment** changes. It's important to keep reviewing the plans to check they're still appropriate. Regular reviewing and updating can help an organisation respond to adverse effects in the business environment, e.g. falling markets, supplier shortages or rising interest rates.

See Section Five for more on the external environment.

Businesses make Corporate Plans which set out their overall strategy

1) Corporate plans set out **objectives** for the business as a whole, and set out the **overall strategy** the business will use to reach its objectives.

2) For example, a corporate plan lays out how the business intends to **survive**, whether the business intends to **grow**, and **how** they might go about growing.

3) The corporate plan will also include an outline of goals for each department. The **fine details** are set out in individual departmental plans.

4) Management aim to have all the parts of the business **working together** towards a **goal**. The idea is that the **combined** effort of **everyone together** is **greater** than the **sum** of everyone's individual efforts. This "whole is greater than the sum of the parts" idea is sometimes called **synergy**.

Businesses produce Strategic Plans for All Areas of their activity

The corporate plan is a long term strategic plan, which doesn't contain all the **fine detail** different departments of the business need. Plans for all the different departments of the business are derived from the overall corporate plan.

1) **Marketing plans** set out **marketing objectives**, and say **how** the business is going to meet its objectives. They give details of **new products**, **new markets**, and **strategies** to increase market share. The marketing plan says how much money will be **spent** on marketing activities, and how much money marketing activities will be expected to **bring in**.

2) **Human Resource plans** set out HR objectives and strategy. They describe how human resources will be **actively managed** to help the business meet its **corporate objectives**. Human resources plans state how **big** the workforce needs to be, and what **skills** they need to have. They set out policies to make sure that the workforce meets the needs of the business — e.g. recruitment plans and training plans.

3) **Production plans** set out the **level of production** that the business needs in order to meet its corporate objectives. The business must produce the **right quality** of goods, as **quickly** and **cheaply** as possible.

4) **Financial plans** set out how much **money** is expected to flow **into** and **out of** the business. Financial plans include the **cash flow forecast**, and **projections** of what the **balance sheet** and **profit and loss** statement will look like.

Contingency Plans prepare for Out Of The Ordinary Events

Corporate plans plan for the **expected**. Unfortunately, **unexpected events** can throw a spanner in the works.

Example: Most businesses have a **contingency plan** in case of **IT** disasters. For example, they might take **backups** of their data at the end of each day. Some of these backups must be **stored off-site** — otherwise if there was a fire at the site, all the data would be lost, even the backups. That would be very sad, and very, very expensive.

1) When you're evaluating a firm's plans for the future, make sure they have some kind of **contingency plan**.

2) Remember, though, that no business can plan for **every unforeseen event**. Some adverse events are hard to plan for. It could actually **cost the business less** to let them happen than it would cost to **plan** for them.

3) Managers must decide **how likely** a particular adverse event is to happen, and how **badly** it would damage the business if it did happen.

4) Contingency planning means **constantly questioning assumptions** about what's going to happen.

Business Plans

New Businesses need a Business Plan to show them where they're going

1) The start-up business plan includes details of the organisation's **objectives**, which **market**(s) it will trade in, estimated **profits** and the time it'll take to maximise **profits**.

2) The plan includes information about the structure of the **market**, who and where the **competitors** are, where the business will **position** itself in the market including a **defined customer profile**, and what the **unique selling point** of the good or service is. Evidence of **market research** is essential.

See p.120 for more about product positioning.

3) The **human resource requirement** is outlined in the plan, including the **size** of the workforce, their **skill** level, the wage **cost** and the **availability** of suitable workers.

4) Proposed operations, including **production** (if appropriate) and details of how the finished product and/or service will reach the customer base need **explanation**.

5) **Financial forecasts** of costs, sales and revenue provide investors, including the owner(s)/directors, with ways of evaluating the viability of the plan, before and during the start-up period. The figures must be realistic.

6) An effective plan explains how the business will **survive** during the start-up period. The plan will then need **updating** as the business grows.

Plan: Sell copper pots and pans.

You may need to **produce** a business plan as part of your **coursework**. You may find yourself **evaluating** a case study business plan in the **exam**.

Once a small business has started up, the owner/manager may not **bother** writing out a formal strategic plan. The strategic plan will exist in their **head**, communicated to staff members through **instructions** and **informal** discussions. The owner might only write a strategic plan when they want to **grow** the business or get extra **capital** from the bank.

A Business Plan helps Stakeholders to Evaluate the business

An effective business plan is a useful tool for different potential **stakeholders**.

1) The **owner**(s) or directors are forced to research, analyse and justify their business idea in written form. This makes sure that they've really thought things through. It's vital for financial plans, where good, thoughtful planning may result in an unprofitable project being abandoned before launch.

2) **Investors**, usually banks, need to be convinced the business idea is viable and potentially profitable. When getting a **loan** from the bank, the bank's **business advisors** will take a cold, hard look at the plan.

3) **Potential employees** need to know the organisation or project they are joining won't go under in a few months. Information from the business plan can be used to ensure employer and employee expectations are likely to be met.

4) If the new business is looking for a **grant** from central or local **government agencies**, the business plan provides evidence of potential success. Government agencies usually want to see **evidence** that the new start up has secured **external funding** from the private sector, as well.

Practice Questions

Q1 What's a situational audit?
Q2 What are contingency plans for?
Q3 What would you expect to find in a start-up business plan?
Q4 What is the purpose of a business plan to an expanding company?

Exam Questions

Q1 Pancho Toys Ltd wants to expand its business and has drawn up an appropriate business plan to attract potential investors. Evaluate the criteria you would use to judge whether or not to buy shares in Pancho Toys. (14 marks)

Q2 Suggest the likely contents of a supermarket's contingency plan to cope with a potential lorry drivers' strike. (8 marks)

Get with the plan, people...

For all three exam boards, this section is tested in a "synoptic" paper that gets you to apply strategic thinking to any area of the A level syllabus — organisational structure, human resources, marketing strategy, production methods, etc. So, you've got to think about themes that have come up in other sections of the book, and in the AS course, while you learn this lot.

Decision-Making Models

*There are a number of decision-making tools used by managers to help them determine the most profitable business strategy. These pages are for **AQA**, **OCR** and **Edexcel**.*

Decision-Making is essential to Planning

A business plan is a **collection of decisions** about what to do. Without decision-making, you can't make a plan.

Senior managers make **strategic decisions** to set the **long term direction** of the business.

Junior managers make **tactical decisions** about how to implement the strategy on a day-to-day basis.

Decisions can be made Scientifically — or based on Gut Feeling

Scientific decision-making means **collecting** data, **analysing** it to arrive at a **conclusion** and then **testing** that decision to see if it works.

The **alternative** to the scientific approach is **inspired guesswork** based on **experience** or **gut reaction**.

Various factors influence how managers make decisions

1) The **type** of problem is a factor — it could be a **routine** problem or a **one-off situation**. Routine problems can be handled with an experience-based approach. **Unfamiliar** problems call for research and analysis.

2) The **personality** of the decision-maker is a factor — some people are better at accepting risk than others.

3) The **decision-maker's job** might be in danger if they get the decision wrong, or the **survival** of the business might be on the line. The **bigger the decision**, the more likely a manager is to do plenty of **research** first. This is common sense stuff if you think about it.

4) Decisions that can be **easily changed** can be made by educated guesswork. Decisions that can't be reversed are by definition more **risky**. They need some serious thought.

1) You've probably looked at some methods used in scientific decision-making before, e.g. **break-even analysis** (p.46) and **investment appraisal** (p.50-52).

2) Most methods of scientific decision-making are **costly** and **time-consuming**, but they **reduce** the risk of making **expensive mistakes**.

3) Research methods used are highly dependent on the **quality** of the data collected.

4) The **quantity** of data has an affect too. Given a limited amount of information, most people make a good, reasoned decision. When there's too much data (**information overload**) a lot of it's ignored.

Businesses analyse their current situation using SWOT

A business's strategic analysis model should deal with the **internal** and **external** environment. Managers use SWOT analysis to help determine strategy. **SWOT** is a kind of **situational audit** — it tells managers **where the business is** in terms of its strengths and weaknesses, and the opportunities and threats that the market currently offers.

1) The business must look at itself to identify its **strengths** and **weaknesses**. An internal audit must be **factual** and **objective** — wishful thinking isn't helpful.

2) The **external** environment provides the **opportunities** the business wants to exploit and the **threats** that might prevent success.

3) SWOT lets the business know where it has a **competitive advantage** over its rivals. (See p.120 for more on competitive advantage).

Strengths
Weaknesses
Opportunities
Threats

PEST analysis shows what's going on Outside The Business

The **PEST** model is used to complete the external audit of opportunities and threats. PEST stands for **P**olitical, **E**conomic, **S**ocial and **T**echnological factors — things which can influence the way the business operates.

1) **Political** factors include **legal** and **fiscal** ones too, for example, changes in laws, customs duty on goods, taxation levels and, of course, changes of government.

2) **Economic** factors include **inflation**, **budget changes**, rising oil prices and **unemployment**.

3) **Social** or **cultural** factors cover **lifestyle changes**, **educational reform**, **environmental changes** and **population movement**. These affect the consumers of the product or service, and the labour market.

4) **Technology** is constantly changing as new materials and products are invented and energy saving substitutes and production methods are introduced.

Decision-Making Models

Marketing Decision-Making usually uses a Scientific Approach

1) The **scientific marketing model** consists of a series of **stages**: setting **objectives**, **gathering data**, **analysing** data, forming a **hypothesis** (a **marketing strategy**), **testing** it out to see if it works, and **changing** it if necessary.

2) **Market research** is **fundamental** — it's impossible to form a hypothesis or test it without **good data**.

See p.12 for more about scientific marketing.

Marketing also uses decision-making Models

Several tools are used by marketing managers to help them **adapt** to changing situations and develop **new strategies**.

1) Market analysis tools like **Ansoff's Matrix** (p.13) help to evaluate the comparative risk of differing strategies.

2) The **AIDA model** for advertising sets out four stages that advertising communication should go through to ensure the customer makes the important decision to purchase. See p.12.

3) The **DAGMAR model** sets out five stages that consumers move through when buying a product, from unawareness through awareness, comprehension, and conviction to action. See p.13.

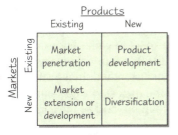

Products
Existing   New

	Existing	New
Markets — Existing	Market penetration	Product development
Markets — New	Market extension or development	Diversification

AIDA = Attention, Interest, Desire, Action.

DAGMAR = Defining Advertising Goals for Measured Advertising Results .

Other Departments use Scientific Decision-Making

1) **Operations managers** analyse and evaluate **productivity data**. They use various **planning tools** to improve the decision–making process to achieve higher efficiency and quality — e.g. **Critical Path Analysis** (see p.90-91), **product life cycles** (p.18) and **Gantt charts** (see p.93).

2) Accountants and financial managers analyse **financial data** and performance measures to develop the business's financial plans. They use **investment appraisal** techniques, **ratio analysis**, **budgeting**, variances and **break-even** (see p.40-53).

3) Human Resources managers use data on workforce needs, availability and training costs / benefits in their **workforce planning**. They use **performance measures** to analyse the success of their activities.

Practice Questions

Q1   Explain how the decision-making process can be influenced by the decision-maker's personality.

Q2   What four things does PEST analysis tell managers about the market situation?

Q3   Give an example of a way that information technology has improved decision-making.

Exam Question

Q1   Look Lovely Ltd is a small player in the UK cosmetics market. In the past ten years it has concentrated its sales efforts on its mail order business. The aim was to reduce distribution costs and sell products at lower prices. A website has also been developed. The current product range includes a budget range of cosmetics aimed at the teenage market and an "anti-ageing" skin care range aimed at older customers. A business consultant's report commented that the firm, "must grow just to maintain its position in the changing, highly competitive cosmetics market," and recommended that it should, "broaden its distribution channels" or "introduce new product ranges".

a)   Prepare a SWOT analysis for Look Lovely Ltd.   (10 marks)

b)   How can Ansoff's Matrix be relevant to solving Look Lovely Ltd's lack of growth problem?   (8 marks)

c)   What other information, apart from financial data, would you require to access the likelihood of Look Lovely Ltd surviving in the UK cosmetics market? Justify your selection of data.   (16 marks)

When you can't decide, just ask a model. They know a lot...

Decision-making models can help with any business decision, whether it's to do with marketing, production, human resources or whatever. SWOT and PEST are the basic one-size-fits-all ways of working out what the situation is — after that, managers still have to come up with the best plan. Experience can be extremely useful alongside the scientific approach.

Decision Trees

*Decision trees are a mathematical model used for decision making, incorporating probability. They're for **AQA** and **Edexcel**.*

Decision Tree Analysis *combines* Probability *and* Expected Benefit

The outcome of any decision is rarely guaranteed — it might NOT happen. Decision tree analysis is used in business to balance the **probability** of an event occurring against the **expected reward**.

1) **Probability** is the **likelihood** of an event occurring. Some probabilities are known for certain, like the flip of the coin which is 50% probability of heads, 50% tails. If a probability is unknown an **estimate** is made by managers based on **experience** or **past data** — this estimate is **subjective**.

2) **Expected Value** is the **probability** of an event occurring, **multiplied** by the **benefit** the business can expect to gain. For example, a business launching a new product wants to decide whether to invest £100,000 in an advertising campaign. The campaign has a 0.7 chance of success. If the campaign is a success it will make £200 000. However, if it fails (with a probability of 0.3) it will make only £20 000. The expected value is therefore 0.7 × 200 000 + 0.3 × 20 000 = £146 000. In this case this is higher than the cost of the campaign (£100 000). So the campaign should be done.

Learn these Features *of* Decision Trees

1) A **square** represents a **decision point**.

2) **Circles** (or **nodes**) mark where there are **alternative outcomes**, which are shown by **lines** coming out of the node.

3) The **decimals** on the lines are the **probabilities** of each event occurring.

4) The **values in £s** represent the **income** to the business if that outcome happens.

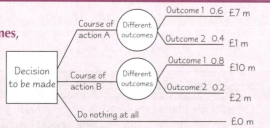

Decision Trees *show which* Course Of Action *is Best*

1) When creating a decision tree, managers first identify which courses of action are open to the business.

2) They then outline the **possible results** of each course of action.

3) They assign **probabilities** to each of the results — filling in the probabilities they know for certain, and estimating the probabilities they don't know.

4) The next step is to **calculate** the "**expected values**" of each result.

5) Managers choose the course of action with the **highest expected value**.

Case Study — Decision Tree for Launching a New Product

A business wants to **launch a new product**.

1) **With a market research budget of £15K** the chance of a **successful launch** is estimated at **75%**.

2) **Without market research** the chance is estimated at **50%**.

3) A **successful** launch would earn a profit of **£100K** — but if it **failed**, profit would be **£20K** at best.

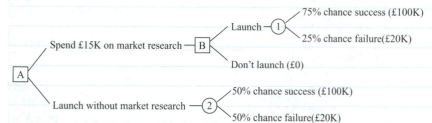

Expected values are calculated for each node point by multiplying the benefit by the probability:

Node 1:(£100K × 0.75) + (20K × 0.25) =
£75K + £5K = £80K

Node 2:(£100K × 0.5) + (20K × 0.5) =
£50K + £10K = £60K

Compare the decisions — the decision at square B is the most straightforward, so start with that one.

Square B   The decision at square B is whether to launch or not. Compare the **expected value of the launch (£80K)** with **not launching (£0)**. After market research, it's best to go ahead with the launch.

Square A   To **compare like with like**, take off the **cost of market research** from the expected value of launching after market research. This works out as £80K – £15K = **£65K**. Compare this amount with the expected value of launching without any research, which is £60K. So, it's better to do the research than to not do the research.

So, the final decision is... to **launch after carrying out market research**.

Decision Trees

Decision Trees have Advantages...

1) Decision tree analysis makes managers **work out** and **think about** the **probability** of each outcome, and the **potential payoff** of each outcome. Managers have to come up with real numerical values for these — much better than vague statements like "this will increase sales".

2) Decision trees are a nice **visual representation** of the potential outcomes of a decision.

3) Decision trees allow managers to compare options **quantitatively** and **objectively**, rather than plumping for the fashionable option or the option they thought of first.

Stay small. The expected benefit from growth is lower than you think.

...and Disadvantages

1) Decision trees are **quantitative** — i.e. they're numerically based. There's a wide range of non-numerical **qualitative data** which a business must take into account before deciding on a course of action.

A business should never rely on one single tool as the basis for determining its long term strategy.

2) **Probabilities** are very hard to **predict accurately**. **Estimated payoffs** are also assumed to be accurate — in real life things may work out differently. If either of these estimates are based on **dodgy** information, the decision is **flawed** too.

3) In reality there's a **wider range** of potential **outcomes** than the decision tree suggests. For example, a new marketing campaign might increase sales for a shorter period than predicted — the decision tree might only allow for success or failure, not for short-term success versus long-term success.

Practice Questions

Q1 Explain the difference between the circles (nodes) and the squares on a decision tree.

Q2 Outline the five stages used in decision tree construction.

Q3 Define expected value and say how it's calculated.

Q4 Give one disadvantage of decision tree analysis.

Exam Question

Q1 Cruse plc is a multinational electronic defence systems organisation. It has won a contract to overhaul the electronics on an ex-Royal Navy submarine. Three other submarines require similar work in the next four years but Cruse plc does not have the current capacity to complete these contracts in the time available. To win the subsequent contracts Cruse has three options: increase capacity, use existing resources but take longer, or subcontract two-thirds of the work. Expected outcomes are as follows:

Option	Outcomes	Probability	Profit (£m)
Increase existing capacity	Success	0.4	700
	Slight success	0.5	400
	Failure	0.1	-100
Use existing capacity	Success	0.4	400
	Slight success	0.3	200
	Failure	0.3	-30
Subcontract	Success	1	300

Answer on p.138.

(a) On the basis of the information given, construct a decision tree for this problem and label it showing probabilities and forecast pay-offs. (7 marks)

(b) Calculate the expected value for each option. Advise Cruse as to the best option. (15 marks)

(c) Assess the usefulness of constructing a decision tree in this case. (6 marks)

(d) Discuss other factors which Cruse plc might consider when taking the decision. (14 marks)

An oak and a fir go into a bar, and the barman says "so, what'll it be"...

Decision trees are a really nifty way of working out what the best option is, when a manager is faced with an important decision. It's based on the potential benefit if things work out well, and the likelihood of it working out well or badly. Practise working your way through a few decision trees to get the hang of it — don't leave it all until the day of the exam.

Porter and Generic Strategy

*Once upon a time, there was a chap called Michael Porter, who was what you'd call a business guru. He came up with a few rather simple but powerful ideas about business strategy. These pages are for **Edexcel**.*

Businesses should Try to get the Edge Over their Competitors

Porter put forward a theory of **competitive advantage**. It's based on the idea that **all businesses** will want to **gain an advantage** in their market. There are two main ways they can do this:

Cost advantage

1) **Competitive advantage** can be had by selling more or less the **same product** at lower cost than your rivals.

2) For example, **low cost airlines** such as EasyJet and Ryanair use a "no frills" strategy to keep their costs at a **bare minimum** — they use cheap airports such as Luton and cut out travel agents by using online booking.

Differentiation advantage

1) Businesses also get competitive advantage by offering **better benefits** at the same or slightly higher price.

2) Offering a product that consumers see as **different** from competitors' products can make the consumers think it's **better**. This is called **product differentiation**.

Porter suggested Three Generic Strategies to Gain Advantage

Cost Leadership

1) **Cost leadership** strategy calls for the **lowest cost of production** for a given level of quality.

2) In a **price war**, the firm can maintain profitability while the competition suffers losses.

3) If prices decline, the firm can stay profitable because of their low costs.

4) A very **broad market** is needed for this strategy — preferably a **global** market, with huge production facilities to take advantage of **economies of scale**.

Differentiation

1) **Differentiation** strategy requires a product with **unique attributes** which consumers value, so that they **perceive it to be better** than rival products.

2) The value added by uniqueness allows the business to charge a **premium price**.

3) Risks include **imitation** by competitors and **changes** in **consumer tastes**.

Focus Strategy

1) **Focus** strategy concentrates on a **narrow** market **segment** to achieve **either** cost advantage or differentiation.

2) A firm using this strategy usually has **loyal customers**, which makes it very hard for other firms to compete.

Porter also said that Market Positioning is Important

1) Product positioning maps, or **perceptual maps**, place a brand neatly in a market.

2) Product position maps plot brands on **two axes**, which each represent a **variable** which differentiates brands in the market — e.g. young/old, economy/luxury, edgy/traditional, convenience/gourmet.

3) The data for brand mapping comes from **market research focus groups**. Consumers are asked to **rate** brands from, say, most traditional to most modern.

4) These maps help identify **gaps in the market**. Any area on the map without a brand name on it — that's a gap in the market, ripe to be exploited by a business.

5) When bringing out a new product, it's very important to have a good idea of where to **position** it in the market.

6) **Mature** products may need to be **re-positioned**, if the market has changed. For example, Lucozade was repositioned from a children's health drink to a sports drink.

Brand map for women's high street fashion retailers

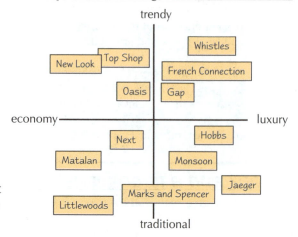

Porter and Generic Strategy

Porter's **Five Force Framework** shows **Influences** on an industry

Porter's **Five Force Framework** shows an industry being influenced by **five competitive forces.** It analyses the state of the market, and helps managers figure out the **best strategy** to gain competitive advantage in that **particular market**.

① **Barriers to entry — how easy it is for new firms to enter the market**

1) New entrants to the market will want to compete by selling similar products — it's in the **interests** of existing firms in the market to make it **hard** for new firms to get in.
2) **High start up costs** (e.g. **expensive equipment**) are a way of deterring new firms from entering the market.
3) **Patents**, **trade marks** and **licensing** make it hard for new entrants to sell similar products.
4) Established businesses may control **distribution channels**, making it hard for new entrants to sell.

② **Buyer power — buyers want products at as low a price as possible**

1) **Buyers** have **more power** when there are **few buyers** and many sellers.
2) Buyers have **more power** when products are **standardised** — it's easier for firms to charge a premium price for differentiated goods and services.
3) When commercial buyers (e.g. retailers) have little power, producers can **buy them.**
4) Businesses can try to tie buyers into **long term contracts**.

Remember, this lot applies to business customers, wholesalers and retailers, not just Joe Q. Public.

This is "forward integration".

③ **Supplier power — suppliers want to get as high a price as possible**

1) **Suppliers** have **more power** when there are **few suppliers** and lots of firms buying from them.
2) A supplier's **main customer** can **negotiate special deals** and lower prices.
3) Firms with **power** over their supplier can **buy the supplier out** — this is "**backwards vertical integration**."
4) Suppliers with power over their buyer can **forward integrate** — e.g. by setting up their own retail outlets.

④ **Threat of substitutes — how likely it is that consumers will buy an alternative product**

1) The **willingness** of customers to substitute is a factor affecting competitiveness.
2) Relative **price** and **quality** important — buyers are less likely to change to a poor value substitute product.
3) There may be a **cost of switching** brand — e.g. buying all new computer software. Firms try to make it **expensive** for buyers to get **substitutes**.

⑤ **Rivalry within industry — how much competition there is**

1) Rivalry is **intense** where there are lots of **equally sized competitors**.
2) Industries with **high fixed costs** are **competitive**. Firms cut prices to raise demand and use up their capacity.
3) Industries producing **standardised** goods (e.g. steel, milk, flour) have **intense** rivalry.
4) Rivalry is **intense** in **young industries** where competitors are following **growth strategies**.

Businesses with high fixed costs don't want production to sit idle.

Practice Questions

Q1 What's meant by the terms "competitive advantage" and "product differentiation"?
Q2 Describe Porter's generic strategies.
Q3 What is a product position map?
Q4 What are the five forces in Porter's five force framework?

Exam Questions

Q1 Describe how a generic differentiation strategy allows a business to pursue competitive advantage. (6 marks)

Q2 Evaluate how useful Porter's Five Force Framework can be to a business manager. (10 marks)

Porter conveniently ignores the force of gravity...

... which isn't a luxury most of us have. Darn pesky gravity, making things fall down. Anyway, the Five Force Framework is a rather useful tool to analyse the market and see where threats and opportunities are. Porter also came up with three generic strategies which can be adapted to suit absolutely any business — you do need to know what these strategies are.

Implementing and Reviewing Strategies

*Once a strategy is decided, that's not the end of the story. Managers have to get it working, and change it if it isn't right. These pages are for **OCR**, and they're also useful for **Edexcel** and **AQA**.*

Strategy *is the way in which* Objectives *are achieved*

1) Business decisions must fit in with **corporate objectives**. Objectives must be **measurable** — vague objectives are useless, and don't help managers make decisions that move the business forward.

2) **Short-term plans**, known as **tactical plans**, contain precise, detailed and measurable objectives. This level of planning is done by **middle managers** and supervisors.

3) **Long-term plans** are not as detailed or measurable. The longer the time scale of the plan, the less certain the outcome can be. Long-term plans are drawn up by **senior management**. They're also known as **strategic plans**.

4) Objectives provide **direction** and **unity of purpose**, and they also allow managers to **measure performance**. For example, a measurable objective set by senior management may be to increase market share by 15% within 3 years. This target can be used to control and measure the activities of junior managers. Each month or each quarter, market share is checked to make sure things are on track.

5) The objectives of a firm's **stakeholders** influence the firm's own corporate objectives. For example, **shareholders** might have an objective of quick return on investment — the firm might aim to please the shareholders by having an objective of **profit maximisation**.

A strategy is a plan for how to achieve objectives. A strategy plans out the tactics that a business will use to reach its goals. Tactics are the actual activities that the business uses to work towards its objectives.

A Strategy *is* Not For Life *— it must be continually* Checked *and* Reviewed

1) It's very important that the managers who devise a strategy also **monitor** it for **effectiveness**. There needs to be **constant monitoring** of whether all the parts of the business (marketing, production and human resources) are **meeting** the targets they've been set. If they aren't, then it's essential to find out why not.

2) When producing the plan, the organisation will include a series of **planning horizons**. This is the time scale by when each part of the plan will be met. The **financial objectives** will be set and the actual performance will be measured against a **forecast** made at the start of the planning cycle.

3) The results may not be meeting expectations. A **difference** between a strategic target and reality is called a **strategic gap**. By **analysing** the gap, managers can find out **why** there is a difference between the target and the reality, and take corrective action.

Businesses use *Various Techniques* to Monitor *how the strategy is going*

Businesses use **market analysis**, **financial** analysis and **management information** systems to work out the **starting point** for the strategy — and then to monitor progress towards financial, marketing and production **targets**.

Market analysis shows if assumptions about the **market** are correct.

1) Firms use both primary and secondary **market research** to check how the strategy is proceeding.

2) They **audit sales levels**, concentrating particularly on the **target markets**. If a strategic gap appears then the business will want to know why. The techniques used are described on p.12-13.

The **management information system** provides most of the information.

1) **Management information systems** are computer systems that constantly collect and process routine financial, stock and production data, to give a picture of the current state of the business. This data is used to see if the business is on course to meet its objectives.

See p.125 for more about management information systems.

2) Managers use **mathematical techniques** such as moving averages and scatter graphs to interpret the data.

Even the *Best Laid Plans* of (mice and) Managers *can* Go Wrong

The business environment is **changing** all the time. External and internal changes can mess things up — they mean that a good plan suddenly isn't so good any more.

1) Changes in **technology** can **increase the productivity** of **competitors**. Changes in technology can make a product **obsolete**.

2) **Consumer tastes** can change **quickly**, which reduces the length of the product life cycle.

3) Improvements in **communications** systems can benefit competitors. Businesses may feel forced to make changes to keep up with competitors — e.g. by outsourcing customer services to India or other low labour cost countries.

Implementing and Reviewing Strategies

Successful **Implementation** of a plan requires **Motivation** and **Communication**

1) Successful implementation of a strategic plan relies on the **people** employed by the company.

2) It's very important that senior managers **communicate the intentions** of the strategic plan clearly to all sections of the business, so that everyone knows what they're supposed to be doing. There should be as few **barriers to communication** as possible. Chains of communication shouldn't be too long. Communication overload should be avoided. See p.60-61 for more on communication.

3) The **middle** and **junior management** will be very important in **interpreting** the plan into the day-to-day actions of their different departments and sections.

4) It's important that everyone is motivated to push forward with the strategy — everyone from top to bottom of the organisation needs to know what's in it for them.

Implementing a strategy means **Changes** have to be made

1) A new strategy requires **different ways of working**. This involves **retraining**, which might be costly, or take a long time. Not all staff can be trained at once.

2) **Mistakes** can occur during the transition period, and these can affect relations with customers. Customers may **resent** a change in the way they're dealt with, unless it's clearly hundreds of times better than the old way.

3) A new strategy might mean making some **staff redundant**.

4) Staff might have to change their **attitude** towards their work. They might have to work **harder**, or **longer** hours, or **shorter** hours, or be more **customer service** oriented.

5) The management structure might need to be **restructured** — departments could be split up, or merged, or moved to another senior manager's control. This can **cause friction** between managers.

Juliet's view of the new customer service strategy had taken a recent downturn.

All the above changes can have an effect on the **morale** and **motivation** of employees.

Good managers can implement change in a way that doesn't seriously hack off their staff — which of course means that staff put their weight behind the new strategy faster.

Practice Questions

Q1 Give two differences between long-term and short-term plans, other than "one's long-term and one's short-term".

Q2 What is a planning horizon?

Q3 What is a strategic gap?

Q4 What are the external factors that could affect the success of a strategic plan?

Q5 What internal factors affect the successful implementation of a company's strategic plan?

Exam Questions

Q1 Margaret Smith is responsible for ensuring that all departmental managers and supervisory staff in XYZ Ltd understand the company's plan to become the most successful company in their market. The targets for customer service calls answered in a target time are 95%. After six months into the implementation phase the following figures for two customer service supervisors are:
Supervisor A: 98% of calls answered within target time.
Supervisor B: 85% of calls answered within target time.
Explain why Margaret's implementation strategy may be working with one supervisor and not another. (8 marks)

Q2 Outline how four different departmental (functional area) managers might help close a firm's strategic gap. (12 marks)

This is you, implementing your revision strategy...

A lot of this topic is common sense — obviously implementing a strategy would rock the boat, and obviously it makes sense to check up on a strategy and see if it's working or not. It is good to have it all spelled out for you like this, because in the OCR exam you could be asked questions about what a business could do to make sure a strategic plan is successful.

Corporate Culture and Strategy

Corporate culture affects the way a business sets its objectives.
*These pages are for **AQA** and **Edexcel**.*

Corporate Culture is the Way a business Does Things

1) **Corporate culture** is the way that a business does things, and the way that people in the business expect things to be done. It shapes the **expectations** and **attitudes** of staff and managers.

2) Because corporate culture **shapes staff behaviour** and how they make decisions, it has an effect on planning, objective setting and strategy.

3) Corporate culture is created and reinforced by company **rules**, **managerial attitudes** and behaviour, **recruitment** policies that recruit people who "fit in", **reward** systems (e.g. how bonuses are calculated and allocated), and "**ceremonies**" such as office **parties**.

Mission Statements give Clues to corporate culture

1) **Mission statements** are written **descriptions** of corporate objectives. They set out what the business does, and why they do it. Mission statements are intended to make all **stakeholders** aware of the corporate objectives, and to **encourage** all employees to **work towards** them.

2) Mission statements give **clues** about culture. For example, a mission statement that mentions ethics and principles gives a big hint that the corporate culture is focused towards ethical practice as well as profitability.

3) Some mission statements **explicitly** state what the business believes its corporate culture is. After a short statement of corporate aim and vision for the future, there may be a **statement of shared beliefs**, e.g. "We believe in providing outstanding service to customers", "We believe that we gain strength through our diversity".

4) Businesses can have underlying cultures within **departments**, known as **subcultures**. For example, a design department might be relaxed, whereas the head of sales might run a very tight ship. One benefit of a mission statement is to try and **prevent** this by creating a **unifying**, visible culture for all employees to **identify** with.

5) **Changing** the mission statement can help change corporate culture.

There are Four Main Types of Corporate Culture

1) **Power culture** refers to organisations where decision-making authority is limited to a **small number** of people —perhaps just **one person**.

2) In these businesses, objectives reflect the wishes of the guy or gal at the **top**.

1) **Role culture** refers to **bureaucratic** firms where authority is defined by job title.

2) These organisations tend to **avoid risk** for fear of failure so they develop **cautious** aims and objectives.

3) The danger here is that over-cautious companies can lose out in the long run, especially in **new** or **expanding** markets where strategies need to be developed and implemented quickly. Organisations with role culture often fail to exploit opportunities before their competitors do.

1) **Person culture** refers to loose organisations of individual workers, usually **professional partnerships** such as solicitors.

2) The objectives of these firms will be defined by the **personal ambitions** of the individuals involved. Care is needed to ensure individuals actually have **common goals**.

1) **Task culture** places an emphasis on tasks and **getting things done**.

2) Task culture gets **small teams** together to work on a project, then disbands them. There may be **conflict** between teams for resources and budgets. This can led to confusion if a firm has too many products or **projects**.

3) This culture supports objectives which are based around **products** (e.g. make Product X the market leader).

4) Task cultures respond well to **management by objectives**. Management by objectives translates corporate objectives into **specific targets** for each **department** and for each **individual employee**.

Corporate Culture and Strategy

Corporate Culture is linked to Management Styles

1) The **power** culture matches up with the **autocratic** style. An autocratic leader doesn't like to let anyone else have responsibility for making decisions, let alone setting corporate objectives.

2) The **role** culture can be linked to a **paternalistic** style of leadership. It's not compatible with a fully democratic style of leadership, because big bureaucratic firms aren't good enough at communication to consult and delegate decision-making.

3) The **person** culture is linked to a **laissez-faire** style of leadership. The workers are generally individual **professionals** and can be **trusted** to make their own decisions and generally **get on with it** by themselves.

4) The **task** culture is linked to a **democratic** style of leadership, with **delegation** of responsibility. Teams working on tasks need the responsibility to make their own decisions, and the freedom to organise themselves in the way they think best, in order to meet corporate objectives.

Management Information Systems (MIS) help managers to Keep Control

1) **Management information systems** (**MIS**) **collect**, **process** and **organise** information using **computers**.

2) MIS usually collect **routine numerical data**, for example sales and production information. This information can be presented in a form that's easily **understood** and **analysed**, for example a report for shareholders.

3) **Managers** use MIS to make business **decisions**, **monitor progress**, or identify and resolve **problems**. MIS help senior managers to **know what's going on** in the business, which gives them a stronger sense of **control**.

4) Accurate, up-to-date information can provide **competitive advantage**. For example:

   • The use of MIS in **production** can improve **quality**, identify **problems** and increase **efficiency**.

   • Data can be used to compare **estimated** and **actual** figures, so managers can take corrective action in time.

   • MIS help businesses to **communicate key data** between **departments**.

5) MIS have **shortcomings**. They aren't good at dealing with **non-numerical** or **unpredictable** information. Also, the quality of information provided depends on the **programming** of the system and the **accuracy** of the **data input**.

Business Culture affects how Useful an Information Management System is

1) For example, say a **steel manufacturer** pays a consultancy firm a large **fee** to design them a **fabulous computer system**. The system **monitors** all aspects of production and allows **fine control** of things like blast furnace power and air/oxygen mix, steel roller pressure, the whole nine yards.

2) The problem is that the steel plant doesn't have a **culture** that **rewards** individual **responsibility** or training. Production staff get a day's training on the system, and they don't really **know** how to use it. They're scared of pressing the **wrong button**, so they prefer to do things the way they know, with the skills they already have.

3) Result — the steel manufacturer doesn't get the **full benefit** of the information management system. The money they paid for the system is **wasted**.

Practice Questions

Q1 What is corporate culture?

Q2 Describe the power culture, and its approach to setting objectives.

Q3 Which culture is best suited to management by objectives?

Q4 Which culture is linked to the democratic style of management?

Exam Question

Q1 Filton Electronics is a medium size manufacturer of diodes. Until recently, it was run by owner Jim Filton and a small team of department managers, in a strict functional hierarchy. It has been taken over by a firm who practise Japanese management methods such as kaizen, JIT production, teamworking and quality circles. The parent firm's mission statement says "we will improve our standards every day, and communicate excellence throughout the business". Suggest changes that Filton must make to their corporate culture, and explain why they should be made.   (14 marks)

Look for clues about culture...

The exam boards give you a case study of a business (Edexcel's is v. v. long), and they may ask you about strategy, staff motivation, external influences or corporate culture. The case study will be full of clues about the culture — it'll probably tell you a story of how the managers acted in a particular situation rather than saying "this firm has a TASK culture".

Managing Change

*Businesses must take care to manage change so that it goes smoothly. There are links to sections on organisation and human resource management — well motivated workers cope better with change. These pages are for **OCR** and **Edexcel**.*

Change can be either Planned or Unplanned

1) Change in business can be **planned** change — part of a strategy decided by management.

2) Changes can occur after some **disaster** or other event which is **outside** the firm's control, such as a **fire** at a **supplier's warehouse**, or new **legislation** banning the use of a material, or the launch of a **rival** product.

3) Change can also happen as the result of a **takeover** by another business.

Change can be Incremental, Catastrophic or somewhere In Between

Incremental change is gradual

1) It's usually the result of a **strategic plan** being put in place.

2) Managers decide a **timescale** for the necessary changes and then **timetable strategies** for achieving them (e.g. training, closures, product development, promotional activities and all that sort of palaver).

Catastrophic change is sudden

1) Management of catastrophic change forces firms to suddenly do things in a way that they might not normally do. They may have to **close or sell off subsidiary companies**, spend heavily on promotions to raise customer confidence or **totally restructure** the way the firm's organised.

2) When you think of catastrophic change, you usually think of a sudden negative event that destroys a lot of stock or makes it useless (e.g. a product is found to be dangerous and taken off the shelves), or makes a whole lot of customers suddenly go elsewhere (e.g. a rival brings out a competing product). It's also possible for **customer demand** to **increase** and force the company to expand even though it wasn't planning to.

Changes in the **law** can be **incremental** or **catastrophic**. Sometimes, the government gives businesses **plenty of notice** that they're going to change the law, so that businesses can **plan ahead** for the change and put a strategy in place to implement the change. Sometimes governments change the law **suddenly**, e.g. in response to a health scare.

Catastrophic change isn't always Chaotic

1) Even catastrophic change can be planned for, up to a point. Businesses may have thought up **contingency plans** in advance — they'll have thought up various "what if?" scenarios, and made plans to cope with them. These contingency plans help them keep on supplying customers with the minimum of disruption.

2) For example, IT businesses (e.g. web hosts) may have **backup systems** in different geographical areas, so they can keep on running if something happens to their main location. Also, businesses may have contingency plans of what they'd do if they were threatened with a **hostile takeover**.

Some businesses say that Change should be Carried Out Quickly

This argument is often used when a business is faced with **an unanticipated shift** in market conditions such as a sudden fall in demand for their products. For example, Corus, the steel producer, was faced with a world **oversupply** of steel and responded with the rapid **closure** or **restructuring** of a number of plants in the UK. This reduced capacity and returned the company to profit within two years.

1) Change is **disruptive** and disruption is **minimized** by getting it over and done with quickly.

2) Customers would see **improvements** in services **sooner**.

3) Change strategies are **expensive** and affect a **company's cash flow and profitability**. Shareholders will see **reduced profits** for a shorter period of time.

Any Change in business operations is Unsettling for Employees

1) Employees naturally **resist change**. Change is **uncomfortable** and **stressful** for people.

2) People tend to find things more stressful when they don't **understand** them. Any business undergoing change needs to **communicate** the reasons why **change** is taking place. For the changes to succeed, staff must not only **know what's happening** but also **understand why** it's happening.

3) **Managers** at all levels will be expected to carry out this communication. They must make every effort to overcome **resistance to change**.

Even "nice" changes can be stressful.

Managing Change

Resistance *to change makes it difficult to implement change*

Managing change well makes the difference between **success** and **failure**.
To manage change well, employers will need to be aware of the ways in which employees can **resist change**.

1) Employees may not want to learn **new routines** because this may take them outside their "**comfort zone**".
2) Staff will be worried about their **pay and conditions**.
3) When **restructuring** is part of the change process, staff worry about their **status and security**.
4) Staff working in teams develop **good working relationships**. These could be broken up.

Managers need **Strategies** *to* **Overcome Resistance** *to change*

1) The most **successful changes** happen when all employees have opportunities to be **fully consulted**.

2) Staff don't like being **kept in the dark**. They cope better when they have **information** about what's going on. **Lack of information** can lead to rumour and **distrust** of management's **intentions**, which affects **motivation and morale**.

3) Employees also don't like to feel **powerless**. They cope better when they're given the opportunity to **have their say**, and **influence decisions** in some way.

The Japanese call this approach "ringi".

There are **two strategies** commonly used:

1) Everyone who may be affected by the change is expected to **become involved** at the **planning stage**. This helps them to understand **why change** is necessary. When a decision needs to be taken, all employees affected have an opportunity to **comment** on the proposal, **suggest** changes and eventually **agreement** will be reached. This is easier to achieve when change is incremental but more difficult at times of crisis.

2) All staff affected by change are kept **informed** at each stage of the process, but don't get the chance to become involved in planning the change.

Management must **Understand** *the* **Organisation** *for change to* **Succeed**

1) Senior managers have to take into account the **culture and values** in the organisation. This often comes back to the leadership styles that are commonly encouraged in the firm. Theory Y managers are more likely to be **consultative** than theory X managers. Theory X managers will often **impose** changes in working practices.

2) Existing **communications systems** must be effective enough to help employees understand the reasons for change and what new objectives need to be achieved.

3) Managers should make sure that the **technology** used in the company will still be appropriate after the change. Computer systems may need to be upgraded or replaced, which requires additional investment in both equipment and training.

4) As part of the process, firms will need to carry out a **skills audit** to make sure that the company has the correct mix of people best qualified to meet the needs of the organisation now and in the future.

Practice Questions

Q1 Why does change need to be "managed"?
Q2 Define the term "catastrophic change"?
Q3 What are the arguments for carrying out change quickly?

Exam Question

Q1 (a) Analyse the problems that could arise if a business experienced an unanticipated shift in demand. (9 marks)
    (b) Evaluate whether a rapid change strategy would be useful in this situation. (11 marks)

Is a change as good as a rest? Ask a bloke who hasn't slept in days...

In general, people prefer stability to change. Change is stressful — the bigger the change, the more stressful it is. A little stress can be beneficial, and there's a school of thought that says managers should keep changing things to keep employees on their toes, which is fine up to a point. Taken too far, change for the sake of change annoys everyone and wastes time.

Impact of Change in Size

*Growth causes a lot of changes to a business. It's not just that there are more people employed there — organisation may need to change, and a business may even take a different approach to long term planning. For **AQA** and **Edexcel**.*

Businesses can **Decide** whether to **Grow** or not

Growth doesn't happen by **accident**. It's up to the owners whether to **restrict growth** or **strategically plan** it. Business owners may choose to **restrict** growth for the following reasons:

1) They may want to maintain the culture of a small business.

2) If the business over-markets their products they could let customers down — the productive, administrative or distributive capacity may not be enough to handle the increased demand.

3) The business will become more complicated to manage as it gets bigger.

4) Growth requires the business to secure additional financial resources, which can be complicated.

5) They may not want to put too much strain on their cash flow position.

If the owners do decide that they want to **grow** the company, they must **devise a strategy** to **raise money** to pay for growth, and **plan** the growth process.

Growing Businesses must find sources of Finance — either internal or external

Whether the business finds it easy to attract the finance needed to grow will depend on a number of factors:

1) The business plan must be realistic, and must give an idea of when investors will see a return on their money.

2) The previous reputation of the business and its management affects how easy it is to borrow money.

3) The type of ownership of the business is a factor — e.g. whether it's a private or public limited company. A sole trader or partnership may have to become a limited company, so it can raise funds by selling shares.

Internal Finance comes from Profits or Owners' Capital

1) Sources of finance for growth depend on the **amount of capital** needed to implement the strategic growth plan. If the amount required is within the firm's own resources then expansion can be **funded internally**.

2) **Retained profits** are where the firm reinvests its profits back into its activities. This may work well as a firm expands from small to medium sized, but the funding available at any one time **could be too limited**.

3) **Owner's capital** is another source of growth funding. If the owners of the firm have the resources they could agree to **increase** their investment into the company. This source of funding is also limited.

4) In most cases, firms need some **external investment** to fund their growth.

The way External Funding is raised depends on Original Size and Ambitions

1) If the business is relatively **small** or **medium sized** then the opportunities to raise finance are more **limited** than for a large or multinational company.

2) Established **smaller businesses** can raise finance through **loans from banks** but these may be **limited** to the purchase of new **capital equipment** or funding the opening of **new branches**.

3) If a small business has unlimited liability they'd be **unlikely** to attract external funding without becoming a limited company. This allows them to issue shares to raise capital. They may go to **venture capitalists** who would invest in the business for a limited period of time, say five years.

4) **Medium sized companies** could also convert from a private limited company to a **public limited company**. They could then raise finance through the **stock exchange** on the Alternative Investment Market (a stock market for medium size companies).

Venture capitalists are people who invest in businesses for a living.

5) **Large** and **multinational businesses** are usually PLCs, already listed on the Stock Exchange, often in more than one country. They would be more likely to use a mixture of **substantial bank loans**, **rights issues** of shares (shares offered to existing shareholders at a discount), **sales of subsidiaries** and **retained profits** to fund growth.

6) Businesses can apply for **regional aid grants** if the expansion involves providing substantial additional employment in **deprived** areas.

Impact of Change in Size

Growing Businesses *must manage their* Cash Flow *particularly carefully*

1) Just like at any other time, during a period of growth and investment it's essential that there are funds available to pay for the current **day-to-day expenses** of the business.

2) Fast growth increases the risk of **overtrading**. Increased **demand** means the business needs to buy more raw materials and employ more people. This **reduces** the amount of **working capital** available to pay the bills, and the business runs the risk that they'll go bust before they have the chance to get paid by their customers.

3) **Additional borrowing** may be required to manage working capital, which adds to the **costs** of the growth plan and therefore reduces the value added of the whole growth strategy.

Growing in Size *brings its* Own Problems

1) When a company changes from a **private limited company (Ltd)** to a **public limited company (PLC)**, the original owners won't find it so easy to maintain **control**, as they'll be responsible to a wider range of **shareholders**.

2) Once a company becomes a **PLC** then it's more open to being **taken over**. Anyone with sufficient resources could buy its shares in sufficient quantities to take a **controlling interest**.

3) Becoming a **PLC** can make managers more **short-termist**. Shareholders often want a **quick return** on investment through **dividend** payments, so they're **unlikely** to favour investment in **long-term projects**.

4) The process of **floating** the business on the **stock market** is **expensive** and **complicated**. The business would need to employ a **merchant bank** to apply for a stock market listing and handle the share offer for them. They'd need to use some of the finance raised to **fund** this.

5) When companies **expand overseas** they need to be familiar with the **commercial law** of the host country. They need to know the **employment regulations**, deal with the problems involved in carrying out transactions in **other currencies**, and comply with any regulations which cover the **product specifications** for those markets. Companies operating abroad may also have to deal with **different languages** and **cultures**.

Businesses *may become* Smaller — *this is called* Retrenchment

1) Businesses can choose to become smaller if they are suffering from diseconomies of scale (p.79).

2) They can **retrench** if they've lost focus. Doing too many different activities makes it hard to stay competitive.

3) Businesses can be forced to get smaller if they're **forced out of a market** by a larger competitor. They can also be forced to stop making some types of product by changes in **consumer taste**.

4) Also, changes in the **economy** such as recession or high interest rates may force a business to downsize.

Practice Questions

Q1 Why might a private limited company be reluctant to become a public limited company?

Q2 What is meant by the term "retained profits"?

Q3 Why is it important to manage cash flow during a transition period?

Q4 Why might a business take a short-term approach to planning after becoming a public limited company?

Q5 List five problems that a national business may have when it becomes an international business.

Q6 What is retrenchment?

Exam Question

Q1 Matthews Engineering Ltd., a private limited company, is a successful machine tools manufacturer. The Board has decided to open a factory in China as part of its strategic plan to expand into emerging markets. The set up costs will be substantial and the company will need to raise additional finance to fund it.
a) Briefly state two methods that Matthew Engineering Ltd could use to raise funds for the China project. (2 marks)
b) What problems should the Board be aware of when expanding overseas? (4 marks)
c) Evaluate the risks and benefits that the company faces as it implements this strategy. (14 marks)

Could a fertiliser business ever choose not to promote growth...

You need to know how businesses finance growth — there's more about sources of finance on p.24. There are various potential problems that come with a change in size. Some of them are specific to mergers and takeovers, and they're covered on p.132-133. The rest of what you need to know is here.

Readjustment After Growth

*When a business grows there's always a period of adjustment afterwards. Staff need to learn to work using different equipment, procedures and possibly in different teams. These pages are for **AQA** and **Edexcel**.*

Growth usually means that Organisational Structures have to Change

1) Most businesses start off as a **sole trader** or a partnership. These businesses are easy to manage — the **boss** can take all the **decisions**, and **organise** all the work.

2) As the business starts to grow, the boss **hires people** to help out. To start with, employee job descriptions can be quite **fluid**, and staff can take on tasks on an ad hoc basis (doing whatever's needed, whenever it's needed).

3) The next step is to move to a more **formal** structure. Employees are organised in **departments** under the control of a **department manager** and job descriptions become more **formal**. It's difficult for the boss to have control over the **whole organisation**, so some control is **delegated** to departmental managers.

4) As businesses get even larger, a simple formal hierarchy becomes an **ineffective** way of organising things, for the following reasons:

- Often department managers work in **isolation** and don't know what's going on in other departments — e.g. sales departments may promise delivery dates which can't be met by production departments.

- Management usually needs to **improve** the internal **communication** system to cope with this. There's a **danger** that businesses can become **over-bureaucratic** if they try to make communication foolproof. They can end up in a situation where **nobody's willing** to make a decision in a crisis because there's no **written permission** from above.

5) A boss who's been used to having **full authority** and control over large groups of employees, may have to learn how to become a **leader** or manager. **Senior managers** such as owner/manager or departmental managers who were **autocratic** by nature will have to learn to **trust** their subordinate employees. When a boss can't let go, and insists on knowing every little thing that's going on, the business can't grow very large.

During growth Managers Delegate More

1) As the business becomes more complicated, owners and managers have to **delegate** more tasks.

2) New **communications** systems are introduced to keep everyone in touch with what's going on. Departments must become less **isolated**. As tall hierarchies grow larger, communication chains get longer, which makes communication less effective.

3) Frequently the organisational structure will change from a **tall hierarchical structure** to a **flat** one (see p.54 for more on tall and flat structures, and it's also covered in the AS course). **Layers** of the hierarchy are removed, in a process called "delayering" (a bit of a predictable name). Senior managers take **responsibility** for **whole divisions** of the business — for example, a manager who was once responsible for only the production department may take responsibility for all aspects of producing and marketing a product.

4) There's often an emphasis on **teamwork**. It becomes the **responsibility** of teams to **manage** their work in such a way that they **meet targets** for quality, utilisation of equipment, customer service, training and budgeting.

5) Team leaders and managers can't be experts in all aspects of the processes involved, so they'll be expected to take **advice** from **subordinates** at whatever level they are employed.

6) Some businesses will encourage **Total Quality Management (TQM)** (p.87) where all **operatives** are made **responsible for quality** at all stages of business activity. They are delegated the authority to remove a product from production lines if they notice a fault from the previous stage of production.

7) Businesses often take the opportunity to develop operational methods such as **kaizen** (p.87).

Managers Need Training to cope with growth

Even experienced managers may need **training** to learn how to effectively manage the changes that come with growth.

1) They need to be convinced that the changes are **necessary** so that they can explain them to subordinates.

2) It takes time for managers to **change attitudes** and learn to take a "hands off" approach to management, if they're used to an autocratic system.

3) Managing change in a business leads to **additional pressures** on managers and more work. **Time management** is an important skill to learn.

4) Managers will need to learn how to encourage subordinates to **contribute ideas** that may help improve the processes used in the firm.

Readjustment After Growth

Management must Keep Control of the growing business

1) As a business grows, and changes its organisational structure, it's **harder** for managers to **keep control** of what's going on.

2) In **flatter** structures, managers have **more subordinates** to manage, and they're ultimately responsible for **more activity**.

3) Larger businesses need good **planning systems**. **Budgeting** and **target setting** becomes particularly important.

4) **Management information systems** help managers keep **in touch** with day to day activities. All the relevant information is available to them, and they can call up any data they need.

5) **Management by objectives** helps businesses to **control** activities, and keeps everyone working towards the same **goals**.

6) **Formal appraisal** systems allow managers to keep tabs on what their staff are achieving.

> Management by objectives is a management style that sets targets for everyone in a business, and then checks to see if they've met their targets.

Management must try to Avoid a Loss of Direction

1) During a period of growth and change it is management's responsibility to ensure that the **current aims and objectives** are met. For example, if service **falls short** of the standards expected by customers because of the organisational changes taking place, it's **no excuse** to say "Sorry you didn't receive your order and sorry that the new customer service staff didn't have a clue who you were. We're going through a period of growth and organisational change."

2) Staff must be **trained** into the new ways of working, to make sure that they all do things according to the new methods.

3) **Management by objectives** gives every single employee clear targets to meet, which are derived from the corporate goals. This makes sure that everyone is working towards the same goals, and going in the same direction.

An 18th century business strategy map.

Practice Questions

Q1 Explain how old working methods might become ineffective when businesses grow.

Q2 What is the difference between a hierarchical and flat organisational system?

Q3 What new skills would a manager with an autocratic style need to learn to encourage a team approach?

Q4 What is the most common type of integration when a large company buys a similar company in the same industry?

Q5 Why do communication systems become more complicated in a larger organisation?

Exam Question

Q1 During the restructuring of Castle Foods Limited, the Managing Director is concerned about the possible problems that could occur with one of the company's older managers. A firm of management consultants has identified that value added is falling in the production department. Delays are happening, as staff have been discouraged by the manager from doing anything without his authority. The manager has skills valuable to the company, and they do not want to lose his expertise.

a) Briefly explain the type of management structure and leadership styles
   that have been used in Castle Foods before the restructuring. (6 marks)

b) What strategy do you think the Managing Director should follow to change the attitudes
   prevalent in the Production Department if it is to run efficiently after the restructuring? (6 marks)

Readjustment after growth — buy some new trousers that actually fit...

This all links neatly into the section on People in Organisations. P.124-125 will also be helpful. Change management is needed after growth to cope with changes to the way the business is organised, including who reports to which manager, who has responsibility for quality, etc. It can be tough for managers to keep a growing business under control.

Change in Ownership

Changes in ownership of businesses can occur for several reasons and in several ways. For **AQA** *and* **Edexcel***.*

Changes of Ownership can be Takeovers or Mergers

Watch out with these terms, because they're often used incorrectly.

1) The definition of a **takeover** is when one business buys enough shares in another, so that they have more than 50% of the total shares. This is called a **controlling interest**, and it means the buyer will always win in a vote of all shareholders.

2) A **merger** happens when two companies **agree** that they should join together. To do this they have to **form** a company with a **new name**. The **shares** of this new company are then **transferred** to the shareholders of the old companies. There will be an agreement between the companies as to what these shares will be **worth** on the first day they are traded on the stock exchange.

Takeovers can be Agreed or "Hostile"

1) **Hostile takeovers** happen when one **public limited company (PLC)** buys a **majority** of the shares in **another** PLC. It can do this because the shares of PLCs are **traded** on the stock exchange and **anyone** can buy them. The company will encourage existing shareholders to sell them the shares by offering a good price for them. This is called a **premium**.

2) **Agreed takeovers** happen when shareholders or other types of owners such as sole traders **agree** that they'll sell the business to someone else. This is usually because the owners believe it would benefit the **survival** of the business.

There are Many Reasons why companies Take Over or Merge With others

1) Some businesses will decide to **diversify** and buy **existing** businesses operating in the **market they want to enter**. They **gain** from the **experience** of those employed by the businesses they buy, so they can **make profits faster**.

2) They may want to buy out companies that **operate in the same market** so that they can **reduce** the amount of **competition** that they face.

3) Other companies will want to **extend** their market in the **same industry** but in **other countries**. Examples of this: T-Mobile (a German mobile phone operator), bought One-to-One (a British mobile phone operator), France Telecom purchased Orange for the same reason.

4) Some large companies buy **suppliers** so they'll be sure that supplies won't be **disrupted** . They'll be able to **control** production of their supplies. This is becoming less common — large companies find it more **cost effective** to place **big contracts** with a **number** of suppliers. If there are **problems** with one they can use another.

5) Some businesses make profits from "**asset stripping**". They buy poorly performing businesses **cheaply** and then sell off the assets at a profit. The land on which the original business had its factory may be more valuable as building land, and could be **sold off** by the buyer at a nice profit.

6) Two large companies in the same industry may merge so that both could benefit from increased **economies of scale**. This is called **corporate integration**. In the car industry, companies such as Ford, Peugeot, BMW, and General Motors have bought out car manufacturers overseas. They can **switch production** from country to country where labour costs may be lower but the expertise already exists.

Takeovers and Mergers can be Horizontal, Vertical or Conglomerate

1) **Horizontal integration** happens when a firm buys out another firm in the **same industry**. It's the **most common** type of takeover or merger. It **reduces** the **competition** in the market. For example, the Morrisons supermarket chain bought out Safeways to extend its branch network and reduce competition.

2) **Vertical integration** occurs when a firm merges with or takes over another in the same industry but at a **different stage of the production process** e.g. a component supplier, or a distributor that delivers its products to customers.

3) Vertical integration can be **forward** or **backward**.

> **Backward vertical integration** is when a business buys its supplier.
>
> **Forward vertical integration** is when a manufacturer buys the **outlets** where its products are sold. This allows them **direct access** to the retail market. They can then **control** what is sold and exclude competitors' brands.

4) **Conglomerate mergers** are between **unrelated** firms — they aren't competitors of each other, and they aren't each other's supplier or customer. **Pure conglomerate mergers** are between totally unrelated firms. **Product extension mergers** are between firms making **related products** (e.g. hairbrushes and hairspray). **Geographic market extensions** are between firms in the same industry, but competing in **different geographic markets**.

Change in Ownership

Management Buy Outs are... when firms are bought by their Managers

1) When the owners of the company want to **close** a division because it **no longer fits** in with its **strategic** plan (e.g. when a retailer no longer wants to own its suppliers) the managers of that division may buy it out.

2) When a company goes into **liquidation** because most of its subsidiaries are no longer profitable, the **liquidators** of the business may offer the management of a **profitable subsidiary** the opportunity to buy it.

Mergers, Takeovers and Buy Outs can be Expensive

1) PLCs can **finance** the purchase of another company in several ways — retained profits, loans, share issues etc.

2) PLCs can act in partnership with other companies **in return** for a **shareholding** in the company they're buying.

3) They also get **private investment** from major shareholders through **rights issues**. This is where extra shares are issued and offered at a **reduced** price.

4) The potential buyer may buy shares from **existing shareholders** of the company. Often they have to buy them at a **premium** (a better price than the existing shareholders would get otherwise).

5) They might also make a **cash/share** offer where they pay cash for part of the share purchase and the rest of the price will be in the form of **shares in the new company**. With a cash/share offer, the buying company doesn't need to **raise** as much **finance** to complete the purchase.

Taking Over other businesses is Not Risk Free

1) Both businesses need to "learn to live with each other". There can be **tension** between staff of the merged businesses as they try to **establish** their **status** in the new organisation.

2) It will take **time** for staff to **learn** new procedures — **mistakes** could lead to **poor customer service**.

3) Some parts of the new organisation may need to be sold off or closed. This could mean additional **redundancy costs** which will **reduce profitability**.

4) When one business buys another, it **takes on all the liabilities** of the other business — this could include things like claims for long term disabilities suffered by ex-employees of the other business.

5) The **Competition Commission** investigate whether the proposed merger will **restrict competition** in the marketplace. If this is found to be the case the government can **stop** the takeover taking place or place **restrictions** on it. The finance used to **plan** a merger or takeover would then be **wasted**.

6) If a takeover is part of a **diversification strategy**, the purchasing business will have **limited experience** in the new industry and it will take time to **learn** how it works. Mistakes would **reduce profitability**.

Practice Questions

Q1 When would you consider a takeover to be "hostile"?

Q2 What's the difference between a takeover and a merger?

Q3 Why do you think a company would encourage a management buy out?

Q4 What is the most common type of integration when a large company buys a similar company in the same industry?

Q5 What's "asset stripping"?

Q6 What is the difference between vertical and horizontal integration?

Exam Question

Q1 A high street fashion retailer is concerned that the overall group profits are falling yet turnover is up. The Board of Directors receive a report from their management consultants which indicates that the problem is one of rising costs. There have been delays in receiving deliveries from suppliers through delays at the supplier's factories. After some discussion the Board decides that they should buy two of their suppliers, both of which are small PLCs.

a) What form of integration is this proposal an example of? (2 marks)

b) Why do you believe that the Board took this decision? (6 marks)

c) Evaluate the risks involved in taking this approach. (12 marks)

Holy cats, it's the end of the book...

That was a big section — not so much in terms of pages, but it covered pretty much everything. Rounding things off, here's yet another page on growth and change management. This one's about mergers, takeovers and buyouts, which are a topic on their own. You know, I can't quite decide whether "backwards vertical integration" sounds rude or not...

Do Well in Your A2 Exam

*This page is about what you're **actually marked on** in A2 Business Studies exams.*

You get marks for **AO1 (showing knowledge)** and **AO2 (applying knowledge)**

AO1 marks are for **content** and **knowledge**. You'll only get about 2 marks for this, whether the question is a short one worth 2 marks, shortish one worth 6 marks or a long one worth 15 marks. At A2 level, they assume you know the facts.

AO2 marks are for **applying** your **knowledge** to a **situation** — e.g. thinking about the type of ownership of the business in the question, the product or service it's selling, the type of market it's in. You usually get 2-3 marks for this as well.

You get marks for **AO3 (analysis)** and **AO4 (evaluation)**

AO3 marks are for **analysis** — thinking about benefits, drawbacks, causes, effects and limitations. Analysis questions usually start with words like "**Analyse**", "**Examine**", "**Explain why**" or "**Consider**".

1) Use your knowledge to **explain** your answer and **give reasons**.

2) With data, say what the figures **mean**, what might have **caused** them and what the **consequences** might be.

3) Write about **context** — compare a business' situation with the industry as a whole, or with a competitor.

AO4 marks are for **evaluation** — using your **judgement**. Evaluation questions usually start with words like "**Evaluate**", "**Discuss**", "**Recommend**" or "**To what extent**".

1) Give **two sides** of an argument, and say which you think is **strongest**. Consider **advantages** and **disadvantages** and weigh them up.

2) You don't need a definite answer. You can point out that it depends on various factors — as long as you say what the factors are, and say why the right choice depends on those factors. Use your **judgement** to say what the **most important factors** are.

3) Relate your answer to the **business described in the question** and to the **situation in the question**. Give reasons why the business would make a particular decision, and how and why the particular circumstances might affect their decision.

A2 Material is Based on AS Material — your AS Work is Relevant

Even though you're taking the A2 exams, you'll still be expected to **use information you learned** during the AS course:

1) As **background knowledge** to help you **apply knowledge**, and **analyse** and **evaluate** business decisions.

2) As part of a "**synoptic**" paper which tests knowledge from the AS part of the course as well as the A2 part.

You get marks for **Quality** of **Written Communication** in essays and coursework

1) You have to write a **well-structured essay**, not a list of bullet points. ← *Jotting down a quick essay plan will help.*

2) You need to use **specialist vocabulary** when it's appropriate, so it's worth **learning** some of the **fancy terms** used in this book.

3) Write **neatly** enough for the examiner to be able to read it and use good **spelling**, **grammar** and **punctuation**. Out of the whole paper, you only get **2** or **3** marks for written communication — but remember that if the examiner can't **read** or **understand** your writing, you won't get the **other marks** either.

The **Marks** are **Shared Out** differently by **Different Exam Boards**

1) For **AQA**, all the skills are marked **separately**.

2) For example, an **evaluation** question has some marks for **content**, some for **application**, some for **analysis** and some for **evaluation**. You can **lose marks** for poor content, application and analysis. If you evaluate possible pros and cons **without** specifically stating the **obvious facts**, and specifically **relating** them to the **actual business situation** in the question, you'll **lose out**.

1) With **OCR** and **Edexcel** the mark scheme is like a **ladder** with **AO1 skills** at the **bottom** and **AO4 skills** at the **top**. You get marks according to how far up the ladder you get.

2) For example, in an **evaluation** question worth **11 marks**, you can get **1-2 marks** for only giving **content**, **3-5 marks** for **applying knowledge** but not analysing, and **6-7 marks** for **analysis** but no evaluation. Even if you give a **half-baked evaluation**, you can actually get **8 marks**. A really **good evaluation** will get you the **full 11 marks**.

Do Well in Your AQA Exam

*This page is all about how to do well in AQA exams. So don't bother reading it if you're not doing **AQA**.*

There are three **Exam Units** at A2

1) There are **three examinations** at A2 — units 4, 5 and 6. **Units 4** and **5** are both worth **15%** of the total A level marks. **Unit 6** is worth **20%**. Each examination lasts **90 minutes**.

2) **Unit 4** is based on a Case Study. It assesses **Module 4** (Marketing and Accounting and Finance) and **Module 5** (People and Operations Management). The questions on Unit 4 are **compulsory** and require you to analyse written information and numerical data. There are normally **four questions** on this paper each worth **20 marks**.

3) **Unit 5** assesses **all three A2 modules** and comprises two sections. **Section A** has a single compulsory question worth **40 marks**. It gives you data in the form of tables, charts and lists and requires you to write a report justifying a business decision. **Section B** contains four long essay questions. You must answer **one question** which is again worth **40 marks**.

4) **Unit 6** is also based on a **Case Study** (given to you in the paper). It assesses **Module 6** (**External Influences** and **Objectives and Strategy**). The current pattern is for five questions, each worth **14-18 marks**. **Unit 6** is called the "**synoptic**" paper, which means it assesses your ability to build an argument by drawing from your knowledge about **all parts** of the **specification**. So, for unit 6 you need to revise everything, not just the External Influences and Objectives and Strategy stuff.

Here's an **Example Essay** to give you some **Tips**

> To what extent is marketing irrelevant to a manufacturer supplying nails to the construction industry? (10 marks)

Don't waffle. Start by making a point. → Marketing is the management process responsible for identifying, anticipating and satisfying the needs of customers profitably. ← *This is straight to the point. It picks up "knowledge" marks straight away.*

There are two markets in which a business can sell its product, one being the consumer market and the other the industrial market. Constant changes within consumer markets make it vital for businesses to undertake market research when deciding upon a possible new product or when analysing the success of their existing product. Marketing is therefore very important. ← *This shows understanding and develops an argument that's carried on in the next paragraph.*

Nails could be classified as product-orientated and are more commonly sold in the industrial market. Because the industrial market for building materials is not subject to differing trends and fashions, one could argue whether marketing is as important as in consumer markets. Nails are commodities that are not affected by changing fashions or consumer attitudes. Because of this I feel marketing is to some degree of little use. ← *This gets some analysis (AO3) and evaluation (AO4) marks.*

Good points, but not explained well enough. → Above the line promotion is an important aspect of the marketing mix in consumer markets. However, for industrial markets below the line promotions are more important and customers are more likely to be concerned about specification, functionality, delivery and price than image. Marketing concentrates on satisfying the consumer's needs. With this in mind, I would say that marketing is important to a nail manufacturer, as it will provide them with knowledge of the economy. For example a decrease in interest rates will prompt people to take out loans and engage in home projects such as conversions or extensions; this would lead to an increase in the demand for nails from wholesalers or large retail chains. Additionally, marketing will be useful in analysing competitive prices and specifications. ← *This is good application of knowledge to the business in the question.*

I would conclude, therefore, that marketing is of relevance to a nail manufacturer, although not all aspects will be as important as others. ← *You should put in a conclusion to sum up your argument. This one is a bit weak.*

This is a good answer. It would get about **8 marks**. The candidate has a good understanding of the nature of marketing within industrial markets and has demonstrated the ability to **analyse** and **evaluate** reasonably well.

In order to **improve**, the candidate could have explored the **similarities** and **differences** between marketing in consumer and industrial markets in **more depth**. Some parts of the answer could be more **specific** to the business to business market. The conclusion could summarise the reasons for saying that marketing is important in a business to business industrial market.

Here's a sample **mark scheme** for a 10 mark AQA question:

Content	Application	Analysis	Evaluation
2 marks: Good understanding of industrial markets.	**2 marks**: Factors specific to the business applied in detail.	**2-3 marks**: Good use of relevant theory to analyse marketing in industrial and consumer markets.	**2-3 marks**: Judgement shown in considering the relevance of marketing to industrial markets.
1 mark: Some understanding shown of industrial markets.	**1 mark**: Some application to industrial sector.	**1 mark**: Limited use of theory.	**1 mark**: Some judgement shown in answer.

Do Well in Your OCR Exam

*This page is all about how to do well in OCR exams. So don't bother reading it if you're not doing **OCR**.*

There are **Three Exam Modules** at A2 — *One Compulsory* and *Two Choices*

1) The compulsory unit is **Module 2880 – Business Strategy**. It covers objectives, strategy, planning and external influences. It can ask you about these in the **context** of marketing, accounting and finance, or people in organisations. So, you need to revise the whole of your course for this paper.

2) The module 2880 paper measures your ability to analyse and evaluate, using all of your business knowledge. It's a **2 hour exam** at the end of your course and it makes up **20%** of the final grade.

3) You also need to complete **one** module from **Modules 2874-2877**, which go into more depth on topics covered in the AS level part of the course. These modules are: Module 2874 — Further Marketing, Module 2875 — Further Accounting and Finance, Module 2876 — Further People in Organisations and finally Module 2877 — Further Operations Management. These modules are assessed with a **90 minute exam** which makes up **15%** of the final grade.

4) You'll also need either **Module 2878** (a piece of **coursework**) or **Module 2879** (the **Business Thematic Enquiry**). Either of these units will give you the other **15%** of the final award. Module 2879 is a **90 minute exam** based on an **unseen Case Study** — your teacher will only know the theme of the case study, not the content, and they'll tell you the theme in advance, so you can get some research done before the exam.

5) For both the **coursework** and the **Business Thematic Enquiry**, you have to **analyse data**, make a **decision**, and write a **report**. You'll be marked on explaining the situation, setting objectives, doing research (for the Thematic Enquiry this means both beforehand and using the data given in the exam), using Business Studies knowledge, analysing data, evaluating data and making a decision, writing a good report, and your use of English.

> The exam board suggest you should attack module 2879 (the Business Thematic Enquiry) like this:
> 1) Spend 10 - 15 minutes <u>reading the case study</u>, think about <u>how</u> you're going to use the data to answer the question.
> 2) Spend 5 - 10 minutes <u>choosing appropriate evidence</u> from the <u>case study</u> and <u>previous research</u>.
> 3) Spend 10 - 15 minutes <u>planning the report</u>.
> 4) Spend 45 - 50 minutes <u>writing the report</u> itself.
> 5) Spend 5 - 10 minutes <u>checking your work</u>.

Here's an **Example Answer** to give you some **Tips**

> Munir Abbas is the managing director of MTA Electronics. The 31 January balance sheet of MTA Electronics shows the amount of debtors as £85 000. During the year to 31 January, the total turnover was £310 250. Discuss the methods that Munir could use to reduce the debtor days ratio. (12 marks)

It's a good to get marks for working out the debtor days ratio straight away.

The debtor days ratio = (debtors × 365) ÷ turnover = 31 025 000 ÷ 310250 = 100.

Munir could reduce the debtor days ratio by offering discounts for cash payment. This would encourage people to pay cash instead of buying on credit.

This is a good evaluation point.

Munir could also charge interest on late payments, or include a penalty clause for late payments. Credit terms are an important factor that influences customers' decisions of where to buy from. By charging interest on late payments, MTA Electronics might find that they lose customers to rival firms. Giving a discount for cash is a better option, because it would encourage cash buyers without making MTA Electronics' credit terms uncompetitive.

Good knowledge of customer credit as a marketing tool.

This shows Business Studies knowledge.

Debt factoring is another possibility. This is where a bank would take the unpaid invoices from MTA Electronics, in return for instant cash payment of part of the value of the invoice. The bank collects the payment from the debtor, and keeps some of it as a fee. The advantage of debt factoring is that it provides instant cash. This would be particularly desirable if MTA Electronics are facing a cash flow problem. The disadvantage is that MTA don't receive the full value of the debt.

This could do with more explanation.

This is a good evaluation point to earn AO4 marks.

Doing an aged debtors analysis would help Munir decide which method to use. If there are a lot of very late debts, debt factoring would be a good idea because the alternative would be to write these debts off as bad debts.

This answer is quite good, and is worth about **10 marks**. To improve, it could give more explanation about **bad debts**. It could explain that the best method depends on **various factors**, e.g. the customers, the length of debt.

Here's a sample **mark scheme** for this 12 mark OCR question:

Level 4	Answer evaluates methods of reducing debtors.	9-12 marks
Level 3	Answer analyses possible methods of reducing debtors.	6-8 marks
Level 2	Answer shows understanding of options.	3-5 marks
Level 1	Answer shows knowledge of options.	1-2 marks

Do Well in Your Edexcel Exam

*This page is all about how to do well in **Edexcel** exams.*

The Edexcel A2 syllabus is very different from AS. Instead of each unit covering one topic, each unit concentrates on a set of key business skills. So each unit covers a mixture of finance, marketing, production and HRM.

There are three **Exam Units** at A2

1) **Unit 4** is **Analysis and Decision Making**. It covers the analytical techniques needed to understand how decisions are taken to deal with business issues such as sales, production of new products, cost control etc.

2) **Unit 5** is **Business Planning**. It covers the planning techniques in Marketing, Human Resources, and Finance.

3) **Unit 6** is called **Corporate Strategy**. This unit looks at how businesses develop strategies to manage external issues such as environmental, global and ethical factors. It also draws together the **whole** of the A level course.

4) In **Unit 4** you get **two compulsory questions** on a decision-making and analysis theme — e.g. investment in machinery or managing a project. Each question has a total of **48 marks**, and is made up of several **subparts**. Some subparts are short answer knowledge-based questions only worth **3 marks**, and others are analysis and evaluation questions **worth up to 18 marks**. The exam takes **1 hour and 15 minutes**.

5) **Unit 5** gives you the choice of a **one and a half hour exam** or **coursework**. If you do the **exam**, you get an **unseen Case Study** which will contain a scenario, several appendices, and statistical or financial information. Several options or possible solutions may be offered and you'll be expected to compare and evaluate courses of action. From the information given in the case study, you'll have to prepare a **report** suggesting potential solutions. You'll have **15 minutes** to **read** the case study and **1 hour and 15 minutes** to **write the report**. There are **80 marks** for content and **4 marks** for the quality of your written English.

6) **Unit 6** is a "**synoptic**" paper — i.e. it expects you to include topics from **other parts** of the **course**, including bits from AS as well as A2. It's based on a **pre-released case study** — so you can read it and get familiar with it well before you get to the exam. Of course, if you really wanted to lose marks for being an idiot, you could leave reading it until you're in the exam room. Your call. The case study contains an article describing a business and the circumstances it's in. The exam has **three compulsory questions** which carry **40 marks each**, giving **120** in total, plus **6 additional marks** for quality of written English. They give you **90 minutes** for this exam.

Here's an **Example Essay** to give you some **Tips**

In the Warehouse department, a new computerised system has been introduced. Some staff have not performed well in the new system, and have been disciplined. Also, the Marketing department has been restructured after a consultation process and now uses flexible working. Since these changes, there has been increased absenteeism in the warehouse, but not in Marketing. Evaluate the different approaches to the management of changes taken by Warehouse manager Fred and Marketing manager Elaine. (12 marks)

Resistance to change is acknowledged but not fully explained.

There's resistance to change in all organisations. Managers and employees will need to learn new skills and procedures. Plans can go wrong which can mean that people can't do their jobs as efficiently as they would like. All of these issues can increase stress amongst the workforce. However, from the information given the senior management of the company have not taken these issues into account.

This analyses (AO3) but doesn't evaluate (AO4) — it doesn't say why this approach is good or bad.

The bit about training and discipline is slightly waffly.

Although sufficient training time has been allowed for training operatives in the warehouse the manager's strategy tends to follow McGregor's Theory X approach. The disciplinary situation between the manager and warehouse workers shows evidence of this. Even though the workers have had the training, they haven't had time yet to become fully used to the system. The manager, Fred, doesn't accept this, and thinks they are lazy and need punishment.

It's good to use material from other parts of the course (motivation) and apply it to the situation.

This is a decent evaluation of the Marketing manager's relationship with staff.

In contrast to this, the Marketing Manager has been more fully involved in the reorganisation process of her department and her approach to management has mainly followed Theory Y. She has kept her staff fully informed about the reasons for the changes and has listened to suggestions from all staff. As a result her staff appear to be more motivated and co-operative and they are able to increase their self-esteem as Maslow suggests.

It seems to me that the change process has not been well planned and detail has been ignored. Some managers such as the Warehouse manager have not been properly prepared to manage change. Staff may have been poorly communicated with and it is quite possible that the increased absenteeism may be the result of poor leadership.

The end bit is rather weak.

This answer is fairly good, and is worth about **9 marks**. To improve, it could explain more about the **process of change**, and the need for **change management**. It evaluates, but doesn't do it brilliantly. **Evaluation** of the managers' approaches could more closely reference **resistance** to change, and **demotivating** factors in change.

Here's a sample **mark scheme** for this 12 mark Edexcel question:

Level 4	Answer evaluates different approaches of the two managers.	9-12 marks
Level 3	Answer analyses approaches of the two managers.	6-8 marks
Level 2	Answer shows understanding of managers' actions.	3-5 marks
Level 1	Answer shows knowledge of change management.	1-2 marks

Answers to the Numerical Questions

Section One— Marketing

Page 9 — Market Research Analysis

Q1 Range = highest value – lowest value = 14 – 0 = 14 *[1 mark for working, 1 mark for answer.]* Upper boundary of lower quartile = (n+1)÷4 where n is the number of respondents *[1 mark].* Upper boundary of lower quartile = (52+1)÷4 = 13.25. *[1 mark]* This is between the 13th and 14th values, i.e. 0 cans. *[1 mark]* Lower boundary of lower quartile = 3(n+1)÷4 where n is the number of respondents *[1 mark].* Lower boundary of upper quartile = 3(52+1)÷4 = 39.75. *[1 mark]* This is between the 39th and 40th values, i.e. 2 cans. *[1 mark]* Interquartile range = difference, i.e. 2 – 0 =2 cans. *[1 mark]*

Q2 Mean = (20+18+14+12+24)÷5 = 17.6 *[1 mark]*

Standard deviation formula = $\sigma = \sqrt{\dfrac{\sum (x-\mu)^2}{n}}$ *[1 mark]*

Squares of difference between each datum and the mean: *[1 mark for calculating x-μ terms, 1 mark for calculating (x-μ)² terms]*

x	x–μ	(x–μ)²
20	2.4	5.76
18	0.4	0.16
14	-3.6	12.96
12	-5.6	31.36
24	6.4	40.96

Sum of (x-μ)² = 91.2. *[1 mark]* Divide by number of observations to give variance: 91.2÷5 = 18.24 *[1 mark]* Take square root to give standard deviation = 4.27 *[1 mark for working and 1 mark for final correct answer for standard deviation]*

Page 11 — Marketing Analysis

Q1 (a)

Year	Quarter	Sales revenue (thousand £s)	4 quarter moving total	8 quarter moving total	Quarterly moving average
2001	1	630			
	2	567			
	3	552			605.63
	4	678	2427		605.88
2002	1	621	2418	4845	606.13
	2	578	2429	4847	595.25
	3	543	2420	4849	583.13
	4	600	2342	4762	577.25
2003	1	602	2323	4665	568.63
	2	550	2295	4618	558.50
	3	502	2254	4549	551.88
	4	560	2214	4468	
2004	1	589	2201	4415	

[14 marks]

(b)

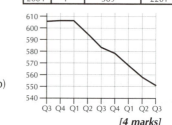

[4 marks]

Section Two — Accounting and Finance

Page 27 — Variances

Q1 (a)Total expenditure = £80k+£30k+£22k = £132k. *[1 mark]* Total variance on expenditure = £12K(A). *[1 mark]* Total variance on sales revenue = £5k(F). *[1 mark]* Total variance = £12k–£5k=£7k(A). *[1]*

Page 35 — Company Accounts: Balance Sheets

Q2 Using straight line method, depreciation per year = (cost when new – cost when sold) ÷ amount of time owned. *[1 mark]* Depreciation per year = (£2500–£500)÷4 = £500. *[1 mark for working, 1 mark for answer.]*

Page 43 — Financial Ratios

Q2 (a) Net profit ratio = net profit ÷ turnover ×100 *[1 mark]* Net profit ratio = (£750 000–£250 000)÷£2 000 000 ×100= 25% *[1 mark for working, 1 mark for answer.]*

Page 45 — Limitations of Ratios

Q1 (a) Dividend cover = net profit after tax ÷ total dividends *[1 mark]* = £300 000÷(6p × 100 000) = £300 000÷6000= 50 *[1 mark for working, 1 mark for answer.]*
(b) Dividend Yield = dividend per share ÷ price per share × 100 = 6p÷300p×100 = 2% *[1 mark for working, 1 mark for answer.]*

Page 47 — Contribution and Break Even Analysis

Q1 (a) Contribution = selling price – variable costs per unit *[1 mark]* Contribution = £5 – £3 = £2 *[1 mark]* Break even output = fixed costs ÷ contribution *[1 mark]* Break even output = £20 000 ÷ 2 = 10 000 units per year *[1 mark]*

Page 51 — Investment Appraisals

Q1 ARR = (average annual profit ÷ investment)× 100 *[1 mark]* Average annual profit = £100 000 – £60 000 = £40 000 *[1 mark]* ARR = £40 000 ÷ £200 000 × 100 = 20% *[1 mark for working, 1 mark for answer.]*

Page 53 — Investment Appraisals

Q1

	Cash inflow	Discount Value (5%)	Present Value
Year 1	£5K	0.952	£5K × 0.952 = £4760
Year 2	£5K	0.907	£5K × 0.907 =£4535
Year 3	£5K	0.864	£5K × 0.864 =£4320
Year 4	£5K	0.823	£5K × 0.823 =£4115
Year 5	£5K	0.784	£5K × 0.784 =£3920
Total Present Value of Cash Inflows			£21650
Net Present Value (total minus Investment)			-£17K = **£4650**

[3 marks for calculating all discount values correctly, 2 marks for calculating 3-4 values correctly, 1 mark for calculating 1-2 values.] [2 marks for calculating all present values correctly, 1 mark for calculating 2-4 discount values correctly] [1 mark for adding present values correctly] [1 mark for working of net present value calculation, 1 mark for answer of £4650]

Section Four — Operations Management

Page 91 — Critical Path Analysis

Q1 (a)

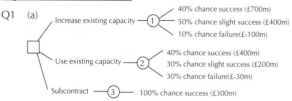

[3 marks for putting (A), (B, C and D), (E), and (F and G) in the right order. 2 marks for one error. 1 mark for 2 errors] [1 mark for B C and D as simultaneous], [1 mark for F and G as simultaneous].
(b) *[1 mark for the critical path — it's a thick pink line on the diagram] [1 mark for the total time — 26 days]*
(c) *Float times at B and F are both 2 days. [1 mark for each]*

Section Six — Objectives and Strategy

Page 119 — Decision Trees

Q1 (a)

Increase existing capacity — 1
- 40% chance success (£700m)
- 50% chance slight success (£400m)
- 10% chance failure(£-100m)

Use existing capacity — 2
- 40% chance success (£400m)
- 30% chance slight success (£200m)
- 30% chance failure(£-30m)

Subcontract — 3 — 100% chance success (£300m)

[1 mark for each correctly labelled probability and payoff]
(b) *Expected value at 1: £280m + £200m – £10m = £470m [1 mark for each correct value, 1 mark for adding them correctly]. Expected value at 2: £160m + £60m – £9m = £211m. [1 mark for each correct value, 1 mark for adding them correctly] Expected value at 3: £300m [1 mark]. Choosing and explaining the best option [4 marks].*

Glossary

ACAS The Advisory, Conciliation and Arbitration Service, which acts as a mediator in industrial disputes.

balance sheet A snapshot of a firm's finances at a fixed point in time.

break-even analysis Shows the point where a company's total revenues equals their total costs.

budget Forecasts future earnings and future spending.

business cycle The regular pattern of growth and recession in the economy.

cashflow Money that comes into and goes out of a firm.

chain of command The number of hierarchical levels a communication or decision has to go through.

cost centre Part of a business that directly incurs costs.

critical path analysis Works out the quickest way to finish a set of tasks.

corporate culture The way a business does things — it affects the attitudes and expectations of employees.

depreciation Losing value over time — fixed assets often depreciate.

diversification Expanding to produce new products or enter new markets.

elasticity of demand Shows the relationship between the price and demand of a product or service.

exchange rate The value of one currency in terms of another currency.

fiscal policy Government policy that sets tax rates and government spending.

fixed assets Things businesses keep for over a year — e.g. property, equipment, land, computers.

fixed costs Costs that stay the same — no matter how much a firm produces.

forecasting Trying to predict what will happen in the future.

gearing The proportion of a business financed through debt rather than equity.

GDP (gross domestic product) The total market share of goods and services produced by a country, within the country, over a period of time.

Human Resource Management (HRM) Looks after all the people aspects of a business — like hiring, firing and training.

inflation The increase in the price of goods and services.

interest rate Shows the cost of borrowing.

kaizen Japanese for "continuous improvement", used in quality control.

lean production Techniques that aim to reduce waste to an absolute minimum.

liabilities Debts a business owes.

liquidity How easily assets can be turned into cash.

marketing mix The four Ps firms use to market their goods / services — price, product, promotion and place.

market research Finding out about customers, markets and competitors.

merger Where two companies agree they should join together into one business.

mission statement A written description of a company's corporate objectives.

monetary policy Government policy that controls the interest rate — this affects inflation and exchange rates.

monopoly Where one firm controls most or all of the market share.

motivation Anything that makes you work harder and achieve more than normal.

multinational corporation A business with its headquarters in one country and bases in other countries.

operations management Planning and monitoring business operations to ensure they're as efficient as possible.

PEST analysis Used to analyse external opportunities and threats — looks at political, economic, social and technological issues.

private limited company (Ltd) A company that is owned by shareholders but its shares can't be sold on the stock market.

privatisation Selling publicly-owned companies to private individuals and firms.

productive efficiency How good a company is at turning inputs into outputs.

profit and loss account Statement showing how much money's gone into and out of a company over a period of time.

profit centre Part of a business that directly generates revenue.

protectionism When a country tries to protect its own companies by making it harder for foreign companies to trade in that country.

public limited company (PLC) A company that is owned by shareholders and its shares can be sold on the stock market.

return on capital employed (ROCE) Shows you how much money is made by the business compared to how much money's been put into the business.

social responsibility The responsibilities a firm has to its employees, customers and other stakeholders.

span of control The number of staff working under one manager.

stakeholders All the people affected by a business — workers, shareholders, customers and the public.

SWOT analysis Used to determine business strategy — looks at the strengths, weaknesses, opportunities and threats facing the firm.

takeover Where one firm buys over 50% of the shares of another firm, giving them the controlling interest.

Theory X managers Managers that think employees are trustworthy, responsible, organised and can enjoy work as long as they are motivated.

Theory Y managers Managers that think employees are only motivated by money, are essentially lazy and require constant supervision.

trade unions Groups that act on behalf of groups of employees in talks with their employer.

variable assets Things that are likely to be exchanged for cash within a year — e.g. stock, debtors.

variable costs Costs that vary, depending on what business the firm does.

vicarious liability Where an employer is responsible for any act committed by an employee — during the normal course of their job.

working capital Money available to fund day-to-day spending.

Index

Index

Index